A PILGRIMAGE OF GRACE

THE DIARIES OF RUTH DODDS 1905-1974

Edited by

MAUREEN CALLCOTT

Bewick Press Tyne & Wear
1995

First published in Great Britain by
Bewick Press
132 Claremont Road
Whitley Bay
Tyne and Wear
NE26 3TX

ISBN 1 898880 02 6

Printed and bound in Great Britain by
TUPS, 30 Lime Street, Newcastle upon Tyne NE1 1PQ
Design, scanning and typesetting (from disc) by Roger Booth Associates
99 Keymer Road, Hassocks, West Sussex BN6 8QL

The Diary of Ruth Dodds.
Begun in the year 1905 on the 19th of
august, when at Alnmouth for the
summer holidays.
August 19th saterday. Fine but very
strong west wind. Molly better.
Went for a dutiful walk with
aunty Poppy in the morning. After
dinner went for a walk by
myself to Bulmer rocks. Went
on with the Wizards Castle. Must
try to think more about the
novel. We did not bathe today
because of the misfortune to
the tent. Elsa went away in
the morning as aunty Looie was
not very well. Hugh arrived
while I was out this afternoon.
Molly was up in the drawrwing
room + Hugh had tea with her.
Hugh has brought a very interestin
looking book called the Convict

The opening page from the Diary

To the memory of Bill Callcott

CONTENTS

ACKNOWLEDGEMENTS

It is with pleasure that I record at last my thanks and debt to those who have encouraged and helped with the publication of this book. Irene and Michael Rounthwaite and their family generously let me borrow the manuscript of the diaries and many of the photographs of Ruth Dodds' Family which are reproduced here. Mabel and Raymond Challinor and Archie Potts of the Bewick Press have provided unfailing support and guidance and I owe them very special thanks. I first discussed the project with Alan Henderson, solicitor (now deceased), who loaned me various family papers, his complete run of the *Gateshead Herald*, and some Ever Circulating Portfolios. He was very enthusiastic, as was Tom Marshall (also now deceased) of Gateshead Central Library Local History Department and his colleague Eileen Carnaffin. Both assisted and facilitated my researches there. Bob and Cecily Murphy helped with the preparation of the text which Bob kindly read in an early draft, as did Elizabeth Pescod. Barbara Davidson read and corrected the final draft and provided much wise advice. Several members of the Religious Society of Friends have shared their memories of Ruth Dodds with me and Stella Clark has helped with this and with other aspects of Friends' history. I have to thank Norman McCord for his direction of my research into local political history and for initiating me into the use of the tape recorder in 1970. Errors of any sort in the book are, of course, my own responsibility.

The publication has received generous financial support from The Joseph Rowntree Foundation and The Reckitt Trust.

Maureen Callcott

LIST OF ILLUSTRATIONS

INTRODUCTION:
Ruth Dodds; Her Life and Her Diaries

Ruth Dodds was born in Church Row, Gateshead, on 8 May 1890, the fourth child of Edwin and Emily Bryham Dodds. She had two elder sisters, Molly and Hope, and one brother, Brian. A younger sister, Sylvia, was born within two years of Ruth. Their mother died in 1896 and a large part was played in the children's lives by her sisters, the Mawson aunts, three unmarried women of independent means, who lived nearby in a large property, Ashfield, built in the 1860s by John Mawson, Ruth's grandfather, a manufacturing chemist. The Mawsons were an important Tyneside family, and Ruth's grandfather was the famous Sheriff of Newcastle, blown up in an explosion on the Town Moor in 1867 while attempting to destroy a cache of nitro-glycerine. Joseph Swan, inventor of the electric light, was a great-uncle. Edwin Dodds owned the printing business on Newcastle Quayside founded by his father in the 1840s. Edwin Dodds shared his own passion for history, heraldry, genealogy, the countryside and Newcastle United Football Club with his children.

Ruth was educated at Gateshead High School for Girls until she was fifteen, and was then sent to Clapham High School in London, where she was a boarding pupil. Encouraged no doubt by father and aunts, the girls were great readers and kept diaries from an early age, though only Ruth's survive. Ruth and Hope both had literary ambitions and devoured poetry, plays, novels and stories and tried their hands writing in all these genres. Hope was a student at Newnham College, Cambridge, from 1902 to 1906 (before women could receive degrees) and was an historian, who later made a substantial contribution to the Northumberland County History. She and Ruth collaborated on a book (published in 1915) about the risings against Henry VIII's dissolution of the monasteries, *The Pilgrimage of Grace*. This was, until very recently, the standard work on the subject.

Ruth lived all her life at the family home, Home House, in Low Fell, Gateshead, as did her two other unmarried sisters, Hope and Sylvia. It was a substantial stone property, with accommodation for the maids who helped with the work of the house, and a large garden where a grass tennis court was maintained. The diaries, which she kept, with a few lapses, from 1905 until 1974, portray a variety of aspects of these sixty-five years. From 1905–1914 they reflect the experience, opportunities, expectations and frustrations of a sensitive and intelligent girl growing up in the north of England in the Edwardian period. After 1914 the diaries reveal the significance of the First World War on the course of the rest of her life.

There had been political interest, if not serious activism, in Ruth's family. One of the Mawson aunts (Camie) was a pacifist and Socialist but was not active in either capacity. Both of Ruth's parents were Liberals, and she herself was strongly so at the age of nineteen. Sketching out, in a 1909 diary, a political play, she observed, about an election, 'It will be rather dreadful to make a Conservative candidate get in.' She was shocked into serious social and political awareness when in 1910 she canvassed for the Liberal candidate among the slums of Gateshead. By 1914 she had joined the Gateshead branch of the National Union of Women's Suffrage Societies, and was then its secretary. In the same year, after the outbreak of war, she worked for the Soldiers and Sailors Families' Association. Her experience of the wretched conditions of her Gateshead clients clearly made a deep impression, for she spoke of it fifty years later in an interview in 1970.

The course of the First World War stimulated her social, moral and spiritual sensibilities, changing her life in a number of ways. She worked briefly on the night shift in Armstrong's huge munitions factory and then, as the men left, in the family printing business. This continued until 1926, latterly in partnership with her brother Brian, when they had what was evidently a very bitter quarrel over their different responses to the General Strike (Ruth supported the trade unions, though she was reticent about the details of the breach). She left the business. This was clearly an impulsive gesture which she regretted deeply. It left a great gap in her life and her sense of loss and frustration pervades much of the remaining diaries.

Although Ruth received an allowance from her father (and legacies from the Mawson aunts), which meant that she was never compelled to earn her own livelihood, she did seek work (even as a theatrical costumier) and for a long time regretted the loss of employment, which had reinforced a sense of her own identity. She threw herself more vigorously into her political work, and after the war the diaries' reflection of a life struggling to be socially purposeful and useful contrast strongly with the pre-war preoccupations with tennis parties, football heroes, dances and clothes. She always loved clothes, fashion and fabrics which she often describes in vivid detail, though later she writes ruefully about her spending which she feels the need to justify.

At the end of the war she joined the Labour Party, to which she devoted much of the next twenty years. She also joined the Society of Friends which became increasingly important to her life in several different aspects. She was a co-opted member of some Gateshead Council committees for several years before being elected as a Labour Councillor in 1929. She held a seat almost continuously for the next ten years and served on a number of important committees, including education, town improvement, housing, and maternity and child welfare. She secured the establishment of four new Child Welfare Clinics between 1920 and 1939 doing voluntary work at the earlier ones 'weighing the babies'. In 1925 she took over the editorship of the monthly *Gateshead Labour News* (later the *Gateshead Herald*). She wrote large parts of it herself and her sister Hope also contributed. It was a quite exceptional paper of its type. It contained full reports of the council and its committee meetings, of local Labour activities, local and national elections, accounts of the doings of local MPs and some contributions from them. There were also literary pieces, poems etc. It was often very difficult for her to meet the deadline at the end of a busy month but she never failed.

She was decided in her condemnation of the defection of Ramsay MacDonald (Labour Prime Minister) and Snowden (Chancellor of the Exchequer) when the National Government was formed in 1931. The heartland of Ruth's political activity, as for many others, was the Independent Labour Party (ILP). When it disaffiliated from the Labour Party in 1932, Ruth joined the newly formed Socialist League established to replace the ILP. Her editorship of the *Gateshead Herald* ensured full reports of the activities of the League in the north east. She became its secretary and regional representative on the National Council. In both 1931 and 1936 she accepted nomination as Parliamentary Labour candidate for Gateshead but was not selected.

Diaries for the period from late November 1931 to late June 1937 are missing, but there are references in later volumes to her concern for those, especially the children, who were victims in the Spanish Civil War (1936–1939) – 'a Spanish food ship collection' (28 December 1938) and a 'Spanish Tea' (January 1940). The former entry also mentions two refugee Basque children. Ruth Dodds was prominent in organising and providing help for refugees during and after the two world wars – Austrian children after the first, and in the 1930s Czechs and Austrians. She supported at least two students through their course at King's College, Durham University at Newcastle and gave unstinting help, both financial and active, to a refugee hostel in Gateshead.

During and after the First World War Ruth, and her sister Hope, became more and more drawn to the spiritual approach of the Religious Society of Friends, or Quakers, initially probably because of its pacifism. There is virtually no mention of religion or church-going in the family before this. Hope was a member of the Newcastle Friends' Meeting, one of the largest in the country, by the end of 1919, and Ruth was occasionally attending meetings from at least October 1918. In May 1925 she applied and was accepted for membership. For many years, from 1930, she was on the Friends' Industrial and Social Order Council for Durham Quarterly Meeting, on the Service Council for the same meeting from 1944–1953 and on the Meeting for Sufferings for most of the period from 1946–1963. After she joined the Quakers the diaries contain a substantial amount of description and discussion of the spiritual life, often with lamentations over her own shortcomings.

Her life-long passion for the theatre found practical expression through the ILP. The neighbouring Newcastle upon Tyne ILP had established its Criterion

Players, supported amongst others, by Bernard Shaw, and Gateshead ILP included among its activities a vigorous amateur dramatic society. In each case they still exist, though without political connections. Ruth and her sisters became zealous supporters both financially and in every other conceivable way. The Progressive Players provided an outlet for Ruth's dramatic enthusiasm and for her socialism. She wrote plays on local historical and political themes; one of the most successful was *The Pitman's Pay*, about the life of Thomas Hepburn and the first miners' union. It was first produced by the Gateshead club in 1920, won a prize in a Sheffield competition in 1922, was published by the Labour Publishing Company in 1923, and toured the mining villages of Durham and Northumberland during the strike and lock-out of 1926. In the late 1930s the management of the Westfield Hall, where the productions were held, wanted the accommodation for other purposes and the Players had to leave. The three Dodds sisters provided the finance and a new theatre was built. The theatre's connection with the Labour movement was severed in 1939, and 1943 saw the opening of the Gateshead Little Theatre, a non-political organisation. She visited the theatre in Newcastle and London as often as possible and saw first productions of numerous plays. She occasionally acted in plays at Gateshead Little Theatre even into her seventies.

She always aspired to be a writer but eventually recognised the limitations of her talents in this respect, at least as far as earning a living was concerned. But she was always writing something. In addition to keeping her diary, writing plays and editing the *Herald,* another outlet was the *Ever Circulating Portfolio (ECP).* This was a compendium of essays, poems and other items; non-political, not intended for publication, but circulating monthly for the pleasure and comment of the dozen or so contributors and friends. Ruth mentions 'the ECP' in her diaries from time to time, and she contributed a number of articles, such as 'Some things I like to look at' (September 1936),' A Great Figure' (Robert Smillie – Scottish miners' leader March 1940).

A shared family passion was the hill and moor country of Northumberland and the Lake District about both of which she was extremely emotional, imaginative and well-informed. Even at her busiest she managed to escape for walking holidays and the diaries contain many detailed and evocative descriptions of her tours.

Ruth resigned from the Labour Party in 1939 because of its support for the Second World War. She then felt forced to give up her seat on Gateshead Council and although she rejoined the party after the war, from then on her social concerns were primarily channelled through the Society of Friends and its Industrial and Social Order Council.

The Gateshead Little Theatre, which had replaced The Progressive Players, was Ruth's major secular interest in the last decades of her life. Her long and strenuous support was recognised in 1975 when she was invited to unveil a plaque in the Theatre commemorating 'the generosity and enthusiasm of Ruth and her sisters Hope and Sylvia'. (*Gateshead Post* 15 May 1975). In recognition of her lengthy and varied service to the life of the borough she was made a Freeman of Gateshead in 1966, the first, and still the only woman to be so honoured in the town. By 1974 she had lost touch with the Labour Party, but in a letter acknowledging this she enclosed a donation to Labour's election fund, and assured the recipient that she had duly cast her vote in the election.

She was very severely affected by arthritis during the last decade of her life, and it was a considerable struggle to maintain the large house and look after her sisters, who both died before her, in times very different from the pre-war years when there had been several servants. She died on 1 April 1976 and was cremated at Saltwell Cemetery, Gateshead, after a Quaker funeral. She was the last of her line, for neither her married sister Molly nor her brother Brian had any surviving children.

Ruth's native Gateshead, with a population of about 127,000 in 1900, was the largest town on the railway between Newcastle and London. Situated on the south bank of the river Tyne, it has always been overshadowed by its neighbour. Across the river, spanned by a growing number of splendid bridges, Newcastle upon Tyne, a fine and wealthy city, from earliest times seized and used economic advantage to the detriment of its poorer neighbour. During Ruth's lifetime, many of the heavy industries which had provided Gateshead with growth and some prosperity during the nineteenth century, declined rapidly. While this was true for the north east in general, Newcastle, with its grand shops and markets a focus for the whole region, its business and commercial centre, its prosperous suburbs, its attractive and varied provision for leisure and culture, its high rateable value, suffered much less. This was regularly observed by commentators. 'Every society started in Gateshead, whether sporting, political or cultural, either moved across the Tyne in search of increased support or quietly faded away' (F.W.D. Manders *A History Of Gateshead 1973*). As Henry Mess put it in 1928, 'an overwhelmingly working-class community ... suffers considerably by living under the shadow of its larger neighbour'. (*Industrial Tyneside*) . As for the appearance of the town, J.B. Priestley's jaundiced comment perhaps exaggerates, 'the whole town seems to have been planned by an enemy of the human race ... if anybody ever made money in Gateshead, they must have taken care not to spend any of it in the town'. (*English Journey,* 1934). But Ruth herself was sadly conscious of the town's deprivation and referred frequently to 'dear, dirty Gateshead.' Her family home was in Low Fell, off the Durham Road, a salubrious suburb at the south end, with sweeping views over the Durham countryside, and a number of substantial properties. Most people were crowded into the northern and eastern parts of the borough in heavily tenemented houses and in industrialised surroundings. Characteristic of the high-density, insanitary housing were areas like Sunderland Road and its off-shoots; ill-lit streets with blackened houses leading from the main route northwards to the factories and the Tyne. While for many years the area of Newcastle near the great bridges had been non-residential, this was not true of Gateshead. Until after the Second World War the cobbled streets of Bottle Bank remained, bordered by tiny houses in a very steep incline – the poorest area of a poor district. The 1923 census defined 36.4 per cent of the population as living in overcrowded conditions. With increasing unemployment in the inter-war period real poverty was on the increase. In 1928 one in ten of the population was receiving outdoor relief from the Poor Law Guardians and in ten years the local poor law expenditure had grown from £109,700 to £486,416 – more than could be afforded from an unproductive rate in a poor town, and which in turn led to cuts in other welfare provision, such as free milk. (Gateshead Poor Law Union. Estimate of Expenditure. In Gateshead Reference Library. Report of Gateshead Medical Officer of Health. *Gateshead Herald*, March 1929). The tuberculosis rate was the second highest for English county boroughs.

Politically, Gateshead had been Liberal from 1832, when it became a parliamentary borough, continuously until 1918. Both Catholicism and Noncomformity were relatively strong in Gateshead (Manders reckoned the Catholic population in the 1970s at about one in four and there were numerous Methodist and other Noncomformist chapels). In 1918 there was a small, but active core of ILP members who were the driving force of the new constituency Labour Party. A number of trade union groups were also important and Gateshead was able to maintain a full-time Labour agent. The ILP was responsible for hiring, and then (with a loan from the Dodds) purchasing, the Westfield Hall, which became the centre of a wide range of social and political activities. When Ruth Dodds joined the ILP in 1918 Westfield Hall became the focus of her social and political life for the next fourteen or so years. It was a meeting-centre for ILP members from the whole region. Public meetings were held, speakers trained, the Socialist Sunday School was accommodated and it was also the home of the Progressive Players. Nightly the hall was fully used for political and social activities, the two often linked. Especially on Sunday nights, big public meetings were held, though if a national speaker, expected to attract a very large audience was coming, the Whitehall Road Co-operative Hall was taken.

Labour first fought Gateshead in 1918 when it was won by a Coalition Conservative (supporter of Lloyd George). In 1923 the Liberals returned to the top of the poll, narrowly defeating Labour by 1.6 per cent of the votes. In

1924, however, Labour gained the seat with 50.2 per cent of the votes. The successful candidate was John Beckett who had fought Newcastle North in 1923. He was a protegé of Sir Charles Trevelyan, a Socialist landowner from Wallington Hall, Northumberland. Beckett left what had become a fairly secure Labour seat in 1929, probably for domestic reasons (an affair with an actress, followed by divorce) and later joined Mosley's New Party. He was imprisoned for his fascism from 1940–1943. In 1929 Gateshead's new Labour M.P., James Melville, was an eminent lawyer, who had become the youngest King's Counsel in 1927, though Hugh Dalton had been approached, as another 'famous name'. Fred Tait, a schoolmaster and ILP friend of Ruth's, the only local nominee, did not obtain much support. The second Labour government (1929–1931) was formed after this election and Melville was made Solicitor-General.

1931 was an eventful year for Labour in Gateshead, and Ruth Dodds' diaries illuminate this. Melville died suddenly in April, and Ruth was one of the two local ILP nominees (out of a total of eight), though she does not mention this in her diaries. The new Labour member, after a June by-election, was a retired civil servant, Major Herbert Evans. His election was followed in August by the political and financial crisis which resulted in the resignation of the Labour Government with its leader, Ramsay MacDonald remaining as Prime Minister of a so-called National Coalition Government. Ruth was on holiday in Sweden at the time but recorded her reactions to the crisis and its subsequent unfolding in Gateshead and nationally. Evans then died suddenly in September and Gateshead was faced with the need to find another candidate very rapidly when an election was unexpectedly announced for October, the National Government simply seeking a 'Doctor's Mandate'. Probably because the Prime Minister's seat was the north east constituency of Seaham, the great 'Dockers' K.C.', Ernest Bevin, was persuaded by the party hierarchy to go to Gateshead. Ruth provides a very graphic account of his selection meeting and his campaign, which like most others was lost by Labour, the National Government gaining a sweeping victory.

Ruth Dodds' diaries are missing from November 1931 to June 1937 but we know that in Gateshead, as elsewhere, the period was one of internal divisions in the Labour Party. When the ILP disaffiliated itself from the Labour Party at a special conference at Bradford in July 1932 there was much heartsearching among those unwilling to sever links with either. Ruth was one of those who elected to remain in the Labour Party but to continue the more intellectual activities of the ILP in a new organisation, the Socialist League, operating inside the Labour Party. A branch was formed in Gateshead in December 1932, affiliated to the Gateshead Labour Party and Trades Council, consisting of ex-ILP members. Ruth was its secretary and representative on the National Committee until it too was expelled from the Labour Party in 1937 for its support of a 'unity campaign' with the ILP and Communist Party. Ruth accepted nomination for the parliamentary candidature again in 1936 when the defeated candidate of 1935, the railwayman, James Wilson, stood down, but she was not selected. The seat was held by a local Liberal National accountant, Thomas Magnay, from 1935–1945, when it was won by Konni Zilliacus. By this time Ruth was not involved with local Labour Party politics.

The diaries begin as a holiday journal when Ruth was fifteen in 1905. They were continued with a greater or lesser degree of regularity according to other demands and preoccupations until about eighteen months before her death in 1976. They are in thirty-one note-books. From time to time in the diaries she provides a variety of reasons for the keeping of this record and was probably content to contemplate their being read after her death, though she would have modestly denied any wider interest. She read sections to me in 1970 and had crossed out sections and even torn out some pages which presumably she didn't want others to read. The only missing diaries are those which would have covered the period from November 1931 to June 1937. They may have been inadvertently destroyed by her executors who had to deal with large numbers of family papers many of which were consigned to a bonfire. It is even possible that she destroyed them herself as they would have provided details of her most politically active and ambitious period which later made her feel uncomfortable.

The selection from the diaries presented here attempts to reflect the weight and balance of the writer's preoccupations. The occasionally lengthy stories, plays, poems, passages copied from other books have been omitted. On the other hand some of the extensive accounts of walks, holidays and clothes have been included to provide an indication of what Ruth chose to relate. As with most historical sources, particularly perhaps those of personal record, there are, of course, frustrating gaps all the time. A major cause of this results from the determination to write 'a sundial Diary' recording only happy hours. She doesn't always do this but does often refrain from making adverse comments about family and friends and relating controversial stories. Where there is much repetition of ideas, aspirations and similar occasions these have been omitted.

In the main the author's spelling, abbreviations and syntax have been retained and only corrected for clarity and understanding. They seem to me to provide an indication of atmosphere, pace, development and present the authentic document. The errors of the fifteen-year-old who began the diaries (e.g. saterday for Saturday) have been left uncorrected for those reasons. Editorial brackets are square [ ]. References are provided at the end to help the general reader place people and events but these have been kept to a minimum.

CHAPTER ONE: 1905–1907

Edwardian teenage. The last school years, holidays, Newcastle United

19 August [*Alnmouth*]. Fine but very strong west wind .... Went for a dutiful walk with Aunty Poppy.[1] We did not bathe today because of the misfortune to the tent in the morning. After dinner went for a walk by myself to Bulmer [Boulmer] rocks. Went on with the *Wizards Castle*. Must try to think more about the novel ... Hugh[2] has brought a very interesting book called the *Convict Ship*. I want to read it as soon as he is finished. I almost wish I was not going to Clapham[3] the aunts[4] do agitate so about my things. I do hope that Aunty Poppy wont come up till after the first term.

Went up the river in the evening. Very windy. Aunty Poppy took two shawls so we sailed when the wind was with us. We met crowds of yachts & people yachting so it made us feel very aristocratic to be "out for a sail dontcherknow" as well. I'm feeling very much annoyed at being turned off the dining room table by that horrid little servant 35 minutes before supper time. Molly[5] & Hugh are sitting on each other in the sitting room so I have been obliged to come to my bedroom. I think this is quite enough for one day, specially as I haven't had any particular thoughts.

20 August. Lovely day. A little heat mist but very blue sky & sea. Went to the other side in the morning & built a sandcastle with secret passeges [sic]. Brian & Hugh bathed. Boys mended the tent & Hope Sylvie & I bathed out of it ... in the afternoon. It was simply glorious. I went in up to my shoulders & there were lots of big waves that took me out of my depth. Hugh bathed again with us & Aunt Poppy came to rescue us in case of drowning. Went up the river in the evening, Aunt Poppy, Hope, Brian & Sylvie. It was ripping though there were crowds of other boats. We saw Hugh crossing the bridge in a trap. Went on with novel a bit after supper. Jolly fine day.

1 September. Things have gone on in much the same way. It has been rather wet for some time but it got out yesterday (Thursday), & we bathed in the morning; it was glorious. In the afternoon we went to Embleton to picnic .... On the 1st we went home for the match on saterday [sic]... .

2 September. Oh! how can I describe this day! Father turned up in the morning to meet us .... We went by the ... train to Sunderland. We had lunch at Mengs .... Then we went to the match. There were crowds going already. We went to the 2/6 seats & had a splendid view. We saw both teams in the little partition just in front. We saw most of them beautifully. Oh! Rutherford [Newcastle footballer].

"Thou needs must be a rake
Thou makest such hay in my autmnal heart."

I won't try to give an account of the match. It will be put in Molly's book.[6]

But I must say that never in all their glories have I loved them as I do now. This is the team that played on saterday [sic] Sep. 2nd at Roker Park against the Sunderland A.F.C.'s first League team:

Gosnell	Orr	Hardings	Howie	Reeth
	Veitch	Aitken	Gardner	
	Carr		McCombie	
	Left Wing	Lawrence	Right Wing	

Oh, how I longed for Bill instead of Hardings, who is new & nervous … . After the match … . Hope & Father & I went to Meng's [a smart tea-room in Fawcett Street, Sunderland] to tea. We had a very good tea. How can I put down all the emotions of the day? On Wednesday they must win. I'm sure they will. They are sure to be a little desperate … .

3 September. Went back to Alnmouth … we saw a lovely sunset & talked about my going away to school … .

6 September. We will see them again today, hurrah. In the morning we missed the train about half past eight … . Then we started for the 11 something in the motor car, but it broke down on the bank. We were too late to get that train & ordered a trap for the 12.44. We waited & waited but the trap never came. It began to rain & that train was missed … . At last we got the very slow train at 3.3 … . We got to St James' Park about 5 I should think … . We saw poor Andy [McCombtrie] introduced to the mayoress … . Then the game began. We scored in the first ten minutes. At half time the score was 1-2. There was no half time except just drinks as the light was failing. The second half was fearfully exciting … . The end was a draw 2-2 … Manchester … certainly didn't deserve to win. It was a splendid game. What will Saturday bring forth?

9 September. Bathed in the morning … . Very cold but lovely … . Walked up to the station to get the 12.49. When we reached the Central [Newcastle] it was raining heavily. We met father … . Then it really began to rain & … Father went & got us a cab & we bought cheap macs at the Indiarubber place [probably Murton's shop on the corner of Grainger Street and Bigg Market] … after some difficulty we got good places at one end. The whole game was played in the wet. Newcastle was by far the best team in spite of results. Donachie was very good, nearly as good as Gosnell. Appleyard was given offside for the second goal Newcastle scored but I am sure this was a mistake. We went home at half time happily believing all was safe … . Then we got the *Chronicle* after tea. Newcastle United 2 Birmingham City 2. Oh! why was that goal given offside by that silly referee … .

10 September. Went back to Alnmouth … . I went out a walk to Lesbury bridge alone in the evening & met battalions of youths, most alarming … .

11 September. Walked along the beach with Hope in the morning. Talked about school & things. Bought *Northern Athlete & Journal*. Went in the little motor car with Hope & Elsa to Alnwick. We went to see the park. First we went & got a pass from the castle. It was quite alarming. We had to go into a room full of clerks writing & papers & typewriters & things to get it. Then we went to the park, after getting some chocolate … . It was a lovely day & the deer & rabbits were sweet. We walked all the way to the tower & had a splendid view from the top. Then we walked back by the heather looking for some white for Andy, but alas! we found none & was [sic] very disappointed at this & was quite tired as we went back to Alnwick for our teas. We went to a place that was very nice except for the chief lady who was horrid … .

20 September. Arrived at Clapham High School boarding house in the evening; unpacked. Nothing much more but confusion. Asked to Mrs Rounthwaite[7] on Sunday. Today Wednesday.

23 September. Got through the day somehow.

Quotation for 21st

When I think of the happy days
I spent wi' you, my dearie,
And now what lands between us lie,
How can I be but eerie.

How long ye lag, ye heavy hours,
As ye were wae & weary
It was not sae ye glinted by
When I was wi' my dearie.

Same 22nd, 23rd

Alone upon the housetops to the north
I turn & watch the lightening in the sky,
The glamour of thy footsteps in the north.
(when thinking of Hope)
Come back to me beloved, or I die.

Went & bought fancy work in the morning. Went to National Gallery in the afternoon … . Had tea at Lyons. Came back & worked all evening. No football news alas!

24 September. Went to church with Hilda. Very funny curate preached sermon on 'peace, perfect peace'. Dinner most dreadfully long … . I am feeling simply furious at not being allowed to go out alone. Made a plain statement on the subject to Mrs Rounthwaite coming back. Had an awfully decent evening. It was awfully nice to be at a real home. Got Hope's letter off.

25 September … . When I got to school this morning I found I had to go on with my entrance exam. I did Algebra Geometry French & Latin in the

morning and History Geography & English in the afternoon. Read the papers & the *Forest Lovers* in the evening.
27 September. Put finally in Lower V.1 yesterday. I have decided that I dont like Mrs Woodhouse & that I like the Babe very much indeed & that Miss Claradge is a jolly decent sort. Also that I may be able to survive this two years or may leave at the end of the term. Got invited … to tea on Friday & leave to go if taken … I love Hope more than ever every night I am away. Oh dearest dearest Hope how I love you & wish I was with you.
28 September. Things went on as usual. Getting accustomed to my fate.
30 September. Went to Johnsons yesterday & had an awfully good time. They said they would ask Hope for next weekend. Somehow I dont feel very hopeful about it. I do hope it will come off. If only I could see her I would feel much better. Just to spend Sunday with her would be glorious. Oh Hope, Hope I do love you … . How I do hate all this waste of time & I dont think I will be able to get on as well as I could at home. I intend to be as good as possible but I dare say I cant bear more than one term.
1 October. Went to Parish Church in the morning. Wrote before going. Awful evening. Little hymns & scripture questions. Awfully dreadful but got through. Longing for tomorrow's news.
3 October. Various things have happened, in particular news of a draw 1 – 1 came yesterday but no letter from Hope yet. Oh I do wish she would write.
8 October. Wrote to Hope this morning tryed [sic] to tell her all about everything but got hardly anything really told. Oh Hope dearest how I love you, how I wish I was with you … . Yesterday I had quite a decent day for this place. In the morning I just read but at lunchtime we had a sort of beanfeast everyone handing round nuts & cakes etc. until no one could eat any more. In the afternoon we went to Tooting Common & saw a fine sight. Simply crowds of football matches going on … . It was glorious. You felt what the national game was then. Clapham Common was just as good. I never saw such a sight though I hope I often shall again.
9 October. Gyms, I do hate them, in the morning & drawing in the afternoon. Drawing was just as bad as before. I was swimming in charcoal … . I decided to join the sketch club though everyone scoffs. Never mind I got a lovely P.C. from Hope together with some views of Gateshead & Low Fell.
10 October. Played hockey in the afternoon. My hockey ardour was entirely damped by watching the practice on Friday. But now I have actually played I think I may in time become enthusiastic.
11 October. School morning. Dancing in afternoon lots of thoughts about home things. Doing *Old Mortality* for literature & period 1688-1783 for History.
25 October. & then only a week till half term. Oh how I do want to see Hope

again … .
3 November. Went to Cambridge by the 2.35. Hope met me at the station & we drove back to Newnham. We had a very good tea in Hope's room & took possession of Miss Lea's room for me but were afterwards turned out into a spare room. It was all too glorious to write about. It seemed too lovely to have been now & it seemed too perfect to be true at the time I think, but I didn't think much it was such a waste of time. We had a very select cocoa[8] … . It was a great success I think. On Saturday morning we went & did some shopping we bought Sylvie the new Andrew Long & I got my new *Old Mortality* & some vases & jars & things for eating. We did some more shopping in the afternoon & some colleges & watched a hockey match for a short time. Then we had a tea party & afterwards dressed for supper & the debate … . After the debate which was on "Whether civilisation tends to laziness" – it was not very interesting – we went to a cocoa in Marjorie's room, given by Myra. It was very nice … .

On Sunday we stayed in all morning and talked about the novel and C.H.S. [Clapham High School] and all sorts of things. Oh my dearest Hope! We were busy making eatables almost all the afternoon. We made toffee and maron glacée but they were both failures. Then we made an extra special dish of chocolate thick cream and chestnuts served with cream. Then we had our supper party and afterwards a short séance which was not much success. Then I walked home through the lovely moonlight night with Mr Smith … .
6 March 1906. The half-term is really over & I have been looking forward to it for such ages. It seems very sad. Oh how I long for Hope, my own elder sister who really loves me. But I was with her the day before yesterday & 5 weeks tomorrow I shall be with her at home. My dearest dearest Hope!

She met … [me] at Cambridge station of course. Then we had a hansom up to the College … . After that we went to our lodgings & dressed & then came back. After dinner we had cocoa with all the usual lot. Before that we went to *Sharp Practice* … . Our lodgings were nice & I had an undergrad in the next room to me which was rather exciting. On Saturday we were called to the high (table) which was rather alarming.
… . Next morning after breakfast we went & explored the dons buildings which were lovely … . Then we went & had a really good meal at the Oriental. Hope says you need one really good meal a term & we certainly had it … . It is not nice to be back again but this time five weeks I shall be kissing her properly. Oh for seeing her again & she loves me as much as I love her. That is the most glorious thing that I can hardly realise. Perhaps she is thinking of me now. I wonder.
16 March. They are in the semi-finals. Oh Joy! Oh Rapture! It is simply superb and glorious. Surely they can beat Woolwich, surely, surely!

11 April. Came home.

12 April. Read *The Scarlet Pimpernel* which I saw with Molly & Hugh on March 31st … .

13 April. Read *A Great Treason* or rather a little of it & finished all I wished to read on Saturday the 14th.

15 April. Went with Hope … to the Roman Wall. We trained to Hexham & then bicycled to Chollerford. Then we walked to the wall … my bicycle went all wrong so I did not enjoy the ride back as much as I should have liked to.

16 April. Went to town with Hope in the morning & went to see *Peter Pan* in the evening. Got a lovely crape de chene [sic] blouse for London.

18 April. Read chiefly. Went to lunch at Ashfield & Aunt Poppy gave a birthday tea at Home House[9] & each of us a black & white tie.

19 April. Hope left for Cambridge … & after that we went on to town & got a new hat from Aunty Poppy & looked at stuff for new clothes.

20 April. Everything ready to start. Oh, if only they win. Surely they can't lose! Three cheers for Andy and all the United! & for the day they win that cup & the day they bring it home to Newcastle … . Arrived late at King's X … . Drove to Waverley & unpacked … . Went to the 'Little Stranger' at the Criterion. It was very funny I am just in bed at 20 to twelve. There are several other cup watchers from Newcastle staying here.

21 April. Left Hotel Waverley & wandered up & down like many hundred other of "us"… . All was lost. Newcastle 0 Everton 1.

5 June. Been at Cambridge since the 1st. Hope's Trip[os] began on May 28th. They say she is pretty certain of a second!

20 June. … . What a lot of goings away I can remember. The first time to Ullswater when the limes were all out, & the glory of driving through that countryside and along the lake, just in the cool of the evening, after the crowded stuffy saloon & the fussing aunts, and the hours of delay. It was a glorious evening with a low red sun. That was 1899 I think.

28 July. Whitby – arrived here yesterday with Doris & Bertha. The others bathed in the morning. Then we walked a short way along the beach & I read *The Crimson Blind.* In the evening we walked along the cliffs towards Sandsend. In the after supper evening we went to some lovely fireworks on the Spa.

30 July. The others bathed in the morning & went to Sleights in the afternoon. Hope's bicycle went wrong so we stayed at home & went up to the Abbey. It is a glorious old place & I enjoyed it very much. Just as we were coming away we saw a great crowd on the cliff & went up to see what was happening. We saw the Channel Fleet. It was glorious. Eleven big ships … .

31 July. Bathed in the morning but it was shingly & unsatisfactory. Read most of the rest of the day. Went up to the Abbey & read in the evening.

Watched sunset after supper.
1 August. Bathed in the morning. Went to Musgrave woods thorough Sandsend in the afternoon.
21 August. … . Went to Yorkshire tennis tournament … .
22 August. Went to Goathland & had a glorious day on the moor though we could not find any white heather.
23 August. Came home.
1 September. The weather has been simply roasting for the last two or three days, & today was hottest of all 91½ in the shade. I sat & embroidered in the garden all the morning. Then we lunched & went in very early to meet father in the St Andrews' churchyard, on the way up to St James' Park … . The Chadwick band played all the usual things & the sun baked down on about 60,000 people who came to see the opening match of the season between United & Sunderland on the hottest day of the year … It was lovely to see all their dear faces again. The cheering was tremendous when Andy won the toss. The team was:

Lawrence
McCombie Carr
Aitken Veitch McWilliam
Rutherford Howie Appleyard Orr Gosnell

It was a glorious match. I can't think how they managed to play so in the heat. Aitken was hurt at the very beginning but though one of his knee bones was fractured he insisted on going on playing, though he looked as if he was in great pain, poor fellow. At half time Appleyard had scored the only goal & (to use a vulgarism) things looked rosy. Then Bridgett having disabled Andy to give himself a chance, equalised for Sunderland. Still we hoped. But when he again scored, giving them the lead, I own I gave up all hope & I think most people did. Little did we know! In the last 13 minutes Rutherford scored two goals & Howie a fourth! Oh! it was too glorious for words! We left the ground to the strains of "Cock o' the North" and marched out to the sound of the "Dead March" mournfully whistled by some who had come far to see the burley [sic] ruffians well beaten … .
5 September. Read & played patience morning. Went to town in the afternoon & bought a lovely new coat. I got a new belt & a lovely lot of gloves as well, besides material for two coloured winter blouses, one plain red & the other green with a white stripe.
5 September. Read & worked till lunch & then went a walk with Hope to the old Fell quarries on the hill & along through Wrekenton to Black Fell. We saw the sea & Durham Cathedral & miles & miles of lovely country & little villages & colliery chimneys. I think we live in the nicest place in the world. But I haven't been far & I like almost every place I go to. Still I would hate to

live in London & the Lakes would be so lonely. So would Yorkshire & the East Coast, & we are really quite near the sea here. Cambridge would be lovely for most things, but the country round is so dull, & it is far from both sea & hills … & in a most interesting cycling country & yet we can … go to theatres at the finest town in the north! Yes, Northumberland & Durham for me; though if I could have them I would take all the five northern counties! Hope & I discussed our literary work a bit. I read most of the afternoon & evening.

7 September. … . It is more than a year since I began my diary now, & I can look back & see what happened this date a year ago. But I wont read the part about school. I dont think I ever shall till after I leave. It made me feel quite funny this morning just to read Hope's letters to me. And I have a whole more year to get through still.

2 November. Went up to Cambridge by the 2.25 … We gave a cocoa that evening … a poem was read at it by a fresher who is publishing a book. Saturday was horribly wet. Poor Hope had a lecture so I sat in the library & read Bradley's *Hamlet* lectures till she came back. I enjoyed it very much; I sat in the big window at the back. Then we went to her room & lighted the fire … .

9 March 1907. At the Ivanhoe Hotel, London … . It is the match today! Oh it is nice to be out on the spree, tra la! but I wish Hope was here … .

They won! they won! 5-1 … . Dinner at the Holborn & the Comedy to see "Raffles" which was lovely.

3 May. Came home on account of swollen neck … it is glorious to be home. Went to W. Hartlepool with Father, who has sciatica in one leg … . Uncle Eustace[10] subscribed [sic] ointment & medicine for me & nuts & exercise for Father. Came home & had a lovely lazy time.

Sunday. Went to Blanchland in the motor with Aunty Poppy, Elsa, Brian & Sylvie. Glorious. Went to W. Hart. & stayed till Monday … . I hope I shall never fall in love. It can't be very nice even if the man loves you too, & must be too horrid for words if he doesn't. And yet it must be rather nice for some things. Theatres for instance & matches & dances. The worst of brothers & sisters is that you cant rely on them. They may get engaged any moment & not care about you any more. I would be quite content with mine if only they would be content with me. Wednesday the 8th was my birthday; I heard from Hope & she sent me Raleigh's *Shakespeare Condensed Novels*. I got a beautiful feather thing from Auntie P. handkerchiefs from Auntie H. & ties from Auntie C. I am 17 years old. It seems a great age. Many girls have been mothers at seventeen. It does seem funny to think of that. I wish I could do something well. What will I do in the H.C. [Higher Certificate]. I wonder. I wish it was over. I wish it was farther off. What I really wish is to get a

distinction in everything which is absurd! I wish Hope was coming home … .
18 May. … Came home & was greeted with the news that Brian[11] had fallen into a police trap & was liable to a fine from £2 to £10. He is quite a local hero. Everyone is very interested & polite. The trap is on a beautiful straight stretch of the Roman Road near Wall houses … . The apple blossom was out when I got home & I got quite drunk with its smell & the lovely greenness of everything & the joy of being at home. Oh I do live in the nicest place in the world! except about everywhere else which is almost as nice.

We had both aunts up in the morning. It was awful. But at length we got safely off. Oh, it was glorious. We went by the Roman Road and Longtown to Lockerbie … . There are hardly any [speed] traps in Scotland so we went better after that. Bri's experience has made him very cautious … the King's Arms at Lockerbie is a very nice hotel & there is a really kindly Scot at the garage half way through the town. He even took a penny off half a gallon of petrol for two rides up the hill beyond the town. The first Scot we spoke to was very stupid.
19 May. We went a beautiful round, along the Solway, up the Nith valley & we tea'd at Dumfries which is a nice town with a good but expensive hotel … .
15 July. I write today bcause it will perhaps influence my real life. This Monday has really come .. the whole week will soon be over & then there will only be a few days till a week on Friday & I shall forget the Higher Certificate & all its horrors until the results come out … . Oh if only I could do well. Just to please Father & everyone & to prove that in some ways I'm not such a stupid as I seem. That was a silly thing to write but its written now & doesn't much matter. I am not very sorry to leave & yet I am just a little bit … .

A croquet party at Ashfield, Gateshead, c.1865, including John and Elizabeth Mawson, their four daughters and three friends

Ruth Dodds, November 1896 aged 6 1/2 years

Ruth and Sylvia Dodds c. 1900

Brian, Molly, Hope Dodds c. 1900

Emily Bryham Dodds – Ruth's mother

Edwin Dodds – Ruth's father

Grandmother Mawson

Ruth and Sylvia dressing up

Play-acting: Ruth and a cowboy

Home House – the Dodds family home – side view

Home House – part of garden which included tennis court

Home House today

Ashfield House – home of the Mawson aunts

CHAPTER TWO: 1907–1914

'A Glorious time'. Hair up, tennis, clothes, dances, Lakes, writing

1 August. A nice thick black line across the page for school gossip & nonsense are all over now, thank goodness. I have started fair with my hair up & half control over a dress allowance & a light heart to face the world! … . But I was going to write about the Tennis Tournament, not myself. We three girls & father have all got season tickets & are making the most of them … .

I have been having a glorious time this week. On Monday it rained so that we only got part of the afternoon at the Tournament & no shopping done at all. We saw quite a lot of good play though … .

From Tuesday the 6th to Thursday the 16th I spent at Seahouses with the Aunts. The house, St Aidans, is charming & on the whole we had a very pleasant time. The tournament inspired Hope & myself with several stories … . Tomorrow we go to the Lakes, Father & I on my first walking tour. It is very nice to be alive.

16 August. Arrived safely at the Patterdale Hotel with Father, Anna[1] Uncle Eustace & Mrs Daniel … . Uncle Fred arrived late for dinner … . I am sleeping with Anna in a nice double bedded room ..

16 August. Went up Place Fell in the morning. Weather grey but fine .. Everything looked lovely … . After lunch we went to Glenridding & bought father a cap & then onto the lake. It was not as nice as usual because the party was rather large & of course three were rather old men & a little fussy … .

18 August. Walked up Deepdale in the morning & Father & I went up to St Sunday gate in the afternoon … .

19 August. Aira Force in the morning. Glorious Styborough Crag afternoon with Father … . Dear dear Father. I am sorry he's going, but I will have a good time anyway of course … .

21 August. Today we went up High Street by Pasture Beck & down by Hazewater. It was simply glorious. Uncle Fred, Uncle E. & I went all the way.

22 August. Went up Helvellyn, mist rain & very very strong wind. Striding Edge great … Swirrel Edge grand & misty … .

23 August. Uncle E. Anna & I went up Fairfield by Hartsop-above-Howe over Cofer [sic] Pike & across St Sunday Crag & down home by the zig-zag Grisedale. … & after dinner a walk on a glorious moon-veiled night … . Oh it was glorious, the smell of the limes & the clear outlines of the hills, the deep reflections in the great smooth lake, the smell of the woods and the hard feel of the ground made it more than words can say of hills & beauty & gentle kindly feelings & content. I love Uncle Fred.

24 August. Went up Glencorn and down by the lead mines with Uncle Fred. In the aftrnoon we watched the sports, hound trail and sheep dog trials. The lead mines were great fun. They are now working them by electricity all among the decaying remains of the old steam engines & so forth.

5 September. Gardened in the morning. Cut strawberry runners. Then practised serves. In the afternoon I went to the free library … . Then I went & met my papa at the Turks Head & we tead & went to the match. It was a splendid match full of life & vigour in spite of its being the first. They did play well though it was only a draw … .

1 October. Went to a glorious Notts Forest Match 3–0.

11 October. Went to town & ordered my evening dress! Oh! oh! My own evening dress! It is white taffeta & will be simply glorious I know. Coxons are the angelic robe makers in question …

27 October. My new dress arrived on Tuesday. It is simply sweet! Pure white with a broad collar of Irish lace with an edging of the stuff & a dear little trimming with hanging blobs. The edge is ornamented with French knots & there is a rosette of the stuff in front & an adorable chiffon tucker with sweet ribbons. The sleeves are short, of course, & puffy finished with a band of the lace, bows & more French knots. The skirt is plain but for two bands of the stuff. The first assembly is on the 19th of November. Oh, just think of it, it will be glorious.

Yesterday I went over to St John's Chapel in the motor to pick up Father … . It was a grey day & drizzled once but still it was a glorious drive. I wore my grey squirrel fur coat & my new grey skirt to match, Sylvie's grey veil & my green motor cap. The woods were even lovelier … . The beeches were red-brown & the elms green-gold & the silver birches & rowans were glorious yellow.

28 November. I am not keeping my diaries as I should. Here I have been to my first dance & made no note of it! .. I had a very nice time. I danced all the dances but three … horrid cold … I don't know what I shall do at the Flower mission dance tomorrow if it doesn't get better at once.

1 December. Went to the Flower mission dance on Friday with Brian & enjoyed it immensely … . I wore my new white & gold shoes & white silk stockings & lilies of the valley in my hair. It was awfully nice, at the Old Assembly Rooms. They looked awfully pretty … . I liked all my partners & enjoyed all the dances, but I enjoyed my dance with Gilbert Atkinson best. I never think about anything but just the music & the motion when I dance with him. And he never collides with anyone however full the room is, though he hardly ever backs & never reverses. I certainly like a glide waltz ever so much the best. If you must hop you ought to have a jolly partner who talks all the time & never has a serious collision but just little ones which you don't

mind because of the beaming good nature of everyone concerned … . Yesterday I did not get up till twelve (we got in at three).
1 December. Today is the day of the dance! My very own dance at Ashfield.[2] It is very glorious. So is the result of Saturday's match 5 – 1 against Everton away! I have been reading *Pride & Prejudice* … . I must be very sparing of her novels. I must read them apart & one at a time so as to enjoy them as much as possible. I want to write acrostics to send with my presents to West Hartlepool.

A nother Year is hastening to its Close
N o more about now blooms the crimson Rose
N evertheless with turkey, wine & song
A nother Christmas blithely comes & goes.

25 July 1909. The spirit moves me to begin a diary again, not at all for posterity but for fun & myself … I am having a good time this summer. Tomorrow the tennis tournament begins. I know I shall enjoy it tremendously … . I expect I shall write some stories when we are in Wales. Perhaps it will be the *Coldham Candidate*. I have just decided that the work shall be about Gateshead instead of somewhere vague "in the South". It will be rather dreadful to make a conservative get in but I am avowed to forswear all prejudice in the writing of this work, & that'll be a good beginning. [outline of play follows].
9 July. Fourth day of the T.T. (Tennis Tournament) & great fun it has been so far … tomorrow the three of us are going in a taxi! A Newcastle taxi! They started last Monday. Hooray!
9 September. The object of keeping a diary is to write things down that interest you, & so get them off your mind without boring other people. I have become obsessed by a love of news & at present all the news is either budget[3] (which bores me to extinction) or North Pole[4] which doesn't. Of course I am sorry that it has been discovered particularly by an American.
9 May. Twenty is very old! soon I shall be "quite twenty eight or nine". I sent a poem to the *Westminster* today. … Sylvie is going back to school in tremendous spirits … . The little wretch thinks it is "funny to have a sister who writes plays" & I'm not to send her any ——
30 July. Tomorrow is Bank Holiday too, & how sorry I am for the people who are not happy tonight. Such a week as I have had too! … On Monday Hope & I went to the *Gondoliers* … . Tuesday was *Patience*, & Wednesday *The Yeomen of the Guard* … There was the Tournament for the rest of the week … .
1 August. The great news of today is that I have finished the *Pirate* play. It is not much good as it stands but when it has been well polished & arranged I

think it ought to be distinctly possible to act … .

17 August 1909. I have finished typing & going over the "Pirate". I have sent it to Myra[5] … . Myra has answered at last … perhaps I shall write a play that is *almost* good. I'm not going to be depressed about it anyway.
8 September. How dreadfully behindhand I am! Not only with my diary, which doesn't matter, but with everything. With darning, tidying, & above all with the *Pilgrimage*[6]. Well I will copy my last chapter out & so get into the swim again. I dare be idle no longer. Not till tomorrow afternoon after a steady morning's work will I go & get the second volume of the *Journal* from the Lit. & Phil[7]. Oh my darling, darling Sir Walter [Scott]! He is so cheerful at the end of the first volume that I feel now as if I could bear the rest … & yet I know that it was all in vain — that the story of my glorious Sir Walter was a tragedy after all … .

It was a jolly time at Harbottle [holiday] … . I did see something of the life of the shepherds on the fells. Our landlady, Mrs Drummond, had been house-keeper at Kidlandlee, the highest shooting-box in England, an immense extremely ugly place which disfigures the pleasant dale of the Alwin. It's set on a high hill & so blights your eyes from many distant parts – but no matter! Nothing can really spoil the Alwin. We went up there one showery day when you were often drenched to the skin & the sun shone between-whiles. We climbed right up to Sting Head at the source of the Alwin & looked down into the dale of the Breamish … . Hope & I went down the hilltop & then over onto the next hill to Milkhope, where Mrs Anderson, Mrs Drummond's aunt lived. She was a splendid rosy-faced woman, mother of sturdy sons, & made us very kindly welcome though I'm afraid we broke her afternoon. She made us dry by the glowing peat fire & gave us warm stockings while our own hung before it; then she gave us tea – & much we needed it; talking to us the while … she had a jolly, rosy-faced little lad who had never been to school, for the nearest was six or seven miles away. A queer lonely life they lead in the fell farms, & yet not lonely as far as human companionship goes. For they have fiddlers or pipers in every family & go from house to house for snug evenings with neighbours. But they get in supplies of flour only twice in the year & the grocer's cart comes only once in three months. Their fuel they dig on their own hillsides, & often they kill their own mutton & pigs. Poultry & cows they keep, for eggs & milk & butter; if you want beef, the man arranges to meet the butcher at some village in the dales. The neighbours go round & help them in with their hay. And then at other times maybe, the men are called out to help to beat for the shooting parties, from Kidlandlee or Clennel or Biddleston hall. They were carrying the hay at Riddleshope, the most shut in & abandoned place I ever set eyes on. At Riddles, lower down the burn, is a big farm-house, with kitchen garden & hay-croft on the hillside, very trim & prosperous it looked. They were driving in the sheep & many a hundred were bleating about the place as we went by. The farm's big in more senses than the house, & rich & well stocked. They kill all their own mutton. Four shepherds live in the big house & the young master, Ord by name. The only woman about the place being a housekeeper & a dairy lass. I wonder if the lasses set their caps at this rich young Ord! Well we had some taste of his kinsfolks manners – the Ords of Shillmoor. Over the hills we went to Bygate Hall, which for all it's so near Coquet Dale is out of the world enough in all faith. And between shyness & fear of stopping & hindering hard-working folk we didn't stop there for tea. But hardly were we down in the Coquet dale than the rain came on, straight & heavy so that every drop seemed to sink in; & there on the other bank we saw a big farm. The garden was full of roses & the house front bowered in purple clematis. The door was open & an ash-tree all covered with berries stood before it. A very big place it was, with no lack of dairies & coach-houses, very trim & sweet with bright polished windows. And what with our weariness & the wet, Hope said to us other two, "Let's beg shelter there & maybe they'll offer us tea". We gladly agreed. So we crossed the bridge & Hope knocked at the door while the Heathers & I sheltered under the ash tree. But no-one answered the knocking for long, & the Heathers [friends of the Dodds] pointed out some blinds were down, & suggested cheerfully that there was a corpse in the house. At last a servant lass came & we made our petition, to which she said she would ask the mistress if we might shelter. We might have said … "Here's sorry cheer" as we waited in the rain. Back came the lass & bid us go round to the back door which we did with some shame, & were led through stone passages, scrubbed wondrous clean, where our wet feet betrayed their passage. And so into a fine old kitchen. Gleaming brasses hung on the white walls & on the dark beams of the ceiling hams & herbs in bunches, & bacon. The smooth stone floor was rubbed so clean that it was near polished, & white deal tables, creamy to see stood by the long wondows. A great fire blazed on the hearth & beside it sat an old woman on a single chair. She was terrible to see, very very old, in a black silk dress & an immense white cap; & all the while we were there she never moved nor spoke, nor as much as glanced at us. For we were greeted by a second old lady, maybe not more than sixty, with iron-grey hair & bright black eyes, & to her I talked. She bade us sit down & dry us by the fire & even took our coats to dry them. But here things went badly from the start. Hope wore a long skirt which, when wet, dipped badly & hindered her walking, so the Heathers had made her an elastic band, to raise it round the waist. As ill-luck would have it, Hope had forgotten this, & when the young mistress of Shilmoor took her mackintosh it was very plain to be seen that

Hope had "kilted up". Our hostess made no effort to hide that she was very shocked … . My shoes she said were too thin. Nothing daunted I told her Id just worn out a thicker pair. I told her the way we had come. What I said should have pleased her, for I praised the size & appearance of her nephew's farm at Riddleshope … . I made no secret we were very weary & that we were wet she could see. But I pleaded indirectly a losing cause. "It was but four miles to Harbottle", she said – a very short way. And somehow her Northumbrian tongue seemed to give point & emphasis to her speech; & Hope said that the rain was stopping & hastily put on her coat again. So we went forth, & indeed I think even without Hope's skirt our quest had been hopeless.

So we went forth of Shillmoor with a much poorer opinion of it than when we went in. There was no honest handshake at our parting with the black-eyed mistress, & I hope she heard some of her own scorn returned in my too emphatic thanks. Very very long & weary were the miles home. Sore were our feet & stiff our legs & the rain ran down our uncovered hair, & trickled uncomfortably in little streams over our faces. And every hill I doubted I could climb & every descent seemed no easier than climbing; & when we passed Barrow Peel, I thought I could go no further; & when we passed Angryhaugh I knew I could never get home to tea – … . Only the shame of being a coward, & the wonder what the others would do with me prevented me sitting by the road-side & saying I could go no further. The others, as I suspected at the time, felt the same. How it was done, I know not, but in spite of my firm conviction to the contrary we reached Harbottle at last. We could take the shoes off our sore feet, & the coats off our wet backs, & oh! we sat down & … such a tea! Never had I had the like – no not even in Easedale Tarn Hut! New bread there was, made by our adorable Mrs Drummond, & soda scones, & sponge cake, & apple pasties & spice loaf & oh! the heather honey, from her sister's at Angryhaugh, & her own apple jelly redder than rubies, & blackcurrant jam & marmalade, & fresh butter from Milkhope on the fells! Balm, too, for our other wounds. For Mrs Drummond told us all about the Ords – very rich they were & very mean. Ill liked through all the country side, & seldom well spoken of. "If you'd gone to a shepherd's house" said she "they'd have given you tea & welcome." And indeed I believe it true. Witness our welcome at Milkthorpe … .

4 September. I've sent away my dear Napoleon play! … .

15 September. Miss Horniman sent back my play with a note which I can only regard as intentionally insulting! Still, I would like to meet her – to see if she has a nose.

25 September. Swaledale. Here I am in the dales & the ghosts of the Pilgrims are all about me. Oh Aske, Robert Aske[8] you are my patron saint at present

… . Oh if only I could write your story as it should be written.
26 September. After terrible rows at breakfast, I am able to withdraw into the garden & write a bit … . Days like today I've pledged myself by my motto not to write about. ["I only count sunny hours" – sundial motto]
27 September. Today has gone much better – swimmingly in fact, and tomorrow, thank Heaven! I go home. But oh! how I wish it wasn't so hard not to be bitter with the Aunts. My beautiful plan of having one good day – of seeing Richmond & Easeby is entirely crushed, spoilt & made worse than if I'd never thought of it. If it's fine all the Aunts are coming too. If not, they've made me promise to go straight home without seeing anything. Oh I do think they're mean! if Poppy is not so bad as Harry in malignancy, she's worse in other ways. And to have to go with all three in one miserable landau! And then to have to get them lunch! It's enough to turn one grey! I'm ashamed to pray for a shower tomorrow morning, yet somehow I hope there will be one.

12 September 1910. So I begin a new diary without finishing the old – a highly characteristic proceeding! Oh if only I could keep pace with my life on paper … my thoughts are so frightfully interesting to me now that surely they will always be worth a smile. The great thing in my life at present is Sir Walter Scott … . I spend my days in a kind of dream at the wonder of the world – but too much I fear at the world as revealed in books. But the (Scott's) *Journal* at least is pure human nature. Still I must take heed not to become too bookish. For then my people [in Ruth's story and play writing] will not be people as seen by me but shadows of other writers ideas of people … .
16 October. I am being disgustingly lazy. What have I done to the *Pilgrimage*? Not looked at it! What *have* I done then? Oh read … books on the South Seas … & eaten sweets & slacked about. Disgraceful! I feel just like a South Sea islander, so comfortable & happy & well-fed, though not so well exercised.
22 February. The Dance is over at last, after all our planning & toilings! My twenty-first birthday dance – a reality, it went very well. The Aunts looked sweet & Ashfield charming – I never saw either look better, & I think almost everybody enjoyed themselves … . I had my hair done a new way – in bandeaux over my forehead & with my silver lattice band across the front. Hope thought it made me look sadder – like Mary Queen of Scots ..

Of course I wore my new dress that Aunt Poppy has given me – by the way the bill has not come yet – I wonder what it will be! It is a dewdrop & blue rosebud chiffon over a white satin underskirt, with a deep band of crushed pearl trimming & a waterfall fringe of crystal beads round the bottom. Little white satin bows down the left side. Crushed pearl & chiffon bodice, sleeves with a slash on the outside showing arms through the chiffon,

& caught up with tiny bows & finished with the fringe. Hurrah!

The Cotillion went splendidly. Mr Forster gave me my fan … . I gave Gilbert my favour because he seemed a little left, but really Mr Mountain was last, so I wished I had noticed him … .

I am so glad it was successful. Bless the dear little Aunts! How good they are to us! Molly made all the sweets, which were very much appreciated, & Harriet's turkey was all eaten, which was a triumph for the Aunts, for we all foretold that people wouldn't want it.

8 May 1911. This is my 21st birthday, & like any sentimental person at such a time, I am just in the mood when a diary seems almost a necessity of life. Yes, this has been the most – what shall I say – the most troublous, serious year I have ever lived through. Sorrows & sickness have been very near people that I love & it is very different when they come near from thinking of them beforehand … [but] … . I have the power of putting the thought of it out of my mind – of reading & dreaming & living in another age – in another world – almost of ceasing to be myself. I have always encouraged this power – it has been such a comfort & joy to me … I will try to live & dream & do both well … . I don't know why I write like this but I can't write about the things that press on my heart … .

4 June. God save the King! It's Coronation Day. Things change a mighty deal between the ages of twelve & twenty one. Nevertheless I still believe in the King as an idea, & the Constitution, which however clumsy, is still the best way of governing yet evolved. And I believe in ourselves – the Nation – & the territorials who are off to camp … . And I believe very much in being a good citizen & paying your taxes honestly & being just to your neighbour & loving your country … .

25 June. Patterdale Hotel. Mawson brought me over in the white car yesterday … . We went by Alston full in the face of a great West wind that chased great clouds across the sky & now & then brought up a bar of blue & a gleam of sunshine went scurrying across the moors. Oh, it was glorious, glorious! … Hartside … there at our feet lay the country stretching – stretching to the silver line of the Solway – to the clear blue outlines of the hills we came to see. And beyond the Solway faintly we saw the outline of Criffel – the king of the Scottish side.

2 July. I've been doing my accounts. I've kept them very carefully for the last two months & I've made the horrible discovery that I spend about £6.10s a month! And my allowance is £28 a year – & a very good allowance too! What am I to do! Of course if it wasn't for the Aunts I would be bankrupt. Well I'm determined to learn to keep within my income after all. I've just been having a birthday burst & I won't count the big bills that have just come as an ordinary thing – though one has to get new clothes sometimes. *But I swear*

1 I will spend no more on sweets except for other people.
2 I will spend no more on *expensive* books nor on novels.
3 I will buy no more coloured shoes & stockings (woe is me!)
4 I will take better care of my gloves.
5 I will only go to the pit – unless I go at somebody else's expense.
6 I will take no more snacks at Tillies [sic][9] – at least I'll try not to.

Six pounds a month is no less then £72 a year and I *ought* to be able to live on that! Instead of which I spend it on clothes, books & sweets & holidays. Oh shame!

3 July. I have paid my bills. I will spend nothing this month except on trams & stamps & will walk to & from Shipcote [Picture Hall] every night to economise … In future I will pay cash *whenever possible* … . Another resolution – rather a premature one. I will try to have something – at least ten shillings over at the end of every quarter & this I will pay in. As to resolutions about not spending things they are legion – too many to put down. The only things I know I must spend on are the D'Oyly Carte Opera Co. & the County Tennis Tournament & they are hard at hand!

24 July. Hurrah I've found a new sport – flying! … . I saw my first aeroplane! It was beautiful to look upon like a big dragon-fly & we saw it about five minutes after the time when it could first possibly have arrived – about a quarter to nine. I heard some people cheering & looked out of the breakfast-room window & there it was! We were all sitting round after breakfast & some people were getting ready to go to Gosforth & see them land. I rushed to the door shouting to Olga & Hope to look too … . It was very near, just over the top of the hill & it did make me feel so excited to see it going so smoothly & fast & high; afterwards we found it was Vedrine's – he is a jolly little French mechanic & was first all the way to Edinburgh. He only stopped a few minutes at Gosforth & the others weren't in time to see him … Hope & I went up to the old church quarries. There were crowds of people – we seemed to meet everyone we knew. And there we sat & watched half the morning … we saw one more plane … . And these are the only planes I've seen. I did hope for some today, but though it is very fine & clear it's so dreadfully windy that I'm afraid they'll all be delayed again. All the others went to Gosforth. They saw one Frenchman start (the second) & Valentine, who they say is very beautiful, both start & fly away again. Then towards evening they saw Hamal arrive in a car. He had left his plane slightly damaged at Backworth … . He too is extremely handsome interesting & also English. When he alighted at Harrogate the poor thing fainted, but insisted on going on as soon as ever he could … . I am quite air-mad

3 August. Ten days since I last wrote & such a lot has happened. I've been six times to the D'Oyly Carte Opera Company – *Iolanthe, Pinafore, Mikado, Gondoliers, Princess Ida* & the *Yeoman*. Also I've got the money from the *Westminster* for my W.S. Gilbert Examination [an article] – a whole guinea – but the paper hasn't appeared yet & I wonder if it will on Saturday. Very useful it will be too, for Hope & I are going a walking tour up the Northumberland Coast with Myra & the Heathers … . [at the tennis tournament] lovely dresses, particularly grey quaker costumes with white collars & cuffs, & black velvet, which must be dreadfully hot this weather. Of course there are lots of other colours too – particularly blue. Blue & grey are *the* colours this year … . I'll describe my own dress. It was only a coat & skirt, light serge, rather a pretty soft blue, with a black watered silk collar, black buttons & braid in straight horizontal lines on the side breadths of the skirt & coat. There's almost something military about it. Of course the panels front & back are plain & the skirt is narrow – though not so *very* – but enough to be in fashion. I wore a black crinoline Napoleon hat with it with a black ostrich feather on the left side. Blue silk stockings (with clocks), black shiny patent leather shoes, with round American toes & square American heels, black gloves & vanity bag, & a *very* slim umbrella. Not a gay outfit perhaps, not startlingly beautiful or up-to-date but still neat & natty –
… . I'm surprised to find how little I've written in this diary about my dear play – *The Ratisbon Milliner* . My last summer's diary is full of the *Pirate* which I'm now revising whenever I can find the time … . On Tuesday … . Aunt Nellie sent back my play. In point of fact she didn't like it at all. I can't deny I was a bit disappointed … . I spent all Tuesday morning writing to her; I'm afraid I didn't take it in quite the right spirit; I'm afraid I let bitterness creep in & Aunt Nellie (the dear!) sent me a delightful letter, afraid she'd hurt my feelings … . Mean to revise … . Hope has been a perfect sister these days (when is she not?) and let me pour forth to her all my sorrows … .
7 August. My head is full of new ideas for my *Pilgrimage* play. I must make it a real tragedy, not a mere chronicle. It shall be the tragedy of Robert Aske. [Plan of the proposed play]
8 August. … . Yesterday I learnt *Bonny Dundee* by heart. I'm glad I did, I shall never forget it now & it's well worth the knowing. But it does run in my head. … .

[Most of Diary 4 consists of poems copied & composed, plans for plays etc & a booklet of a walking tour in Northumberland glued into the back.]

27 May 1914. Lakes. There is nowhere in the world like How Grayne for bluebells. High upon the Rampsgill side they almost cover Gowk Hill; the lower slopes are all blue – bluer than the sky and yet yesterday was a blue day too, with wonderful white clouds and bright sunshine almost all day long ... I came over from Bannerdale to Boredale Hause ... . Sylvie & Uncle Eustace went by the hilltops so I was alone. I almost think I like this best, though it is very solitary of me. It is so nice & selfish to consult no one's feelings but your own. The day before I went up Place Fell three times! The first time was out of mere lightness of heart before breakfast, I little knowing what was before me ... . The second time I carried Mrs Bremmer's [another visitor] painting things. She settled down to paint Kirkstone and the valley head from the very top of Place Fell. So I went down to fetch her sandwiches ... . After lunch & the cutting of sandwiches I started on that weary second ascent. I thought I should never get up. Even the Marseillaise failed me & I could only prevent myself resting every three steps by counting my steps up to a hundred & not stopping in between. By this scheme I got on faster. I got up in an hour and a quarter & found Mrs Bremmer happy as a queen quite unconscious of the fact that it was nearly three o'clock.

24 June. I have had no time for journals & trifling with baby[10] here, & tennis, & the Suffrage[11] Oh dear! ... .

3 August. The Tournament is over. This used to be a great event for description in my Journal, but now that "seven long years are past & gone" since my first ... well thing are different. It is not that the gilt is off the gingerbread exactly; I am really singularly like I was then, & I enjoy it much the same as ever, & if I'm not quite so excited that is partly because we don't seem to have such queer & amusing characters just now. It was a quiet tournament this year ... . My dress was the one I got for Elsa's wedding done up. All the black is taken off & over the cream-coloured silk & lace foundation I have a panier tunic, cream ninon with tiny flowers in orange, yellow & amethyst – especially the last. The panniers are short in front & fall almost to the bottom at the back, very full, in a kind of soft box-pleat. So the lace shows almost all round; the overskirt is finished with a narrow net ruching. The bodice is all covered with the ninon, very full magyar sleeves finished with a flounce & a deep lace cuff at the elbows. The sash is perhaps the triumph; I got it at Fenwick's by the greatest piece of luck, for the salmon pink & amethyst roses tone quite beautifully with the ninon; it has a long tail in front. My new hat is black lace, quite transparent with a dull blue ribbon round & an amethyst bunch of poppies at one side. Shoes & stockings white, of course, white gloves, black bag & Sylvie's amethyst pendant at the neck. Other people were far more gorgeous.

On Friday we saw the first soldiers guarding the High Level [bridge], & Father laughed at it so much that we all laughed too. But now Germany has invaded France without declaring war, & no one knows what will happen.

Perhaps we were butterflies dancing on the brink of a precipice after all … I for one don't give up hope. Countries have mobilised & not fought before now, & I seem to remember the calling out of the Naval Reserve not very long ago. It may not be all true one hears of Germany. Sylvie says it makes her feel very creepy … .

4 August. The Conservative papers say that we are as good as committed to war, but I can't help thinking that it isn't quite so bad as that. After all we haven't declared against anyone, nor anyone against us. Germany may still withdraw from Luxembourg & leave France in peace, though they say that the French & German ambassadors have left Berlin & Paris & I suppose it is not very likely, for Germany doesn't seem easily frightened. Sylvie & Margaret were in town this morning & all grocers are shutting & crowds of people around them & round the newspaper offices. We are having some trouble ourselves; Hunter's haven't sent the butter, but we think this is only owing to the rush of business & it will arrive alright tomorrow … .

High Street, Gateshead, in Edwardian Times

CHAPTER THREE: AUGUST – DECEMBER 1914

War changes everything

5 August. So war is actually declared against Germany, & now for the life of me, much as I hate it all I can't see what else we can do as Germany has attacked Belgium. Belgium would probably not have dared to insist on her neutrality if she hadn't believed that we would uphold the treaty. I feel a confidence which I hope will be justified in Sir John Jellicoe. It is wonderful how everyone trusts Sir Edward Grey. We know he wld not commit us to war if it could be avoided with honour.

I am so glad Father keeps urging us not to show panic, & be frightened, or alter our plans. Sylvie (as a young housekeeper she is naturally anxious) wanted to get in stores, but Father says no; we must act sensibly even if no one else does. MacGorram wanted him to put the people on half-time already, but though he thinks it will come to that he is not going to do it in a hurry. I am so proud of him; he isn't one of those employers whose one idea is to save themselves … . I am worried about the autumn suffrage work too … .

It has come so suddenly. A week ago we never dreamt of it. There was a small war far in the East, that was all … .

Father went to Durham today in a carriage full of the 8th Durham Territorials. They got in at Chester-le-Street – pit-hinnies all who had never obeyed any man's order, rowdy lads, with the pitman's bow-legged slouch to serve for marching strong & short & ignorant but all in the highest spirits. The sergeant was a better educated man, who herded them in, but then let them hang about the window shouting to their people. At last as the train moved, he shoved the lads into their places, & leaning out shouted "Tak' care of the bairns!" to his own wife. There was another civilian in the carriage. "I suppose you're dying to meet a German?" he asked one of the lads. "A German? By! if a meet a German A'm off!" In Durham station Father saw a train with field-guns & munitions bound north.

Father can't think how the pitmen are ever to be drilled into shape; but they are better guarding the coasts than at home, for all the pits are laid idle.

6 August. I went into Town in the morning. There were a fair number of soldiers about but everything was very quiet. In the evening we went in again to Dr Williams'[1] for a meeting about the action of the Union. We are to offer help & I must get out summonses for a committee meeting.

7 August. It is all lies about the great naval battle. Yesterday came the true news that a German mine-layer was sunk, & I felt bad, almost worse I think than if it had been a British ship, for I had decided we were in the right – & yet to kill people to prove it! This morning we learnt that the Amphion was sunk by one of the mines. & I felt different. But now I could cry over both of

them. Thy saved about fifty Germans & about half the Amphion's crew. How I pray for Peace! Almost all day I am a kind of unhappy wail inside, a mere feeling of protest against War. And yet I believe us right. When Belgium appealed to us how could we say "Peace is dearer to us than your freedom, dearer to us then our promise: we stand aside." When Germany offered us peace if she might work her will on France, & walk as she pleased through the neutral states, kindly adding she wld leave their boundaries (but not their colonies) when she had quite finished with themselves could we have said "yes, peace before all! We truckle to you." I don't care for national prestige but I do care so much for honesty & right; & as God made the world force can only be met by force at the last. We cannot make Germany behave by moral force for how is it to reach her? All the neutral states think her wrong, but an armed nation looks at public opinion – for a while. And yet can anything be so wrong as to sail out, in the sunlight, on the sea & look for an enemy to destroy her? … . To die like the men of the Amphion in defence of our honour – yes, our honour, a tattered, torn, dirty rag, perhaps, a thousand times denied reviled & cast down, & yet a flag still flying, never altogether lost – & surely, surely worth dying for. Yes, it is worth dying for, but is it worth killing for? How can I tell? Men have always held it so. How can I tell?
8 August.

Heavy my heart as lead:
And the grey sky rains:
Mourning the blood new-shed
Mourning the helpless dead:
It is our grief wide-spread
And the South wind plains.

Out on the wild North sea
The squalls are flying.
Down in my garden dear
Shiver the flowers like fear
And in the height of the year
All seems dying.

This is the sort of thing that ought not to be given way to. I am thoroughly ashamed of myself as I ought to be. And in a sundial Diary too!
10 August. Aunt Edie has come & I feel much better, though Father is as gloomy as ever. She says it will do us good, make us more unselfish; though of course she thinks it silly & useless in theory, like everyone else.
14 August. … at this point Father said he heard cavalry. We were all sitting in the breakfast-room after supper, there certainly was some rather faint cheering from the direction of the George 1V. I slipped on an old waterproof

over my best dress & hurried out down the Lane, Sylvie following me. There was a convoy passing – endless it seemed, great waggons pulled by huge strong cart-horses, one after another. At first they were regulation waggons covered with karki [sic] tarpaulin, but by & by the square boxes [of ammunition?] were left quite naked on trolleys, & finally farm carts – anything that would do. They were not heavily laden to the eye, but two great horses pulled each, with a third at the tail, for hills, Father thought. There was always a man driving & one walking with the leader & another with the tail horse, besides one or two walking beside. Between each cart was a mounted man, & officers rode up & down, shouting orders, which were generally "halt". There was one long halt – twenty minutes I should think & I went up to tell the maids. We had all come out before this. It is very exciting to have seen a real convoy. They were all so hot & tired poor things – both men & horses.

All the public houses close at 9 p.m. now. They say that the first night the soldiers were in Newcastle it was a disgraceful sight. The Chief Constable put his foot down with a bang. "You say you're here to guard the bridges" he said to the military authorities. "My men would guard the bridges twice as efficiently without any fuss; & what's more they would keep the town in decent order.

"Take away your drunken soldiers," he said," and let me do the work they can't stand to do; or, if you won't, at least make them behave." We went to the Picture Hall tonight, but we didn't escape the war. We saw the King reviewing troops. But first of all they shone on the King & played the National Anthem & we all stood up & cheered. Then followed popular characters – Sir John Jellicoe & Lord Kitchener & Sir Edward Grey; Roberts & Beresford & Winston Churchill. Not the German Emperor to boo! We keep ourselves respectable at the Shipcote; not that I've heard of it being done anywhere; I hope not … .

18 August. I've been visiting the Reservists wives, & it is dreadful but thank goodness I feel as if I was doing something & it is such a comfort … .

21 August. What a blessing it is to have a garden & books! I really don't believe I could have borne these last few days if it hadn't been summer & all the flowers … anything beautiful & strange is cheering, I find, however sad. It is commonplace things like dirt, & fleas, & pawning your clothes, & 20s/ a week being as much as anyone can expect, however many children there are that put me in the dumps. Then again I have to work because of the S.S. [Suffrage Society] scheme of children's clothes & I hate work. Still I have much to be glad about. Blessed be the name of the *Common* Cause! [Suffrage Journal] … By its means I have conquered the difficulties of "separation pay" "compulsory allotment" & "voluntary allotment," together with other useful things, & now I can look the world in the face & give a reason for what I do.

What depresses me most is to be lectured on the duty of not giving way & not doing anything but spend lots of money on ones own clothes & amusements. How I hate the *Times* with no sympathy for any but the well-to-do! Men are so apt to be like that: to think that if youre comfortable youre worthy, & the poorer you are the worse you must be. And no relief is to be given to women who are found to drink! What about their children? And would I (for one) drink if I lived in one of those holes? I should think so! … . I don't know what to think of the German advance so I think nothing.

26 August. I couldn't have believed that any public event could have changed life as the war has done. After all your thoughts & doings are so utterly changed, even a German invasion would only intensify it – it wouldn't really be so different. Now the Germans are victorious I feel as if the worst had really happened, & yet we all go on calmly enough & the papers have not lied to us about it after all – unless it isn't true that the British fought well & are not to blame for the retreat … I should like to pray for victory but somehow it seems a contradiction to expect God to interfere in a war … God is God of all the world & how can he fight for Germany or England? May he be with the women of all who fall? And yet – O God send us better news. Our hearts are so sore with failure … . I am not behaving well myself. I tire myself over the Reservists wives & the children's clothes business & then I am cross, depressed & the others tell me so & make me worse. I must try to be cheerful, but I do see the worst side of war (& of peace too) down Grosvenor St. & my cases run in my head so that I dream of them at night.

… . Hugh volunteered for the Navy – as an engineer of course; but they say they don't want him. How lucky we are. Conscience satisfied & all well. It took him a fortnight to persuade Molly to let him go. If I was a man I think I should join the transport. One wants to do something, but it would be so beastly to kill people … . Whatever folks may say about patriotism & a righteous war how can it, individually be right for a man to kill another? The Holmses are taking in a Belgian baby. I cant help thinking that we ought to. Of course it would be horrid if it was a nasty child, but if one got it small enough that would hardly show.

… . Hope is doing the *Pilgrimage* index & Sylvie mending sheets. They are both splendid at "Business as usual" & put me to shame. I can hardly even read proofs through with patience now. I must try to be more sensible.

6 September. Bad news today. Of course it comes from the Admiralty – apparently we are never to hear anything more about the Expeditionary force, except occasional casualty lists, & from German news, the towns that the English & French have lost … .

10 September. With good news for two whole days I feel quite bucked. I do admire Sir John French's dispatch & I want a good full copy of it to keep for myself … . The Walkers have heard from Bert, & he is a long way off on the Loire, with his hospital, & dying to get back to the front. He says the Germans do shell hospitals, but I feel sure it must be by accident. It must be so difficult to recognise a hospital on a large field of battle … . In the same way with many other "atrocities." Both sides say the others use dum-dum bullets, but I have heard of no real cases, on the sworn testimony of surgeons … . Then the driving of women & children before them – that may be a mistake; fugitives on their own hook being mistaken for shields … .

I am trying to judge the Germans exactly as if they were our own troops, for we may invade Germany (I hope) & there may be English outrages then, though I really do think our men are kind-hearted & decent on the whole. But when men are mad with excitement dreadful things do happen, like the German who took a revolver from a surrendering wounded Englishman & shot him with it. That sounds to me like a man in battle fury quite unconscious of his acts in any ordinary sense … . The Indian troops are a bit on my conscience, I must own, but they are probably better disciplined & more under control than any European troops, & we have a free press to watch them (no, not exactly …) Perhaps if it comes to invading Germany they will send them back to the border, as Wellington did the Spanish troops after the Pyrenees. I hope so anyway … . I mean it would show that we respected German feelings, for any white race could not help disliking coloured men entering their country as conquerors even more than folks of their own colour. It may be a silly prejudice but there it is. And to be as horrid as possible to Germany because of what she has done to Belgium would only make matters worse, though I'm afraid no one will ever see it. To burn Nuremburg will not give us back Louvain. To punish German women & children for what Germans have done is nothing but injustice, & as bad as thinking that to send Germans in England to sea in leaky ships would be a just return for the laying of German mines.

10 October. Yesterday we sent off our first parcel to our soldiers. They were a great mix-up of little things. I do hope that they'll get there eventually … .

What have I been doing today? "De luxe!" as Flambeau said. And it has been so nice. All the morning I read at the Lit. & Phil. … it was so pleasant & peaceful. I went out & had my usual baked beans & cup of chocolate – an excellent but not very sustaining meal for ninepence. No, I will not compare it with the 2d meals of the mothers. For one thing it wasn't worth it. For another it was much less in actual bulk, if that goes for anything, & can hardly have been so feeding, as it was strictly vegetarian. And then what about the poor waitresses; I wonder how much they are paid. I always assume not enough, though it means 2d extra; & they don't love me a bit the more for it.

After that I hung about to see the soldiers marching to the recruiting meeting in the Tyne & Pavilion [theatres]. We did see one lot … with pipers playing *Tipperary*. Nice little boys they were.

11 October. … . I wonder if it is true that the Germans will soon be here.I heard some sort of explosion in the middle of last night & wondered if it was a Zeppelin bomb. But I didn't believe it & never will till one drops.

15 October. For the first time in my life I am travelling to London First [class], & it is so wonderfully comfortable & smooth that I really thought I could write … & Aunt Poppy will be so much less tired this way. I cannot really believe that I will see Bob tomorrow …

17 October. Baby is, of course the most beautiful boy in the world. For the rest I don't want to say much about my visit here so far – in a sundial diary. I will let off steam to Sylvie tomorrow, as I may be as pungent as I like to her … .

24 October. Today I walked to Selsey – ten or eleven miles each way. It was a perfect day & I saw it right through from daylight to dark. Mrs Stag had come to clean the rooms, so I had a day off … .

2 November. My last night here; my last tea with Bob wriggling on my knee; his farewell bath … . My last moonlight walk on the long grey beaches; it was a perfect night, & I bade a tender farewell to the English Channel & the Owers Light … . Also I have swept the stairs for the last time … . I am dreadfully sorry to leave, yet how I hated it when I came! That was partly my monthly time coming on. Not that I shan't be very glad to get home again … .

9 November. … . Go where I will I can't leave the war behind. Today I went to the mothers & babies welcome & the mothers told me stories of their husbands at the War. Poor souls! They are such nice women too … . I met a wounded soldier in the Lane & talked to him. He said it was terrible at the Front & hadn't even one good word for it. He was a dear. He thought the Germans very wicked (& he had seen what they did) but he gave his great-coat, in bad weather, to a starving German prisoner. Oh, why doesn't the war end?

14 November. Today I got a letter from the Front. I am so pleased & altogether above myself. It is nice of Lance Corporal Bustard to write to me just because we sent him a parcel. He wrote on Oct. 20th & I got it today. So of course he had only got one parcel, the one we sent on the 16th. It is rather a formal letter, but that is quite correct in writing to a stranger. I shall stick it in here when I get it again. With wild generosity I sent it on to Sylvie who's at West Hartlepool for the week-end. Of course it was partly for swank, so that they could all see it. Besides it really is partly Sylvie's, for we all sent the things & all paid for them. I have been making up letters back to him all today

.... Days we sent things to Bustard & Bartley
Oct. 9th
Oct. 16th
Nov. 13th

16 November. Bartley's first parcel has come back marked "unable to trace." It is such a disappointment & I hope nothing has gone wrong with him .... The great happening of this week is that I have found Joseph Conrad. When, I wonder, did I last discover a great author? It is wonderful, like falling in love .... It was *Lord Jim* I brought home ....

22 December. Myra (a VAD) ... says the men are just splendid & laugh & joke when they are "all to bits" & never grumble. The VAD live in two cattle trucks on a siding. She describes trying to feed 400 hungry men on bread & butter & tea, with only one small spirit stove! .... "... they inspect our bedrooms at 9.00 a.m. every morning (or say they do) & play around with our collars & waistbands as if we were 13 instead of all over 30 & many over 40 & put up notices to the effect that the credit of the Detachment depends on the use of the clothes brush you may form some idea of what we are putting up with "pro patria" .... Of course they have put us in a cleft stick as it were; once we have had a sight of our men return as they do we wld sell our souls & give our bodies to be burned for the sake of giving them half a glass of milk, so if Mrs F. or the CO choose to inspect our toenails or make us repeat a hymn before retiring for the night we shall do it, but my God! It isn't as if they hadn't enough to do with the things that matter, e.g. store & food without waist-belt parades & clothes brush drill". She is 12 hours on duty & 12 hours off & finds it difficult to get enough sleep.

12 December. We have had a p.c. from Bustard, saying that he received the tobacco parcel & "distributed the cigarettes among his comrades".

17 December. Yesterday, Wednesday, The Hartlepools were bombarded by German cruisers. And they got safe away! It seems almost as well as if we might have no Fleet. They keep on saying "If only the Germans would come out – " & when they come they never catch them. The Swanicks are safe, although we didn't hear till this morning when we got a p.c. from Aunt Edie .... I never knew the news until I got in late for dinner, as I had been down in New Gateshead & then up at Wrekenton, giving out clothes. I met such a nice pitman there with a family of eight & a ninth expected. He had been working all night up to his knees in mud, on hard stone & coal, & he thought the trenches couldn't be worse. I agreed with him. He showed me his pay packet with the offtakes – such a lot, sharpening pick, weighman's fee, doctor, stone in the coal he had hewed & heaps more. The family were all in rags & very dirty, but there was plenty of the rags one over another, & they were fine healthy-looking boys & girls, well-nourished & quite content. They didn't in the least want anything; they looked at the clean clothes I brought with interest but without desire. However they were very kind & accepted what I brought rather than let me think I wasn't appreciated.

I will put down all about the great news when I hear it at first hand. I am going over on Saturday.

20 December. I have heard so much about the bombardment that I don't know however to describe it – it is much too confused in my head. But I must try. To begin with the Swanicks:- Everyone while in bed heard loud noises & whistling which they attributed variously to trams, timber-movers & the town's own guns. Anna went to Margaret's bed to ask her what she thought it was & Margaret said "Nothing, go to sleep again." However everyone began to dress & the firing became so much worse that they guessed at once that it was the enemy; so they began to pack & have breakfast. But before the bombardment was over the surgery was full of injured & they all set to work to help. They filled the dining-room, drawing & kitchen. They had all sorts of cases & two people were brought in dead. The worst injured were sent on to the hospital & the slightly wounded Uncle Eustace attended to & Anna helped him, & Aunt Edie & Margaret boiled kettles & comforted the ones waiting their turns & warmed the shaken ones by the kitchen fire. It must have been a terrible time, but they were so busy that they hardly noticed when the firing ceased … . When it stopped they were told that it was only a lull & wld begin again soon much worse. They seem to have been busy all the morning at least. Three shells fell within a hundred yards or so of the house – one at the station, one up at the "Mail" Office, & one in Church St. On the whole they seem to have been less scared than merely excited & worried & they are all very well & brisk. They really got a worse fright on Friday morning when news went round that there wld be another bombardment, a Zeppelin raid & heaven knows what. They all got packed again & when I arrived early on Saturday I saw their baskets waiting in a neat row in the hall. Very nervous people left the town on Wednesday, But crowds & crowds left on Friday, a regular exodus … . The firing only lasted 30 to 40 minutes but the loss of life was terrible – nearly 100 dead in the two towns, counting those who have died since. I went round to see all the damage here yesterday, & all the worst places in Hartlepool this morning. … Houses look very disreputable with their plaster gone, & their lathe ribs tumbled loose here & there – with their slates blown off & the roof-beams left gaunt & naked, – with great holes in the walls & all the glass broken, with the whole front of a bedroom gone, & all the pictures, walls fireplaces & furniture exposed violently to the glaring light … the chests of drawers leaned drunkenly forward, their drawers full of things starting out, the curtains flapped about the torn edges of the rooms where no sign of window was left, & some bedsteads were all crushed up. We saw all sorts & degrees of damage, from walls merely pitted by flying fragments, or corners just touched by a passing shell to whole upper stories demolished & houses pierced from side to side. One shell had gone right through the Baptist chapel, across the street & somewhat injured a house beyond. But the chapel was utterly wrecked inside & wrecked plaster & lathes out of all the windows. St Hilda's church had a hole in the roof & a kind of scrape across one side of the tower. The East window had a fragment of shell through it & the stonework was chipped. The Rectory was a perfect ruin. The damage in Hartlepool looked worse because it was nearer together … . There was a thick mist over the pale blue sea & through it we saw a man-of-war moving. Somehow I don't feel so enthusiastic as I did about Britain's watchdogs. Though now I am calmer, I will admit that it was probably mostly bad luck that made them miss the Germans.

If I wrote all the stories I hear I should fill another book this size. … we saw several wrecked houses with little notices on the doors "All safe. Please inquire at the Bank," & "Present Address so-&-so." The engine-house at the waterworks had all the slates blown off; & the gas-works (by the way) were on fire at one gasometer – very pretty the girls said. Wednesday was a lovely morning & everyone agrees that the Germans saw the Hartlepools at their best.

The town was stuffed with sightseers yesterday come to see "the bombardment" as it is called.

… . Today I went to the great Christmas Dinner at the Mothers & Babies Welcome. It was a success; I think the women thoroughly enjoyed it, & their babies, most of them loved their toys. They had roast beef & plum pudding & (I think) turkey & mince pies, but I didn't really see, for I was nursing babies all the time. The tables were decorated, the little Xmas tree looked quite gay & jolly, & the mothers all turned up in their best; the babies were resplendent. There were songs music & addresses. I pretty nearly cried when they played "Its a long way to Tipperary" & all those soldiers wives sang. It was partly the tune, which is somehow very touching, & partly because it did seem such a long way between them & the men they love. I notice the popular version (sung by street-boys) has for the last line "But we're not downhearted yet," which somehow makes it sadder still.

I have forgiven Professor Pollard[2], which I never thought to do. It comes very appropriately at Christmas, & in time for me to go to his lecture & clap if I am pleased. We wrote him a polite letter of thanks for all his "helpful criticism" & added we were sorry he did not seem to like the book[3] He wrote back & said it was he that recommended the University Press to print it! And several almost pretty things about it bringing us better things than money. Also the ghost of an apology … so considering he is rather a little tin god, &

it appears he never meant it to be rude but only has an unfortunate manner, I have forgiven him. Really & truly I did think I hated him very much & more than once he made me cry.

The entrance to the old Quaker Meeting House in Pilgrim Street where Ruth Dodds started attending meetings of the Religious Society of Friends in 1918. This section of the street was demolished in the 1960s to make way for the building of the Pilgrim Street roundabout.

CHAPTER FOUR: 1915 – NOVEMBER 1918

The War, work – the night shift at Armstrong's and the family business

23 March 1915. Fittes has been here – Leading-signalman Edward Fittes. He is rather short but spare & chunky, & he has a nice sailorly face & a beautiful complexion, – ruddy not tanned. He wore a gold anchor on his left arm for leading signalman, & crossed flags on his left, for passing an examination, & a gold star on either side of them for another, & a gold star on the other side of them for a third. He was not at all shy. He came very late to tea, because he had lost his way & wandered up the Lane; … & he stayed to supper & on till 10 o'clock, yawning all the time, so we know something about "the Service" now! We know where the Grand Fleet is. It is in Scapa Flow. And Fittes is on a Flotta at the big signal station in Stanger Head, & he signals for the opening & shutting of the big boom that closes the flow. For the fleet goes out sometimes for a short cruise, & the colliers & armed liners are always coming & going of course. At the beginning of the war the Fleet lay there without any boom to keep the enemy out. If the Germans had only known, their submarines might have destroyed our battle Fleet as it lay at anchor. But now all the openings are blocked except two close to the Flotta, & the big boom is across the Sound of Hoxa. It is made of great pieces of timber, held in place by trawlers, & below torpedo nets down to the bottom of the sea, weighted down. One morning the boom had shifted; there was a dent in it, where the spars had been pushed inwards – by a submarine trying to creep in in the darkness. But she came too late. The grand Fleet lie behind their defences now … .

Fittes spoke a good deal of the view of the lights & the driving storms. The place was stamped deep on his imagination, though he didn't like it. Commander Stukely is head of the signal station on Stanger Head – he is "liked" very much by Fittes. He is very rich & has a big place at Bideford & didn't censor letters when he should because he "understood what nonsense one writes to the girls at home" … . In the Fleet one is always having "spasms". When a lady was seen on the mail boat there *was* a spasm on the *Magnificent*! When news of the East Coast raid came, there was a spasm & no mistake. Jellicoe was on his hands & knees praying the third fleet to get there in time to intercept the Germans!

Jellicoe is very much liked, but when he came the Lower Deck was disappointed in his appearance. He doesn't look a bit like an admiral, Fittes says. He is short; that's why he's always photographed three-quarter length. And he is *quite* bald; that's why he always wears a cap or cocked hat in the pictures … .

Winnie Churchill is much liked now, as he had increased wages & mess allowance & reformed punishments; at one time he was not liked & the crew of one ship mutinied, trying to get at him. ? what wld they have done; hanged him at the yardarm or thrown him overboard? Fisher, I gathered, the Lower Deck can't abide. There is a song about him – how he messed up the Fleet.

20 May. I meant to begin this book on my birthday, but the news of the *Lusitania*[1] came & I hadn't the heart. Since then I think it has been the worst time since the war began – worse than the German advance, much worse than the sea losses, worse than the *Louvain & Rhiems*. Because it was not of ourselves we were ashamed before, only of humanity … . And now not only have the English nation disgraced themselves in that the rulers gave way to the evil thoughts of the mob, but all humanity is lowered. The Germans are worse than we thought – there was not the ghost of a chance for escape for those babies – I wont think of it … . And the gas – that we are to use too. O, if anything could make one hopeless this month would – the month of May when the roses were to have crowned our victory. Alas, alas, what good will victory be if the Germans have dragged us down to their level! What will it profit a man if he gain the whole world & lose his own soul?

7 June. When I was in Murton's this morning & had just bought a nice green waterproof to keep off the soft hill rain [for a visit to Harbottle], & a nice navy blue bathing dress to bathe in the dear yellow Coquet, a young shopwalker dashed into my department to say that there were 14 Zeppelins over Hull, that the whole town was destroyed & 7 porters killed in the station alone. According to Father's latest when he came in this evening, there were only 2 or at most three airships; & the docks were or had been on fire. The evening paper said that 5 lives had been lost in a raid "on the east coast." I hope it is no worse.

Against this we set the sinking of a submarine off Tynemouth, which took place today or yesterday. 14 of the crew are on a ship in the river. It is said to be the U28, an oldish boat … . I'm glad some of the crew were saved; at least I think I am, … .

8 September. First Autumn Suffrage meeting. Miss Tooke on Women under the Insurance Act. I was a good deal stirred, but what can one do?

[*11-18 September* walking holiday – Hexham – Barrasford – Simonburn – Bellingham etc.]

1 October. … . We have heard from our prisoner in Germany & he likes our parcels, especially food, & he writes a good hand & no one else is sending him anything. Today in town we bought him books (which he specially asked for) good long stodgy old-fashiond ones like the *Moonstone & Nicholas Nickelby & The Golden Butterfly*.

2 October. … . hope I shall not find the work at Armstrong's[2] … dull.

However that will only be once a week at oftenest. I am very much excited over the scheme … . Sylvie & I went to Fenwick's to see the munitions overalls. They are both pretty & useful … .

I am very pleased with my new winter clothes. They are not an extravagance as I simply couldn't do without them. Greeny-brown covert coat with wide belt falling to a little below the knee; full very short rough tweed skirt, a good true brown which goes exactly with my shoes & stockings. …. then for hats I have the fluffy brown felt with the yellow scarf (this looks very nice though not a fashionable shape this year) & the 4/6 Fenwick smooth felt … brown with ribbon to match & two little green feathers in front. It is pretty & simple as well as cheap; & its pet name is Budge. Mr Taylor has done up Sylvie's furs & made them beautiful; she looks so smart in her new navy-blue coat & skirt, her wine coloured hat & the furs. She puts me altogether in the shade. But I don't mind. My things are much warmer.

7 October. … . Sylvie & I are to go together to Elswick for our training on Monday & Tuesday (heaven send my leg is better); but these things are as nought except to swank before ones friends, they are of outer life only. Oh, Ruth, Ruth, why dont you buckle to & do some real work.

12 October. Our second day's training at Armstrong's is over & I am too sleepy to write about it.

13 October. If only the *Pilgrimage* would come out this would be one of the most exciting months of my life. Both Sylvie & I enjoyed training at Armstrong's immensely; we were shown how to work the indexing machines for time fuses, & Sylvie was on one or two other processes too. I was on the same machine nearly all the time, learning from a very nice little girl called Annie Peacock; she was only twenty & had worked at Armstrong's four years; she was pretty & fair & very slightly made, much shorter than I am, & she worked her machine beautiful [sic]. She had a sister in another shop & her father had lost the sight of one eye by the explosion of a shell here. She told me lots of things – how one night last winter about eleven o'clock all the lights went out; the buzza had sounded three times, which meant that they were turned off on purpose. For four & a half hours those two thousand girls waited in the dark, expecting Zeppelin bombs any moment. It was bitterly cold with the lights off, some screamed & some fainted, & some sang in chorus & some to themselves, & presently some lighted their gases & heated up their tea on them. As for Annie, she went into the next shop among the older girls & had a good sleep. She says it is terribly hard on night-shift; the girls take it alternate weeks the hours are seven to seven; twelve hours out of twenty-four in the great gloomy echoing shops, where the artificial lights are always on & the rushing of the machinery never stops. Outside the sunlight falls & the winds play on the river, but at this time of year the girls can hardly even see the sun once a day, for they go to work in the morning fog, & dark has fallen long before they come out. Yet they don't seem to think their lives hard; they are full of talk & fun, & all sorts of silly school-girlish little jokes run up & down the shops. Some are pale but others again have the most blooming complexions under their coloured cotton caps & becoming blue aprons. It isn't true to say that working women never smile; all these girls had pleasant open smiles to greet us with; perhaps it is true of older women – married women with big families, & the dinner & the washing always on their minds. You don't see them smile so often but even they haven't really forgotten how. It will be lonely on Saturday when the girls are not there; I had plenty of time on my hands when Annie's machine was being changed by one of the fitters – young men in boiler suits with vast collections of spanners who drift up & down the shops resetting the machines when they go wrong – to look well round at the ones near me. They are all so kind and friendly & a wonderfully good-looking lot of girls too … a few were beautiful. I was told there are 2,000 girls in shop 40, but then one hears many things; certainly there were a great many, several hundreds in the parts I saw, & goodness only knows how big it may be. On my left as I sit at work is a narrow gangway, piled with "bodies" or bits of fuses in trays, unfinished & in all stages of development. Beyond the gangway the benches begin, & at my end they are very full of very young & gigglesome girls packed very tight on the seats & washing in the methylated spirit baths. We were told … one of we weekenders on this job was overcome by the fumes & had to be carried to the cloakroom where she slept six hours; while others (abstainers) became quite tipsy & very gay. At the benches all sorts of filling, polishing, burnishing & fitting together goes on by hand; the machines used there are not machines at all, but are tools or helps to the hand work. It is all very fascinating & one could spend weeks passing from one to another & watching the different workers, if one was learning exactly how a perfect fuse was made. The girls do not know much about it except their own bit of work. Most of them do not even know from whose hands their parts come to them nor to whom it passes on. The benches [end] at the gangway & the machines begin. Behind me is a line of machines on benches, hard to work as the girls on them have to stay all the time & hold a lever in each hand … . Opposite in the corresponding place on the other side of this part of shop 40, is another continuous line of machines, making brass rings, I think, but I never saw clearly; & in the space between are the indexing machines, which stand each one apart, with a seat beside it … they are not difficult to work correctly … but a beginner is very slow & fumbling compared to the perfect ease & precision of the old hand. All beyond on the right of me are more & more machines in great complication so that the men & girls threading up & down with the heavy trays of bodies are always making blocks. And the foremen & fitters drift up & down constantly too, now adjusting a machine, now altering it for a different kind of fuse, now merely eyeing it suspiciously from top to bottom, to see if anything is shaking loose. And if you look up into the mysterious heights above you see all the belts, big & little, broad & narrow, turning, turning, & the dim shapes of the big power wheels above; & all the while the wheels clatter clatter, & the tongues chatter chatter on the benches, & the electric lights in the roof glare with great eyes down on you, while one little light carefully watches each machine. There is an overhead lift in the next shop & you can look over the partition (it is quite low) & see it hurrying up & down, carrying great shells & lumps of metal & all kinds of things, & dropping them gracefully in the right spot … . As for the people who live there they are nice. "We are all friends here," said one of the girls, & indeed they seem to be, with one or two exceptions, such as a Belgian whom the girls are sure must be half German, because he is so unpleasant & called one of them an "English dog," which was certainly just like a German spy in a play. Annie pointed him out to me & he had a horrid face. I am sorry I shan't see Annie again, & so was she. She goes on night shift next Sunday evening, so we shall just miss every time. The rest of the weekenders are nice & I'm sure we shall get very friendly with them, but they are not quite so interesting as the regular girls. Miss Lindsay, our distant cousin, & Mrs Harden, her sister, were with us for training. But unfortunately they have been put on the other shift, so that all the Gosforth people may be together; so we shan't see them; we had tea with them yesterday at the Canadian, the new teahouse in Grainger St (buckwheat cakes & maple syrup)… .

Annie said that before the war there were 250 girls at Armstrong's, & now there are 8,700; I wonder if she got her figures right. We go on night-shift on Saturday – ten until seven in the morning. Goodness knows how we shall get home.

Father is quite pleased about our work & tremendously interested in all we tell. He has been swanking about us to the Quaysiders who are working at Elswick … .

14 October. I hate war & I hate killing & yet I am right to make munitions. I thought once that I could not, but since then I have changed my mind – & the need is much greater, & our men write saying that every shell helps to save their lives. I admire the German women who are working day & night for their men, & shall I not imitate what I admire? I cannot stop the war by holding back, but I & my like may shorten this war by working. And I cannot escape blood-guiltiness by sitting at home idle, for as I honestly think this war unavoidable & our cause just I am in soul as guilty of it as the soldiers who are fighting my battles & the ministers who declared my mind to other nations. Thank goodness I have no time for thinking these things when I am actually at work.

15 October. Today I am almost quite better of my bilious attack. Went into town with Sylvie in the morning & got our pink employment cards at the Elswick Labour Exchange. Had a snack at Coxon's; I know this is a thing we ought to give up, but I really was feeling quite faint this morning. I hope I shall be all right in the works tomorrow night; as a precaution I went down to the Drs tonight & he gave me a new medicine. He also urged me to exercise, & I walked home on the strength of it. There was a bright half-moon but she did not save London from the worst air-raid yet. Well, I suppose she has seen worse things but its hard to remember anything more cruel than dropping death on all those people laughing at the play & forgetting real sorrow in imagination for a few hours … .

Last night I wrote a paragraph for the publishers announcement of the *Pilgrimage*. Poor dear book, how I did love it once. I wish I could write history again … .

October 17. Sunday. I can end this journal with my first shift at Armstrong's. I thought I would have a lot to say about it, but I haven't. It was a dreadfully drunk Saturday night we had to get there through, & pouring with rain. We did not get nearly so tired as we expected, though I admit it was a great joy to see the first signs of daylight through the shop roof. We walked out from the Central [station], carrying our bag & mackintoshes & weren't so very tired. Indeed the way didn't seem long. Some of the weekenders on our shift are nice, some horrid. Everyone of the Wks people has been nice to us so far.

25 October. When I was at work in Shop 40 on Saturday last the spirits of the girls that work there every day seemed all around me, & this common-place, vulgar, music-hall-like song came into my head & I nearly wept over it. On Sunday when I thought of it I felt too ashamed to write it down. But today I got a book of poetry by one Ford Madox Hueffer out of the Lit. & Phil. & the preface is all about writing poetry out of emotions roused by the things you are really in touch with & see & feel every day, even if they are of necessity in vulgar language so I wrote it down after all.

Annie in the Shell Shop

Father's in the hospital,
– There's accident's a heap –
Doctor says he'll save one eye, –
And three at school to keep!

Food & coal & clothing
Are dear as they can be,
But Annie's in the Shell shop
Where Father used to be.
Seven days day-shift,
Six days night,
Twelve hours darkness
Twelve hours light
Far away beyond the sea half the world at stake
Working all the weary day for
England's sake

Tommy's in the trenches
Giving someone beans;
Jack is in the North Sea
Hunting submarines
Mother gets rheumatics bad
She can't stay on her feet,
But Annie in the Shell shop
Keeps the children neat.

Working from before the light
Till after day is done
Annie in the winter time
Hardly sees the sun;
But though amid the roaring wheels
Not a note is heard
Annie in the Shell shop
Sings like any bird.

Are you shocked when Annie
At the picture-hall is seen?
Pray, didn't you enjoy yourself
When you were seventeen?
Leave the old to scrape & pinch
Against an evil day
Annie from the Shell shop
Has earned an hour's play.

"More & more munitions!"
So the soldiers plead,
Armies in their thousands
Are making good the need.
Who says we'll be beaten?
We know it isn't true
Annie of the Shell shop
Is going to see us through!
    Seven days day shift,
    Six days night;
    Twelve hours darkness,
    Twelve hours light.

Somewhere out across the sea
Half the world's at stake;
Working all the sleepy night
For England's sake.

6 November. I had a good day at Armstrong's yesterday & did 108 fuses. I was very glad it was not night shift, as I have rather a cold … . Certainly I was not lucky in my weather for beginning my business life.[3] I am getting more used to the shop now; I secretly wish very much that I could be in the Office with Father; not that I dislike Turnbull, but he is rather fussy & gets on my nerves, & it is always so delightful when Father comes in at twelve. But of course I shall soon get used to Turnbull.

I have learnt some things, but there is heaps to learn. I can post up the Ledgers, & the Bought Ledger from the Cash Book, & keep the Long Day Book, & take orders on the telephone pretty well (but its difficult before one knows the names of all the firms we deal with & all the things we sell). And I am beginning to learn which office-boy belongs to which firm when they come round for things, but this will take a long time coming. How sleepy I am; & I ache; it is very nice just to sit in front of the fire & bake; I stayed in bed till ten this morning. I feel it rather a hardship that I should only have one Sunday morning a fortnight, the night-shift one not being at all the same thing. Yet I enjoyed Armstrong's very much, & I am not half so worn out as I was … . When one is there one forgets colds & all else in the intense excitement of the work. Certainly I never find it monotonous. Every new body is a new thrill; every finished one is a triumph or a disappointment. Then things going wrong & the fitters provide a certain amount of amusement, & some of the people we are with are nice – & some are not, & it all provided matter for conversation. It was very exciting to get paid; I got

11/2 & Sylvie 11/9 – I suppose because I was ragging [finishing the metal edges of the shells] one night, & I don't think one gets so much for that. I lingered to talk to Mrs Harden, so I was the last person to get paid & was greeted with cheers; I afterwards heard that 5 people had never claimed their pay at all. Mrs Watts had rather a nice story about a very proper lady who was much horrified at being told on arrival that she was to spend the evening "ragging with the foreman"!

9 November. Yesterday was Sylvie's 21st birthday, bless her. We all opened banking accounts under Father's direction; I at the Quayside Lloyd's & the others at the Gateshead one. We had a grand birthday tea at Ashfield … besides much money Sylvie got a magnificent dressing case, a brooch, a suade (sic) bag, a railway rug etc. Today was lovely on the Quay, high wind & bright sunshine on a laughing river, & both the towns so clear & bright; but I was not so bright I was very stupid. I must try harder.

11 November. It is very beautiful on the Quay. It sounds rather silly put that way, but how else can one put it? I always did think the two towns rising so steeply from the river were fine, and it always made my heart jump to see them from the High Level, whether it was a fine clear morning gay with blue sky & red steamer funnels on the river, or grey & misty with the sun round & red & solid over the roofs, or fading cloudy evening with a thin white haze on the river & streaks of pale gold & delicate pink sunset behind the Redheugh Bridge. But now I see the two towns & the dear Tyne itself in a hundred new ways. From the Swing Bridge it is not impressive – at best it is quaint; on the Quay it is both quaint & something more – "something quite grand." And then the High Level itself. I have crossed it a million times & never knew (how could I?) that it is beautiful, full of massive dignity & strength, standing firm on its double stone piers, with a kind of heavy grace in the curves of its iron girders,- & yet not too heavy either – it stands perfectly poised & safe, while the passing craft "creep under its huge legs," & the tugs "peep about," it is friendly & majestic & serviceable – more wonderful even than the walls that the gods built to guard Troy.

And that is only the beginning of the beautiful things I see – the square Tower of St Mary's black with age, older even than the weathered rough stones of the keep that, high up the opposite bank, seem to stand shoulder to shoulder with the square solid gravity-laden Moot Hall; & between these two last (if you take the left-hand footway as you cross to Newcastle) in a contrast that fairly strikes your eyes so that you can hardly look away, rises the Spire of St Nicholas, lightly pinnacled, fairly soaring towards heaven, with its intertwined arches & shining vanes. This is ahead to the left; to the right is All Saints, false classical like the London churches, & like them again in having a cheerful homely look which makes up for the lack of beauty … . All Saints stands high too, a great attraction in itself, & below along the Quayside the big blocks of offices tower tall & solemn, with a stately look too, & in front of them the steamers come to berth & the sailing ships (they bring ice) with their slim masts & network of rigging, & all the Quay is littered with kegs & bales & packing-cases, & the trains of waggons on the little railway puff up & down, & the stevedores shout or slouch about waiting for work … . And looking down the river to the bend it seems all crowded with shipping. When a really big ship passes the Swing Bridge with her tugs before & behind she is generally a Gov. boat, all painted grey, for service carrying food & stores to the Fleet. And sometimes a submarine goes up & down & sometimes a German interned liner, painted grey with Government broad arrow mark, working for us too … .

All this I saw yesterday when Father sent me to Mr Richardson's office to get an order for 5,000 memorandums; it was my first attempt as a traveller & the order was really assured already. I went into the wide dark doorway in Dean Street, up in the lift, & after groping along a dark passage came to the office; it was a lovely surprise to find that on this side the building faces onto the East End of the Cathedral, & there outside rose the Spire against the sunset sky. The girl clerk in the office was nice & seemed quite interested when she saw from the card that I was Miss Dodds. I know they gossip a good deal on the Quay (& why not?). I wonder if even a poor humble person like me entering a little firm like ours is a piece of news? I have given a very confused account of a great many different things, but really the Quay is rather like that, very confused & bustling (yet leisurely too), & all sorts of things together, & full of interest & excitement, & always a feast for the eyes, from 9 o'clock in the morning when I first see it, till 5 at night, when it is quite dark & the few faint lights still gleam on the water where there was once such a glow & splendour of them … .

18 November. *The Pilgrimage* has really come at last. It is so very beautiful & big & magnificent that it quite takes my breath away. It costs 30 shillings the two volumes! So no one will ever buy it, that's clear. I wonder if anyone will ever read it? I am tremendously pleased with it, & yet I don't seem excited the way I expected to be. Perhaps the reviews will stir me up. But now I am so busy the days pass by in a kind of gentle dream … . Even the bad news hardly seems to touch me now.

28 November. We had a rather nice time at Armstrong's last night & I made friends with Billy the foreman of the benches. He has been there years & saw the first girls taken on 16 years ago come Easter, & saw them all sent away after the South African War so that there were only four left. "So I know all their ways" he said "I've had some experience of women – I've studied them." "I wonder what the result is?" I asked. "The result is I got married," said he triumphantly. Now was not that a pretty answer & a nice compliment to us all?

3 December. Since Tuesday things have gone wrong & I have been rather miserable now & then – we all have … . Other people's brothers & brothers-in-law are being killed every day. So what if Brian & Hugh have lost their jobs? I hope & believe they will soon get new ones … & it is another comfort that their Knowledge is far more valuable to their country than their fighting abilities.

… . I hold my head far higher now I know I am worth something, if it is only 5/-a week! (And there is the Armstrong money too). And I believe if I set my hand to it I might earn more yet by silly articles for the magazines … .

11 December. This week Father is ill & Brian staying here with a very bad cold; but apart from this things are much more cheerful. Not in the world at large, but with us. For Hugh has got the job at Samuel White's, Cowes, the very first one he applied for, & it is the same salary & a much better position, more future, much larger works & a good old-established firm. So we need not fear that Molly & Bob will starve. Sylvie has gone up (yesterday) to take charge of Bob while Molly goes house-hunting in Cowes … . I am longing to hear from Sylvia; by all accounts Bob is a perfect Terror (though of course very sweet) & I think she will have rather a time. Hope is compiling a book of essays – hers & mine … . They printed my music-hall song in the *Common Cause* – very badly, especially the punctuation & besides made a dreadful howler in quoting from my letter

… . How beastly it all is – this trying to frighten men to enlist. I sometimes wish that I had never been born, or rather that I had been born in the dear quiet Victorian days & died the summer before last when everything was so sunny & lively & no one thought of war. But in those days I used to think if there was going to be a great war I hoped it would come in my time. I did so want to know what was going to happen next. It may be that I will live to be glad yet; for if ever this war is over (& wars do end somehow) we may hope that the generation after us will live in peace … all that has happened will not be so dreadful as conscription in this country. It is all so wrong & wicked. If our men will not fight because they believe it right then we should make peace … . If they take Brian I don't know how I shall bear it … .

31 December. … . I am glad the year is ending tonight. One can't help thinking that the next one *cant* be so bad … .

6 January 1916. How beastly everything is! We are worse than the Germans, really, because we knew better once … . And now "military ends" are getting the better of us, & soon will carry everything before them. And as to the hidden brutality, I have always known at the bottom of my heart that this is in us too … .

16 January. … And what a coward I am! With all the others alive & well I have yet let myself get horribly low once or twice lately, & worried myself over little things of no importance … . I don't count one or two rages with myself for being stupid in the shop … . When a person with no business capacity becomes a clerk it is no use expecting to be a dazzling success all at once.

19 June. Sometimes I have a curious feeling I'm not really alive except when I'm in the country. It seems that every minute that is wasted away from the growing & falling of the leaves – the blooming & seeding of the flowers – is lost time … .

2 August. Why shd I be so miserable? But I can't help it. What is England to me? … . Why does she let herself be led by an evil old man who has brought her to this shame? and yet – & yet how can I help crying – how can I help praying for us all, that we may be saved from sin? … . Oh what wld I give to be able to do something now – something tonight – in time. I pray & pray & pray, but prayers are not answered – for hundreds must be praying like me … if we could speak I know what a shout wld go up for mercy, what a pitiful weak malicious shriek for cruelty. When I wrote the *Pilgrimage* & wept I little thought I shd live to weep for a treason execution myself … I cry easily. I feel as if I'd cried pints for Roger Casement[4] already – & yet I care very little about him really, poor gentleman. It is a finer end than he deserved for trying to induce soldiers from their oath – which take it how you will is a mean thing to do … .

24 March 1918. I want to finish up this book altogether & begin a new one when I go to the Lakes *this* week – yes, it is this week now … . I don't think I'll put anything at all about the War into my new diary. I can't bear it; … how things have changed (since the war seemed justifiable). First the Irish Rebellion – or rather the suppression of it, showed how little "the state" cared for mercy & the rights of small nations. And we – heaven help us, – we were apathetic, many of us consenting. … then last summer when we deserted Russia in her dire need & refused the Stockholm conference,[5] & drove her into the straits we now so bitterly accuse her of being in! I wonder why L.G. changed his mind, first accepting & then rejecting the conference? Oh, if we had taken our opportunity! Certainly I will join the Labour Party, for whatever may be said against him Henderson was statesman enough to see the true state of affairs, & all the time submarines & casualty lists, & food scarcity & paper prices; & far worse even than these hate & despair & cruelty & military despotism getting stronger & stronger… . And now the Germans smashing us in the West, in spite of our superiority in money & guns & everything. It makes me miserable, even more miserable than our offensives last year, & that's saying a good deal … .

Easter 1918. Scale Hill Hotel, Loweswater

28 March. We trained to Cockermouth … . the hills are covered with snow … . Lovely tea by a great fire in the room looking out on the fell, with daffodils on the table – daffodils filling all the vases, & nodding out in the garden in the rain. Such a jolly big double room for Hope & me … .

29 March. Very wet first thing so did not take sandwiches. To Buttermere & back by road … early tea & walked round Loweswater; glorious! Evening got out clear & blue & sunny; snow on all the Fells; Great Gable & Green Gable standing out fine & clear up the dale like Japanese pictures, like the high alps, like dreams … .

31 March. … . Went to Ennerdale by Floutern Tarn. Glorious walk over hills fine views across Buttermere & up the Hause Pass. Other side disappointing at first, but looking up Ennerdale most glorious; it is a very beautiful fine wild lake, with great craggy fells at the head. We had a cup of tea at the Angler's Inn & our own sandwiches, & walked back by Loweswater … .

1 April. Heavy showers but long intervals between. Walked to Seatoller over Honister … started back immediately after tea, & got to the top in 35 mins … against a strong head-wind & heavy rain. We went back by the other side of the lake through the woods; how all the becks were shouting & laughing! Gradually the rain drew off, & as we crossed the fields to Buttermere village the sun came out & lighted up the higher slopes. All the way down Crummock we had the most glorious sky, pink against the deep blue, slowly fading into dusk it was almost dark through the wood, though the radiance still shone in the west over Loweswater, faintly pale & primrose. The owls called in the woods & the blackbirds were still singing round the house when we got in very late for dinner … .

2 April. We walked over to Keswick by Coledale Pass in the first & only really fine day that I had. It was really heavenly, such a wild narrow winding beck-course leading up & up into the inmost chambers of the hills; & then up to the crest of the ridge, leaving the beck as a little waterfall on the right, & there was a slip of Crummock behind & Skiddaw before & such a sense of height & space & hard work done! But we were only at the beginning of our troubles, for we turned out to be in a little attic valley, perched up on top of a great wall of crag – Force Crag – with two fine waterfalls down its face … hard to find the path … lost the first train of course!

7 October. In the train, coming home from West Hartlepool … . It was a Sunday afternoon that Uncle Eustace brought in a "Mail" with the German peace offer. I was simply shaking with excitement, but I had enough self-control not to argue with him when he began to say that we must never sheath the sword while one brick of Berlin stood upon another & that sort of thing. It was terrible; I ran upstairs to pray, but couldn't quiet my nerves … . Even if peace comes it comes too late – so many lives lost; so many hearts broken. None of the men of "my lot" are left alive now, I think. But there are still the little boys. If only we can make peace & save all the little eighteen-year-olds that they are taking every day … .

12 October. A week of all sorts of rumours & unrests. The Thursday lecture was on George Eliot, & all day the town was agitated by rumours of the Kaiser's Abdication. I almost half believed it, because such strange things do happen … . What can ever make up for all that some of us have gone through. How many mothers must think bitterly that peace has come too late for them. Friday Hope & I went to the ILP [Independent Labour Party] hall & heard an inevitably dull address on the League of Nations; … .

7 November. It has come thank God! The Armistice is signed. I write in the shop about five o'clock. A girl from the Brewery brought in the news about ten minutes ago. It is true I suppose; I can hardly believe it yet … .

8 November. And after all, it wasn't true. This is Sylvie's birthday; a dark wet November morning after a wild night … .

Everything has been going wrong at the Quay lately, but I hold on tight & hope for the best. I have a terribly big stock of paper at high prices; but no matter. There is money behind our business, & even if we lose a good deal, we have enough to see us through.

10 November. Today came news of the Kaiser's abdication. Hope & I got a paper on our way in to meeting … & saw it then … .

11 November. The End of the War. It really is true at last; the Armistice was signed at 5 oclock this morning … . Still we cld hardly believe it until we got a paper, & all the buzzas began to go, answering the bells, & the sun shone, & people hoisted flags, & there was such a noise & wonder & all quite true at last. So we all shook hands & announced a holiday, for the war actually stopped at eleven, just before we got the news. For an hour or two or three – I hardly know, I was walking about first with Hope & then with Margaret Joyce, whom we met in Cloth Market – there was such a crowd before the Town Hall all the time, & the bells ding-donging away, so that if the Lord Mayor had made a speech no one could have heard him possibly. Then we went to Lawson's & to Tilleys to get sweets for Hope's Play Centre children. We got two lbs plain for them; & then we all three had coffee at Tilleys – which I don't think I've done since the War – the War that is now over. The orchestra played God Save the King & we all stood up; & followed it by other national airs; & the staff cheered. Then we walked about the streets & Hope went home – such crowds & crowds of people, & little flags, & big flags on all the shops & buildings & crowds of children waving flags, & crowds of children marching with flags & tin cans & guys but I suppose they are Kaisers now. And all the people had flags & red white & blue ribbons, & there was no traffic except now & then a big car or motor dray loaded with munition girls or wounded soldiers or festooned with flags; & the NER [North Eastern Railway] men were letting the little dirty children ride in swarms in the empty rulleys. All the cars had stopped & the tramway men & girls came marching down the street singing, & as I was at lunch at Carricks, fine decorated cars, packed with drivers & conductresses went down Grainger Street, cheering & waving. People would cheer for anything & every here & there were soldiers giving away scraps of paper ribbon red white & blue for favours, & people mobbing round in thick crushes to get a bit … . I went into St John's [church] to give thanks & afterwards into the Cathedral … . And this is my last War Journal.

Three sisters, Sylvia, Hope and Ruth, Spring 1917

'Dear dirty Gateshead' – Bottle Bank in the 1920s.

CHAPTER FIVE: NOVEMBER 1918 – MAY 1920

'I have found a cause'. Working for 'dear dirty Gateshead': political commitment, new comrades, walking holidays

12 November. … . We had another half-holiday & I went up to the Thanksgiving service in the Cathedral with Sylvie at half past eleven. It was frightfully full & we only just got in … . The service began well with "Now thank we all our God," & a beautiful lesson from Isaiah – the "How beautiful upon the mountains" chapter; then prayers & thanksgiving – quite good – but the Bishop's address was frightfully long & dull … . we came out by the big West door, & had a fine view of the Lord Mayor's new coach about which the old Lord Mayor is very angry & envious according to Father… . My first question is always "How did *you* hear the news? I love to hear just how it came to everyone, & everyone loves to tell … . Tonight we went to the pictures, & sang "Tipperary" & the King, of course; & cheered very bad pictures of the Generals shone on the screen instead of advertisements. To think that it has lasted four years & three months! The chief thing now seems to be to feed Germany, & I think President Wilson will insist upon our doing that. The rest of the Armistice terms one takes as they come – some seem rather hard, but after all they are not to last. One can hope for things to be put straighter by the final settlement. If the shops are at all open tomorrow I think I will buy a few things by way of celebration. For it really & truly is over.

14 November. Late afternoon. The little boys are shouting Revolution in Germany. I hope it is nothing very bad; it will be terrible if our Government say the Germans are Bolshevists & refuse to conclude the Peace with them.

15 November. It was all rubbish about the Revolution. Things seem to be going on very fairly so far, though of course you never know. The attitude of the *Times* is: "If they're not Bolshevists, they're not sincere; if they are Bolshevists we must go on fighting them." The General Election is a blow, but an expected one[1] … . By the way the League has had a meeting about reestablishing the Game. I think I must go to St James the first time the glorious Black & White appears again, just for old sake's sake.

17 November. I am so glad that I don't get tired of being so happy about the fighting having stopped. I was afraid the rejoicing wld go off quite quickly & I should begin to worry about other things. But not a bit of it! What are General Elections to me if we are going to have peace? We can always have another when this Gov. becomes intolerable; for its no good their thinking they can keep on Dora[2]. She will have to go; popular opinion will sweep her away … . I did such a shopping today! I spent so much that in future I must certainly rejoice in more economical ways. It was Saturday, of course, & I bought new shoes – slipper shoes, very smart, with buckles for really best; & a lovely warm new dressing gown, rose pink & frightfully expensive (three guineas) instead of the old blue one that I've had ten years or so & swore to make last till the end of the war; I got it at Coxon's, also some camisoles; & a magnificent silk blouse, wine-coloured & kharki (sic) for a present to Molly; I got myself a greenish paisley silk blouse there the week before; & chocs & toffee & some little flags & Christmas toys for Aunt Poppie, at various places, & left my watch to be mended … . Hope & Sylvie are going to share in Moll's blouse with me, as it is so dear. And we had pheasants for supper, & a lovely big roaring fire all the evening to keep out the frost. How jolly it is to live in peace & plenty! … .

19 November. We can never go back, I know. I shall not live to see such a "merry world" as there was when I was young. Or perhaps when I am very old – but even then I think not … . The human race is blighted for my generation, but at least I shall live to see as many young men as young women, again, even in the generation already born – if we have no more wars. For them we must work hard & work now, & abolish Conscription first of all.

22 November. … . I was pottering about the stable (at Home House) the other day – & the stable is rapidly falling to bits. Its so full of us & our childhood – & especially of Brian – it contains a complete biography of BMD, & chapters from the history of the rest of us. The printing press – or rather odd type boxes – the garden tent, the bathing tent, trunks & odds & ends of the Alnmouth & Madagascar Railway, the fretsaw, the supports for the wing of our private theatrical stage – the toboggans – all in the loft; & all sorts of engineering & cycling details in the lower part – the tools, the policeman mascot, pumps & old motor tyres, empty petrol tins, a few gardenig reminiscences of me, an old hose, the basket Molly used to have behind her saddle for lunch & wild flowers; & dumped over all the latest importation – the store of war-time coal … . I am glad the continuity of our house has never been broken – very glad. And yet we are always changing it – constantly. And most of the really old furniture has gone the way of all flesh. If my grandfather could come back, there is not very much that he could recognise – the floors are carpeted that he knew bare – the four posters are not even left in the attic – though there may be a few fragments in the loft; but the clock chest & iron box in the hall, & a pièce de résistance or two of tables & chairs or wardrobes in each room are still the same.

3 December. I'm rather wrapped up in the election at present, & that's a great bore, but thank goodness, the War is over, whatever happens next. All except in Russia; how I wish that was over too. The ships are beginning to come back to the Tyne by degrees. There was such a big one in last night – about the biggest I've seen; she had brought some Czechs from Archangel. I wish she would bring our men back. As she went out the apprentices waved to me & I waved back & wished them god-speed. The Swedish mail boat is in again too; I'm so glad to see her back, it makes me feel lovely & peaceful. Yet when I first came down to the Quay she was coming in as regularas clock-work, & there were plenty & plenty of ships, all painted so brightly with neutral colours on their hulls – but the British boats plain indistinguished grey! ... how many changes in these four years of war.

9 December. ... . There was a great transport in from Archangel one day – about the biggest ship I ever saw. She stretched from Trinity Chare right to the entrance of the Exchange Buildings; but she dropped nothing at the Quay except a pile of miserable old empties. Oh, how I wish she was bringing our boys back now. My heart is sick about Russia. That is the chief blot upon my happiness in peace. That the war should be going on anywhere is bad enough; but that we should be insisting on fighting in such an evil cause is very bad ... in July, when Hope & I began to go to [Quaker] meetings I never thought there was any hope of an early peace

18 December. Everything is horrid at the shop; but no matter, I'm not going to write about that ... .

1 January 1919.

I built upon a rock
But when destruction's hand
Dealt equal shock to tower & cot
My rock had turned to sand.
O faithless rock
My simple faith to mock.

But it is too bad to start the New Year & Peace new year with such a sad quotation. Still the results of the election make me feel like that! To have worked for the suffrage all these years only to have the women's vote return the Coalition by an immense majority! And Gateshead! ... to return a Conservative[1] for the first time in history.

26 January. I joined the ILP about a fortnight ago. I like it. I like my comrades with their Gateshead accents & their jolly practical way of looking at things. I like their way of arguing violently all in the most friendly spirit. I like them because they are Trade Unionists & because they are working men. I like Mr & Mrs Wilson; I am glad that I seem to be about the only "intelligentsia" member – at least the only one who attends regularly; it makes it much more interesting for me than if they were the same old lot of people I used to meet in the Suffrage Society – though of course we had a fair number of working women in that too.

It is amusing too & rather instructive to have to hear first one comrade's

views & then another quite contrary, & then a heap more & finally have to make up your mind how to vote. It shows you, compared to the NUWSS (National Union of Women's Suffrage Societies) that Parliament & similar institutions are quite spoilt by being pledged to vote one way or the other beforehand. The ILP method … is much more amusing & character forming.
5 February. … I daren't make plans for the future. If [Turnbull conscripted into the army from the printing busines] he does stay [in the army] it will be dull to go back to book-keeping & dusting the shop. I still feel very run-down & poorly; but a trip to the country is out of the question while it goes on snowing so.

I have just finished my story about Tuesdale – "Meldon of Meldon or the Pink House."It has taken me nearly – no quite six months to write one little fairy story, but it has been quite a wonderful comfort & pleasure to me off & on all the time. I wonder why making up fairy-tales should still be the delight of my life at the age of 28?
12-13 April. Housing School at Kinnaird Hall Newcastle

It was a funny end to a wild week of cinema films, rehearsals (of Poppa) & Hope's pageant (for the Play Centre children) & generally wild & stage-struck life … . It was all most exciting; I was stirred up through & through & do so long to *do* something. I like Mr F D Stuart the Organiser. He promised to write to me. Oh, if only I could help Gateshead, dear, dirty Gateshead, the most overcrowded borough of all!
16 April. Lake District Scale Hill Hotel Loweswater

Our first holiday since the Armistice; we are all three here; the daffodils are out & there is snow on the high hills; all the hedges are in bud … . We heard the first cuckoo.
17 April. … it rained & rained – Sylvia said it wasn't worth coming for this. But I looked at the glowing red of the wet bracken it Rannerdale & the wonderful lift & fall of the clouds & the bright gleams that came & went behind them, & I knew this was worth while too.
18 April. Good Friday. The Old Gentlemen are very friendly this time; they have an extra one, a little younger than the others called Major Blundell. He is a six foot Yorkshireman, very jolly & rowdy, he came all the way from London & is always shouting. There are five altogether. This day began like the first with clouds low on the hills, but this time without rain. We boldly took sandwiches & set off down the Vale of Lorton, & all the way it brightened & brightened, blue sky appeared & patches of sun on the hillsides … what views we had of Whiteside & Grassmoor, just touched with snow … . The O.G.s were rather quiet at dinner but came to our window afterwards like a circle of elderly Romeos & confessed thy had only been as far as Scale Force & there fallen asleep … .

19 April. We were talking of tackling Red Pike this day … when the Old Dears … actually asked us to go up with them. We had such a perfect day. We set off up Mosedale & it's one of the characteristics of Old Sep (Mr Hedly, The Chairman) that he goes straight across country in fields, climbing or wading all obstacles. Mr Marks, the most silent & queerest of the ODs does not approve this method much & keeps a look-out for gates. They told us that the high path we came along yesterday is called the "Corpse Road" & goes all the way to St Bees because in the old days that was the nearest sanctified ground … keeping well up the valley we began to climb at the next stream above Scale Force – a beautiful beck that comes tumbling down the rocks in a series of lovely waterfalls. Henery (Mr Marks), who doesn't like climbing broke off here, & we saw him no more till evening. The climb was steepish but there was a good path. Once on the top we had a good skirt round the skirts of Starling Dodd, & then a steep pull up the horn of Red Pike & what a view! … Isle of Man as clear as if it was two miles away, Solway, Scottish hills, Penines & all the Lake hills from High Street & Helvellyn on the one hand to Scawfell on the other. Perfect day! Glory of snow-capped hills, & sea & sky & sun! It could not be beaten for clearness & variety, to say nothing of mere expanse. Then we lunched & went on along the ridge … we skirted the tops of the great gullies & precipices that make the face of the mountains here – glorious crags of High Stile & High Crag. After High Crag we went down rather a rough scree to Scarf Gap … . We had tea at the Fish (hotel), where they were rather rushed, but thoroughly understanding the ODs they brought us breakfast cups … . We had a good dinner & were made to drink healths in port, being welcomed as sisters of the Society! Afterwards Mr Townend showed us the sacred books of record – most absorbing.

20 April. Another lovely day. The ODs almost insisted on us going to church to hear Henery read the lessons – so we did. In the afternoon we went to Scale Force … as beautiful as ever in its haunted retired cavern, falling white & cool from among the green hollies … .

21 April. One of the great advantages here is that there is never the smallest delay about boots & sandwiches. If you don't desperately wait for the post … you can easily get off by half past nine or ten. Sylvie & I made an early start to go over Coledale – to the Pheasant Bassenthwaite where the Swanwicks are … . We had a splendid walk & reached the top of the pass in an hour and a half exactly – three hours saw us into Braithwaite … train to Bassenthwaite. It was at Bass station that the crowds began – swarms & swarms of trippers – quite horrid ones – along the road, & quite thick at the Pheasant – all over, outside inside – stuffing the bar, standing in queues along the passages; by great firmness & pressure we could just squeeze in; & found Aunt Edie too in quite a nice little sitting room marked "Private" … . We heard much about the rich fare at the Pheasant & had a most luscious tea. Train back to Braithwaite, & a late start up Whinlatter at 6.30, with the low sun right in our eyes. It was a glorious walk home ... the sun setting over the Vale of Lorton, & we saw all the glorious changes of the sky from golden full rays to the last deep orange after-glow – wonderful, wonderful night, like a dream from fairyland! ... .

22 April. We went with the ODs this day, all the way up Crummock, & along Buttermere by a lakeside path (lovely) and up the Miner's Pass above Warnscale Bottom, across behind Fleetwith & down a quarry railway to Honister ... some hopes of doing Great Gable had been held out. I did not credit it but Sylvie was a little disapppointed ... .

3 April. This was our stolen day; we wired Father the day before that we wanted another day, & he wired back yes ... we each had an Old Dear left to walk with. Grisedale Pike was our "ideal" but ideals are seldom realised, alas. Still we had a topping day ... . We went up Swinside ... over Hobcarton Pike, Sandhill, top of Coldale Pass, Whiteless Pike & down into Rannerdale, – a beautiful round; & such views of the Scawfell & Pillar ranges, & many others beyond on this side & that. There was much snow on the hills ... . It has been a lovely holiday ... .

14 May. I have been in bed five days, feeling thoroughly ill & upset, though nothing worse ailed me to all appearances than a quite ordinary bilious attack ... .

23 May. I had a fortnight mostly in bed altogether, for just when I thought myself recovered I developed mumps.

26 May. Came to the Murray Arms Otterburn for a week's recuperation. [summer: holidays in Redesdale & Teesdale & London]

5 July. ...[in London] we had very heavy showers ... . I couldn't wear my best clothes as much as I wanted to, & the rain came through my blue costume coat & dyed my best georgette blouse! It was grieving. My best dress, which Molly has just made, was constructed from two remnants which I bought last year at Coxon's sale; four yards of dark bottle green poplin silk, & one yard of Liberty silk (figured shantung) in a misty pattern, bright green, dull slate, brown & blue; I also got a yard of bottle green georgette to eke this out & she made it from a picture in *Vogue*; the result is most charming; it has wings & a very wide belt of the dark green, a little flat panel of the figured silk in front of the skirt, & a little coatee of the figured over a very low bodice of the dark, filled in with the georgette in soft folds; the sleeves are dark green silk to the elbows, then a band of the figured, then a deep frill of georgette. The whole effect is quite magnificent, for me, especially with a pretty bead chain that Aunt Camie gave me for the occasion. Hope lent me her lovely green winter coat with the fur collar, for evenings, & Molly a gorgeous black lace scarf embroidered with pink roses, with a lot of green shades in the

leaves, which went charmingly with my things. Aunt Camie had turned this up at Ashfield & given it to Molly … . Really … there is more of everything [at Ashfield] than they could possibly use in a hundred years! And Aunt C. gave Sylvie another scarf, pale rose pink, with raised velvety flowers, just the present fashion, though she bought it at a sale years ago for only 15/-! And it's worth about £10 now. We saw one in Liberty's very like in design, but not half so pretty in material & colouring. Liberty's was *so* lovely. We had a most delightful time there & saw hundreds of things we loved; I do want a pair of moccasins; I wonder if I could make them? They were 29/- to buy!
17 July. We had an amusing Thursday meeting at the ILP discussing the Sunday "Hands off Russia" Demonstration & other things.
19 July. Peace Day … . About ten they began letting off fireworks – golden & silver shapes of coloured stars … . Presently they began to light flares at the old quarry on Sheriff Hill … the future is full of hope, even if the present is full of wrong & shame & dishonour. I have found comrades; & that is much; I have found a cause, & that's something too; I am grown-up & more – I am middle-aged; … .
20 July. Of course it poured for the Russia Demonstration & our last garden tea for the Play-centre children. It was annoying especially as one of the National speakers had actually turned up – most unusual for us. I took Hope & Sylvie; they were very willing to demonstrate against the Russian War. As it was coming down whole water the meeting was held in the Westfield Hall. Mr Warne the aforesaid principal speaker, spoke last, so the meeting was rather spun out & Sylvie got impatient. However when he did come on he livened things up very much, & she said he was a blooming little firebrand. He is very Bolshevick [sic] & extremely good-looking, with just the sort of square-cut ruddy determined face that a labour leader should have; he had also a flashing dark eye & curls; & his clothes were of a fascinating individuality. He was quite young & shouted rather too much, but he made a very clever use of his dialect, which however must have been perfectly intelligble to any audience, as it was mostly intonation, slightly gutteral "r"s & a few local words which explain themselves, "matterless" being a particular favourite.
21 July. Our last elocution lessons; thank goodness they're over. We have got something out of them, I think, but nothing in proportion to the expense. Still acting the *Hat* will be quite fun … . O, I ought to say that *cream sandwich cakes* have come back at Coxon's & are as delicious as ever in spite of the awful price.

[Scottish holiday]

11 August. … went back to work. I must work hard – only its so difficult when there's nothing much to do, & that very dull.

19 September. I have been given a most unexpected piece of pleasure & encouragement. During the Gunn bye-election I wrote some verses down in my diary … then one Sunday night Mr Peacock asked me for something for the *Circular*[3] which was to go to press on the Tuesday. Not much time! … so I hastily copied out the verses & sent them off, true to my inward resolution to do what I was asked, if I could … . "Oakwell Gate" has made quite a tiny local sensation! The *North Mail* quotes it, the *Chronicle* prints it in full … but best of all, & before these things happened, the comrades were pleased & told me so … .

28 September. The Railway Strike! … . The papers quickly convinced me that the men were right; the Government, as usual, are trying to hide the weakness of their case with cries of "Bolsheviks" … . In the afternoon the play-centre children came – such a swarm of rude, noisy wild little hooligans! Heaven send them better manners & send us strength to kill the slums & all the conditions that breed such children! I suppose they will get a bit more civilised as they get older. It is astonishing that Hope's gentleness has so little effect … .

2 November. Yesterday really was a most exciting day. I begin to see how it is that political life grows on you, in spite of the horrors of canvassing in the pouring rain, as I have been doing every evening all the week. On the Friday night I did Earl's Dene very late & it simply sloshed down on me wandering about in the mud … . Polling day was lovely … I wasn't very excited to begin with. I only brought in a very few voters in the afternoon, & shamelessly spent most of my time dosing over the fire. After tea I did go along to the Committee Room, & finding Mrs Thomas there (until that very moment I had been the only woman worker) I went with her to bring in some more. She was great & simply hauled them in; I wish I could; but then she had known them all for years & that makes a difference. The most annoying woman was waiting all the evening for her husband to get back from the football match (United won by the way – victories on every side). At last we persuaded her, at about a quarter to eight, to set off without him; she brought Jacky (aged two) & it took some time to get him dressed; …. but alas! just as we arrived Alderman Clough had locked the polling booth down! I shall believe till my dying day that he was early. I saw Jacky & his mother home & then hurried back for the count. I had quite missed my supper but I didn't care a bit. I was really wrought up by that time. It was rather solemn when we all filed into the Polling Station, Mr Howcroft first. He is *such* a dear – a real big gentle sweet-tempered pitman, with one of those rather solemn long faces & big moustaches that go so well with the humorous twinkle in the kindly grey eyes … . I can't name nearly all – all good comrades & stout workers – a "band of brothers," … . Well we all went into that stuffy little schoolroom with the flaring gases & sat round on the tops of desks, face to face with the other side. I knew Mr Grainger at once from his photograph on his election card, only he was older. There were two ladies with him. I was the only one on our side, of course; & just as the returning officer, Ald. Clough, & the counters took their places at the table I heard Mr Young telling Mr Grainger who I was – "Miss Mawson's niece." … . They did not announce which box was which, but it was pretty evident that Low Fell & Wrekenton had polled rather heavily, Sheriff Hill rather badly; they had to count over twice & even three times until the number of papers tallied with the number of names crossed off on the register. It was all the fault of one counter, who was very slow & generally got it wrong. Meanwhile we sat on our desks, trying to see whether more crosses were in the top or the bottom place, or peeping furtively at each other … . When the last box had tallied, the papers were sorted into Howcroft & Grainger piles, & Ald. Clough told us that the Agents might draw near & watch. I had never been bored, but I was more excited still now. Badly marked papers were thrown out & passed to the returning officer to inspect but in the end only one was found to be really spoilt, which was very good in a poll of nearly two thousand … . Then came the final stage. The sorted papers were counted into fifties, checked by another counter, tied up with red tape, glanced through by the clerk & sometimes by the returning officer & then put in two piles before him. We were all round the tables by now … . the candidates sat still; Mr Grainger chatted with his lady friends; I caught Mr Howcroft's eye once & he smiled in his gentle slow way … . then they came to counting the last packets .. The Clerk counted Grainger's pile 19 packets – 950 votes – then we knew we had 19 packets too … . It was ages before Ald. Clough, busy filling in forms got the result announced, but if I hadn't been too excited I might have seen it in his face, & Grainger's. Howcroft 987 Grainger 981 – majority of 6! It was a good thing it was no nearer. Clough would have loved to give a casting vote against us, I believe & then … . Our new councillor had hardly a word to say; it was a victory for Labour, he said, a victory for the cause, & he moved a vote of thanks to the returning officer & his helpers. Grainger, seconding, glib & polished, though with rather an angry face, said the usual things about a clean fight. I was sorry for the man, too; he had been so confident before … then we were allowed to clap; & then we got to work shaking hands. And we passed our new Councillor out from hand to hand, to the steps where the result was announced to the waiters outside. There were no cheers then; I think they were mostly supporters of Grainger. Our chaps were at the Committee room, & as we later ones hurried along the lane, we heard their welcome ahead. Then I went down with Mr McKenzie to the Westfield[4] to tell the news. Upstairs an orderly elderly whist drive; below, stuffed into the little hall, an election-mad mob. I came in shouting "We've won! Howcroft's in!" … . "Everyone in so far!" people were saying, & it was true, & we might have expected it for ours was the most doubtful seat in the town. Well, I can't write more now! It was good, good, good. One & another came in & always news of victory … . Then we went back to tell our news … . They came down in their dressing gowns to hear the astonishing news. They gave me cold chicken & sausage for supper – & I felt I needed a treat … . But I was too excited to sleep soundly. I kept on waking & praying most heartily for our new councillors & that our victory might bring blessing on the town, on our dear dirty Gateshead.

2 November. My first public speech – took the Chair for Dr Williams at the ILP.

10 November. Wrekenton & Team Colliery. Up Peggy's Bank in a hard frost all alone to speak at Wrekenton Institute for Mr Lawson – the Chester-le-Street Bye-Election.[5] Then down the hill in a driving snow-storm to the Team Colliery Institute – this time with Mr Elder. I didn't make much of a job of it but it was exciting.

17 November. Mr Howcroft took Sylvie & me down the Betty Pit … . can't say all I felt & thought down there in the darkness & the flickering lamp. … . It is a strange life, a strange work down there in the heart of the earth. The heat, the dust, the confined space, & the ceaseless, muscle racking work. It is a world under the world indeed.

February 1920. The Carl Rosa 1st Company were here for a fortnight & we heard *The Miracle* (new, quite good) *Merry Wives* (heavenly …) & *Hansel & Gretel* … . By the way, Hope is teaching Miss Luke's children at the Play Centre two ballad playlets – *The Ballad of Otterburn & Hynd Horn*.

1 April. Scale Hill Hotel [Loweswater] Arrived yesterday afternoon … . Life's a funny thing! … 24 hours before I was at the LP & TC [Labour Party and Trades Council], hearing an impassioned debate on the affiliation or non-affiliation of the Catholic Workers' Union … . And now, and now, – what does it all matter, among the rain & clouds & eternal hills? Only the children still matter – the rest very little. We found Mr Pound & Mr Hedley here; Mr Blundell joined us this morning & two more (Mr Marks & a new one, a Mr Scott) are coming this aftrnoon.

2 April. Hope still tired so we did not want to do too much, especially as it was raining first thing, & we made a late start, taking sandwiches; the clouds … when they rose showed fresh falls of light snow on Grasmoor & Whiteside; we walked up Loweswater through the wood … hillside covered with beds of stagshorn moss … & we picked enough to wreath our caps … .

3 April. This was a great day. We started off … with lots of food for Ennerdale Water … . Then we went up the zig-zag that we prospected yesterday & a breathless but delightful climb it was; I was in my breeks, of course, with only a jersey, not even my short skirt, for my mackintosh, which I wore when not climbing covered me to the boot-tops. Oh the comfort & ease of it! Walking without a skirt is the poetry of motion! … . We lunched on a cold bare hillside looking down upon the meetings of the rocky streamlets that form Croasdale beck … . Then down the dale by the green path & a pleasant dale it is with unexpected cascades & white lines of foamy rivulets down its sides, a fine rocky opening in one place, & a beautiful double slope of larch plantation at the foot, all golden-green in one of the rare hot bursts of sunshine … . It was dull & difficult as usual to get to the Angler's Arms, most cut off of inns, but when we did get there rather before three, they welcomed us hospitably & promised us eggs & tea. The lake looked beautiful … but alas Pillar & Steeple & Haycock were covered deep in masses of rolling cloud; only their great dark flanks appeared … . At the turn for Floutern (tarn) we stopped & Hope & Sylvie both voted for Clews Gill; it was raining a little & rather against my inner promptings we set off up the Lake; it was a glorious walk. Ennerdale has a singularly wild & desolate charm of its own, & even without the crowning glory of the Pillar group, it was not a walk to be forgotten, but the rain fell thicker, the clouds came down; looking behind all was blotted out by the scudding showers, & at the foot of Smithy Beck my heart somewhat failed & I advised that we should go back by the road. Again it was Hope who spoke first for going ahead, & as it was chiefly for her that I was afraid I agreed, half pleased, half with misgiving. Farm or dwelling there is none above the cottage under Bowness Knotts, now out of sight. Smithy Beck is a magic-looking stream, running & roaring over the rocks between beds of russet bracken through an eerie valley tucked in behind Latterbarrow, hidden even from the empty valley of the Liza. We crossed the beck below a fine waterfall, & then into this faerie country of bracken, gorse & heather, little rowan trees & strange rock-shapes for perhaps half a mile, when the stream turned sharp to the left & the climb began. It was steep but the path was well-marked; the clouds had lifted again & for the first time the top of Crag Fell was clear & we could see the rock teeth standing out on its jagged face; right up Deep Gill we looked too into Iron Crag & the recesss of Haycock; but the tops of the great fells were still close-blanketed. Best of all, looking ahead, it seemed that we could see the ridge of the hause, black with heather, standing out above us clear of cloud or mist; so we toiled up with light hearts & good will, Hope leading all the way with great energy. We had reached the highest turn of the beck when the rain came down, while we struggled on in bitter wind past a sheep fold & some strange shaped rocks into the top sources of the stream, deep cracks in the red clay, with black heather above; then the mist began to come down; by a happy chance we reached one of those green dry grooves which sometimes form the very tops of the streams in these hills & we followed it up to the ridge when the cloud had absolutely enclosed us & we had no guide but the slope of the land … almost immediately we came upon a wire fence with a wide hole through which a well-marked sheep-track ran. Now I was very frightened on strange hills in a mist which for all I knew might fill the whole of Mosedale, & I could not tell how near lay the stream I had intended to follow down, nor whether it could be followed, for it might be steep & rocky; but the sheep track gave me more heart, & I followed it forward stoutly enough over good grass ground only gently sloping downwards trying to show none of my tremor to the others, but praying very earnestly in my heart for the mist to lift. For there was nothing to be seen to right or left, nothing before or behind, but white mist, only that thrice-blessed sheep track at my feet … . Suddenly something white glimmered to the left, & I gave a great shout "There's Floutern"; so it was & a great deal more beside, for we passed the bottom edge of the cloud in a twinkling, & saw Mosedale at our feet, & Crummock & Whiteside & the hills of home. It was the most heavenly relief … . I found a way down a steep but possible grassy slope … hard on the knees … none the less it was a glorious day … getting in at 7.30. And was it worth it? All the bodily effort, the panting up the hills, the jarring on the stiffened knees down the hills, the splashing in the bogs, the sore feet, the stiff legs, the mental strain, the anxiety, the difficult choice – to return or not, the desperate fear in the mist, which might not lift? … . Was not all this somehow part of the pleasure? In a strange way it seems to be … .

4 April. Walked over to Pardshaw Hall [for Friends meeting] this morning along the very beautiful road which slopes up the Loweswater face of Low Fell … . There was no one at meeting but us! So we had a little meeting all to ourselves in the lovely old meeting house … . All was open & waiting & not one soul about; there was a fire in the meeting room, a little library, a waiting room, a porch for the Quakers to gossip in … I felt welcome… .

5 April. … . After breakfast it looked so bright that with one accord – "We must try today", but we still had to charter the little horse & trap & our sandwiches. We started about ten … every crag & boulder & bracken frond seemed to stand out in sharp outline under the grey sky & above the still grey lake; clearer far than ever you see in sunshine with the obscuring trick-playing shadows … . We reached Gatesgarth about 11.20 & started out at once up the Miner's pass. Hope, who was only setting us on our way, turned back half way up. A very large party … were on in front; about a dozen of them the ladies wearing breeches walking suits like Sylvia & me … to the shoulder of Fleetwith, where we struck across towards Grey Knotts, & found a very nice path marked with cairns running along its side & also along Brandreth rather below the ridge … We saw Helvellyn, Skiddaw, Saddleback

& the Keswick hills behind, the Borrowdale hills on the right; & on ahead the fine mass of Kirk Fell shut out Pillar & Steeple; beyond Kirk Fell we caught a glimpse of the rugged outline of Scawfell, & it was on it we first saw mist … Great Gable itself stood out bold & bluff & absolutely clear behind Green Gable … but just as we began the ascent by the railing, the first flutter of mist came creeping through the gap between the Gable & Kirk fell stretching eager fingers round the famous crown of crags … half the ascent … the mist pouring towards us all the time, & then we decided to sit down & have lunch just below the summit to see if the cloud would grow worse or lift; before we had eaten much Great Gable was blotted out … our hilltop too was invaded & a white curtain shut us off from all our landscape … we set out for the top still hoping it might be clear … mist showed no signs of clearing … set off down … & as my right boot had already split … we decided to go down … to the western side of Buttermere … .

6 April. … . We were a little late starting because I had to sew up my own boot with black thread & a crewel needle, there being no cobbler nearer than Cockermouth. I made a very tidy cobble of it too & it held out splendidly all day over very rough going … . I was so stiff & sore from the day before that I though I would never get up … . After lunch we scrambled down the green end of Melbrake to the path that runs opposite Scale Force Then along the marshy path between Melbrake & Crummock … oh the colours of everything! Every grey rock with its golden green lichens was a feast of colour … . I plucked one yellow whin-flower & sent a golden boat sailing down a silver river, one of the dozens of little streams that sing & laugh & bubble down Melbrake, from the crags to the clear lake.

1 May. This was a red letter day; it began fine & sunny, though with a cold East wind; … all the papers, except of course our own, have been perfectly horrid about May Day; … and I did think that perhaps the whole thing would be a dead failure; not that I minded that so much … so I was quite prepared to be one of about a dozen ILPers, & had quite decided to urge that we should carry the banners, even if there was just enough of us to carry them to show that though few we were dauntless. Of course I went to work in the morning, but left before twelve, had a snack & went up to the Windmill Hills; things were very quiet when I arrived; two big silken banners, the Allerdene Miners' & the Iron-founders', & one lorry into which they were fixing a green & white maypole; this turned out to be the property of the Irish Labour Party; also the famous fife & drum band turned up early … ILPers were mustering at the Westfield … presently joined up with Mr & Mrs Fred Tait. I suppose it would be nearly half past (one) when our contingent did turn up but it came in style; three brake-loads of children in fancy dress & decorated with greenery, with the "Socialist Sunday School" Banner in front; then the two ILP banners, the new red & white painted one with the name & the green Rising Sun with "Socialism" above. By this time the Irish ILP had fixed up their lorry, with a very pretty dark-haired Erin in a long white shamrock-sprinkled robe standing in the middle & a dozen or more little red-cloaked green-petticoated colleens sitting round about; this made a very bonny load. We had another long wait, for the Redheugh miners & their band this time; but they came in the end, & the Irish band gave us the "Wearing of the Green" & "Swanee River" to while away the time. The Redheugh Band is a fine one, & their banners very gorgeous in purple & gold, but I didn't hear much of them, as they led the way, followed by the lorries, the Trades Unions & their banners & finally ourselves, with the ILP banners before & the "Rising Sun" behind. There was a very good crowd of us of the ILP, nearly a hundred I should think. It was a great relief when we got started at last; the bands played, the sun shone, the banners waved, & all down Bensham Rd there were good crowds of people standing about to see. We must have made a fine show going down Bank Street, indeed one could see that much even in the procession, one banner below another all the way down the hill. (I forgot to say that it was flag day for the children's hospital, & our own people were selling tags & red & white favours … [?] was for the hospital & went all round the ILPers & did well.) It was hot & dusty; I was walking with the two Miss Redferns & Mr Surtees Hutchinson the schoolmaster was on the other side; we reached the cattle market through great crowds & found the Ncle ILP, & Irish contingent in Blenheim St all safe; here we lined up for another wait. But a little after two the fun fairly started … . There were five or six bands, perhaps a dozen lorries, decorated horses & flats, a cycle parade (which we couldn't see at all) & perhaps a score of banners from the largest & most luscious trade union sort that need relays of strong men to struggle with them, to the modest little red shield of the Ncl ILP. We fell in almost at the end, but were followed by a juvenile band in uniform & the enormous purple banner of the General Workers. In front were the Irish with two bands united, a fine inscribed green banner for Ncle, & a smaller one Green White & Yellow (Sinn Fein?). All round the Central Station was packed with people, & they were climbing up the Stephenson monument. But crowds! I never saw such crowds; all the way from the market to beyond the Hancock Museum the streets were lined four or five deep, & packed solid at the corners & places of vantage, as in the Cathedral square, the foot of Grey Street, & at the War Memorial. We stretched about the full length of Grey Street. Every now & then there was a halt; & the people laughed & chattered – such a kindly, good-humoured holiday crowd, full of children, & the banners waved, & the sun shone, & my heart was very merry to be marching with so goodly a fellowship towards the new world … . The white cherries were in flower

along the Spital Tongues road, & presently we turned off onto the Town Moor, & on & on across the grass, & when we reached Cow Hill at last & looked behind it seemed as though all the town were following in their thousands for the whole wide green was black with moving figures. There was a pause after we arrived, while the picnic parties settled down on the grass, & the big boiler in the hollow bubbled with hot water for the children's tea; in a very little while the speakers got going; at each of six platforms a huge attentive audience; & some of the speaking was very fine, I am told, for I was too excited & perhaps too hungry to listen; I wandered from one to another, seeing all the fun of the fair & hailing friends on the way; the sun had gone in by now, & a cold East wind swept across; but I left before the rain which came on a little after four & rather spoilt the dancing. I got some tea at Coxon's & was more than half ashamed of myself for taking off my litle yellow shield which should have been proclaiming to all the elite & respectable that I too had been to the Moor with the crowd … . This was my first maying! I did not get up early to dip my face in the dew, but then I am thirty on Saturday, so it would hardly have been worth worth while … .
25 May. … . On the Sunday night after I came home [from Alnmouth] I heard Alderman Smith of Durham County Council speak. He carried the old story, the great drama of the coal-fields forward another step, later than the Coal Commission. The miners did at last what they have been so often taunted with not doing – they elected a sweeping majority of miners onto the local authority. It was extraordinarily moving to hear this old fighter describe the long awaited, hardly hoped-for triumph. He was not bitter; there was no real malice in his quaint little straightforward smile; but he was glad, glad, overpoweringly … glad that the tyrants should " make way for honester men," that the smart cars that used to fill the road to the Moot Hall on council days should be replaced by old shabby cycles propped up against then railings, as the pitmen councillors had left them after riding in from many a little grubby village at the pit-head; that the rough homely Durham speech should sound from the sacred committee "chairs" where of old the coal-owners sat enthroned … . He described … how at the first meeting they deposed, one after another, chairmen, alderman, committee-men – great men of the old régime & put their own men in their place … .
20 June. Patterdale. Oh heavenly hills … . How glad I am to be back again … . Sunday began wet, soft clouds drifting down the valley, so I went to meeting at Grisedale Bridge. It was so nice; there were only six people; … . The spirit moved me to say "I will lift up mine eyes;" I began quite boldly but the spirit didn't last out very well … & I was rather trembly before I got to the end … .
21 June. … . In the morning, though there was a shower & it looked rather doubtful Uncle Eustace set off with the two Herskind girls … for Helvellyn.

Aunt Edie Mr & Mrs Herskind & myself completed the party, but the two ladies did not keep up with us far. I did not much want to do Striding Edge … a trifle surprised to find that I was not in the least nervous – though rather bored by my Uncle Eustace's well-known patter & very very slow progression. However we did get to the top eventually & lunched … in a bitter wind … . I wore my new five-guimea Amos Atkinson boots – their first long day – & they were perfectly splendid … much admired … I was wearing my breeks on the Helvellyn day, of course, & my green Quartier Latin smock with the black bow … this costume makes my boots & stockings very conspicuous. I generally wore a mackintosh through the village, though only out of deference to the feelings of the elders. I did not see anyone else in breeks, which surprised me a good deal; most of the folks about were very smart, in light skirts & stockings (generally tussore or white) & gay jumpers. But the glory of my boots made up for all my deficiences. And anyone who saw us go along Striding Edge must surely have admitted that my things were not only neater, more comfortable, suitable & efficient, but also infinitely more decent than the Herskind girls' skirts. It's such a comfort that you can't show anything you should not in breeches, do rocks & wind their worse … .
22 June. Went to Angle Tarn in the morning … a terrible cold wind on top sweeping down the valley fit to take your ears off, especially in the exposed part where the path winds round the edge of the hilltop, with fine views of Dovedale, Deepdale & Brotherswater. We barely looked at the tarn … & turned back to seek shelter.
Wednesday

It was finer first thing … so I got up early & walked in the Park. I met a ghost – myself of six years ago – the just-before-the-war Ruth Dodds, & she didn't know me, but walked past with her head full of books & plays & fame … but I didn't let this depress me for long. After all, I am happier now in spite of the bad bitter times between … .

We all set off together … to walk down Boardale Hause & down Bannerdale … . I walked round the Lake path & the rest went home by Boardale … after supper I took the two and a half hours of daylight all for myself & wandered off up the park all alone. It was mid-summer eve … Glenmara is magical at every time, but the magic of evening, with the last cuckoo calling three times & then silent, with the scent of the birches & the scent of the sweet-briar; with everything waiting, tense, finger-on-lip, for the coming of the little people – the toadstools pushing up to their tables at the feast, the rabbits alert & watching for them, the foxgloves nodding, wise, oh so wise! – but discreet; the streams singing for their music, the grass & tiny heath flowers spreading such a carpet. But all this is nothing to the silence & peace & the cool sweetness of the evening.

CHAPTER SIX: OCTOBER 1920 – JUNE 1926

Mainly politics. Quarrel with brother over General Strike and Ruth leaves family business; Pitman's Pay

18 October 1920. It is already the third day of the Coal Strike. I pray God it may not last the week, at any rate without negotations; Peter (Howcroft) thinks that if it is not settled soon it will be a long struggle … . Last night I read a paper at the ILP on Hepburn's Union & the Strikes of 1831 & 1832; It was quite successful. Indeed, who could fail with such a subject? But it was very strange; & perhaps the strangest thing of all was when I was going home with four of the Low Fell comrades. As we stood waiting for the tram Mr McKenzie said – "My father was one of the children who were carried to the Pit; he started at six years old at Redheugh colliery; his mother used to carry him there, & then after his twelve hour day came to carry him home again. "And my father started at seven down the pit," said Mr Howcroft. "And so did mine," said Mr Miller. "And mine," said the silent Mr Thomas, "and I started myself at eight." "Ay, & that's only yesterday, as it were," said Miller, "we have come on a bit after all … ."

23 October. I have been Saturdaying down at the Westfield Hall, cleaning splashes of paint off frosted windows – very difficult; I have got cold too & feel tired … . Then there are the elections … I find it hard to make up my mind to canvassing. I have no store of simple easy propaganda at my finger-ends. I wish someone would write an easy guide to Labour canvassers – quite serious; with various suitable openings, possible developments, answers to likely questions & hints for local applications. Everyone is rather low about it just now … .

28 October. I can think of little except the elections … . Last night we had a meeting … at Low Fell. It was very well attended, the room was quite full; unfortunately Dr Ethel Williams, who was to have spoken, did not turn up. I was in the chair … .

2 November. … our position in the Council is exactly the same as last year – only Peter Hancock, a good man, is out, & John Pickering, another good man is in … . I really knew as soon as I heard the cheer; it was a horrid cheer, not deep & hearty, as our people wld have given it. I remember clinging to Mr Howcroft, more for moral support than for steadiness in the crowd. The Westfield Hall packed, & Mr Peacock's fine call to action. Fred Tait's reception when we all rose to him & sang "He's a jolly good fellow;" the words of victors & vanquished; & the laughter & fellowship & good cheer of it all … . Our people are good in victory; they are perfectly splendid in defeat. Oh, I am tired; I didn't go to bed till 1.30 this morning; & then I couldn't sleep, I don't know why. This morning I felt rather as I used to when we had been on nightshift at Armstrong's – weak & cold & thin-blooded, somehow … .

19 November. Father is rather poorly – worse just when we thought he was better. The Dr thinks he has had a very slight stroke & he complains of loss of power in his right hand … . Dear dear Daddy, I do hope he will soon be better. I wish so much that mother was here. It is lonely for him only having younger people.

27 December. Father is going on well & has got over his stroke wonderfully. He walked both down to Ashfield & up again on Christmas Day. We have had & are having a lovely holiday, with Mutzi & Linschi, two little Austrian girls, with us. The *Doll's House*, our Nov. production went off very well. Then came the Bazaar, which was a huge success. I did passe-partout, & have enough orders to keep me busy another month. Then the Dec. production – *Twelve Pound Look, Carrier Pigeon & How he Lied*; not sufficiently rehearsed owing to Bazaar; & small audiences, owing to holiday time. Then Xmas – ILP Carol party, otherwise Jazz Troup on Xmas Eve – 23 at Ashfield for dinner – Bob & various others with bad colds.

A First Memory

To the miner who asked me how I got my sympathy with the miners?

Born & bred on the coalfield
Where the men work deep below,
Born & bred on the banks of Tyne
How should I not know?
Before my sunny childhood
From the mists of infancy
From the very dawn of consciousness
One memory comes to me:-
There echoes from that earliest time,
Dim & far away,
The tramp of the passing miner's feet
In the darkness before the day
Maybe a mother first recalls
Her mother's lullaby;
The poet's mind may waken
To the deep & stormy sky;
And because I was born well destined
To a task I will not shirk
I remember first the tramp of men
On their weary road to work.
And that echo of passing footsteps
In the ears of a sleepy head

Has become the call to service
The message of daily bread

It calls to share in spirit
The burden of heavy toil
With the workers of forges & factory
The workers of mine & soil
And upon the day of action
When the Red Flag is unfurled
To march as a loyal workmate
With the workers of the world.

26 January 1921. Hugh is gone; & *Candida* for which he did me a beautiful poster as a farewell gift, is over; & Brian is going to Japan in March.
16 April. All this week has been a queer week & yesterday, the 15th, was one of the queerest & most disagreeable days of my life – indeed the whole week since I fell ill of a swelled face & a rash all over me on Friday the 8th [the end of the first week of the miners lockout] – it has been like that – The ILP Dramatic Club were doing *Foundations* on the Tues Wdnes & Friday … the collections were disappointing & I'm afraid we have hardly cleared expenses. 26/- & 22/- & 32/- = only 17/- when the hall is paid for, & we have 7/6 to pay for Jamie's uniform … .

Somehow I couldn't sleep. The talk & the faces of the comrades had convinced me in the end, without my realising it, that the Triple Alliance had broken down … its so unexpected this terrible betrayal. Even the strike would have been better … . The miners' case is lost now, just when it seemed won, & by no action of their own … . And for lack of leaders we are condemned to darkness, probably for my lifetime … . The great trade unions will dwindle & pine; people will lose all faith in each other, in comradeship, in direct action, in political action. The stunt press, & the kinema, because they distract our minds with trivialities, will be the mainstays of a foolish aimless people, who will afford these things when they cannot afford to feed body & mind properly. The Labour Government has faded into a dream. My only comfort is that bad as things are August 1914 was worse. Betrayals, defeats, destitution – these are the lot of man; in a world already made miserable by them it is still possible to add one horror more (war) & as long as we are without it in a world bad enough as it is, there is something to be thankful for. I did not sleep much … . I listened to the trains & there seemed so many of them. Disunion, betrayal, defeat, disunion, betrayal, defeat, they said. And towards morning, when the miners should have gone past but didn't, these verses came into my head. I feel these things more because I have been

reading the Webbs Trade Union History.
19 April. … . Molly & Sylvie are now in bed with German measles! The Dr, who is a dreadful alarmist, said yesterday that it *might* be scarlet fever … . Poor devoted Hope is nursing them, they are very slight cases & not at all ill … & I shall be able to manage the business & go to meetings in reason … . I feel I am not nearly sorry enough for the poor things, but then I have just had it myself & they were not particularly sorry for me. I spent the weekend at West Hartlepool; It was quiet & nice on the whole, though – oh well, never mind. It is very good for me to go back sometimes into my own past & realise what a *thoroughly middle class person I was born & bred*.
2 May. I went to the May-Day procession yesterday. I *was* disappointed that I couldn't join in! But with Hope as well as Molly in bed with measles I was just worn out by nightfall as it was. However I'm not going to write much more about the illnesses! The doctor (pig) says I must go to no meetings for a fortnight. I am quite amused to find out how much the prospect of 14 days spent undiluted with my family appalls me now! The Socialist movement has grown on me much more than I realised … .
23 May. … . On Saturday I had my first outing with the Speakers' Class. Part of the Choir went with us to Chester-le-Street, the idea being that they sing to collect the crowd & then members of the Class give addresses. It was the most perfect of days & we had a fine caravanserai – forty or fifty people men women & children! We had a poor meeting in the afternoon, tea on the Green (bring your own bun) & a fine evening meeting, at which I was chairman. It was quite a field-day & I spent the times between talking to Miss Harrison of the Dunston Branch[1] & Tom Gibb, a Yorkshireman, a LP [Labour Party] organiser at Jarrow.[2] But the best was still to come; about half past nine in the most witching time of evening, Comrades Isaac, McKenzie, Colvin & I set off to walk home; the trees are in their first green; the young corn is inches high; the corncrake & cuckoo were both calling; down in the north west was a great river of crimson sunset. We went by Black Fell & the low blue misty hills of Durham lay all around us, gathering up the falling shadows into deeper & deeper blue. A great red full moon got up over the hill. A vivid flame of orange & scarlet showed a hay-rick in a blaze. The May was full out & the fields full of daises & buttercups & ladysmocks. A magic night … .

I finished Thomas Hepburn … & (Hope) read it & was very nice & interested; but I could see she didn't exactly admire it, or think it much good … .
4 June. … . Today Father is seventy years old; he is well & cheerful, thank God, at present, though his walking has not improved much lately, he is getting down to the Quay every day.
6 July. Everyone is turning on the miners now, saying "I told you so!"… bought a Queen Anne silver spoon from the *Daily Herald* Fund for the

miners children ... I should like to keep it forever as a memento, & to look at it whenever I am tempted to sacrifice a temporary principle to a temporary advantage. And years hence, when the mines are nationalised & the commonwealth almost here, I will tell children the story of the spoon & the miners most splendid strike. The worst of it is that our two pits are closed indefinitely – for lack of a market, so they say, & what will become of our people in the meantime? .... .
8 July. .... Went to the Warwick St meeting; it was dreadful; a very hot night, & that part of Gateshead is only just bearable in cool weather. They made me take the chair; no speaker as usual ... . It took all the heart out of me somehow. Those awful faces! People that I felt *could* not hear the message; they are the wrecks of the present system & so completely a part of it that I sometimes doubt whether they could even conceive anything different, still less come to desire it. And we, we Socialists who are so ready to re-organise the world & put it right, we cant even organise a meeting! I stole away as soon as ever S. started & went to the pictures with Sylvie ... .
11 July. .... Maternity & Child Welfare Milk Sub-Committee at 4 p.m.; as I know next to nothing about it, I am at present confining myself to trying to make a good impression on the MOH [Medical Officer of Health] ... .
15-17 July. [Harbottle holiday] I went to Bellingham with my pack on my back. Such a golden windy walk (wind behind from Bellingham to Otterburn). Spent night at inn there ... . Walked across the fells next day by Hate Cairn to Harbottle. It was lovely as far as Branshaw but rather grey & dark & eerie the rest of the way. This was my first experience of tramping alone; & on the whole I'm not sure I like it. The evenings are so dark & dull. Of course in summer it would be different ... . It was my farewell to summer I went after our first production "Arms & the Man," in which I took part, rather against my will. Sylvie was Raina & I was Catherine. I have taken to the stage too late to play any of the parts I used to dream of in my youth. But Sylvie takes them & that's better still; for after all I've had my fun, & she missed most of hers through the War ... .
April 1922. ... Hope & I came to Sheffield yesterday ... for the reading of my play by the Sheffield Playgoers Society; *The Pitman's Pay* won their open competition for plays of more than one act ... . We reached Sheffield at 12-50 & met Miss Radford, the Sec, a large overpowering & very talkative lady, at the Victoria Hotel where she lunched with us ... everyone in Sheffield talked by the yard ... went to the Church House where the reading took place. It was rather a gloomy room & none of the windows opened, but it has a nice platform. I was feeling rather nervous by this time ... There was only a small audience; not more than fifty or sixty at the outside ... . It was a very middle-class audience, in spite of what Miss Radford had told us about them being so

mixed; but some of the readers had a Yorkshire or other accent … . It only took from 7.30 to 9.30 to read, so it is a good length, say 2½ hrs in actual production … . This one evening is very likely the beginning & end of my success as a playwright! … .

Sheffield is like home only more so; blacker & bigger, with more smoke & more theatres & societies & a larger Town Hall & steeper hills … . I didn't think the theatres seemed much better than ours, though more numerous, but the play producing societies were numerous & very strong. There was a "Little Theatre" that produced "propaganda" plays; I suppose Socialist, though this was never clearly explained. For this reason it was disliked & the Playgoers were apparently started in opposition, & never did "propaganda" if it could be avoided. I think the *Pitman's Pay* is regarded as propaganda & will not be produced for that reason. The Playgoers, however, are democratic, & make no social distinctions among their readers, even if they do among their plays … .

May Day was held on Sat May 6th this year. I have recorded both my other May Days, so I must not miss the third … . On May Day it rose to a perfect gale; dust flew in the streets; the wind went through you; cold flying drops of rain dashed singly from the grey skies now & then. None the less we marched, & there was a fine beat up of banners, only unfortunately it was impossible to keep most of them up. There were five waggons, one provided by the Drama Club, with a tableau from "Much Ado" on it. I walked with the ILP, of course, but as there was a conference at the Westfield it was not such a good turn-up as it ought to have. There were crowds to see us in the streets; but not so many on the Windmill Hills, which were terribly bleak & windswept; my eyes were so full of dust & my face so black & my hands so cold by this time that I fairly turned tail from the meetings & got home in time for tea … .

8 May. My 32nd birthday.

16 June. … the day we started on our walking tour … . Hope & I took our packs & started off for Newbiggin-by-the Sea from Manors [station] at 9.30 a.m. … .

May to September 1922. This summer was about the busiest of my life, as I was organising the Summer Campaign, two open-air meetings a week in different parts of the town. It went fairly well. The speakers really turned up quite finely on the whole – at any rate better than I dared to hope

29 July. I organised a No More War Demonstration this day. It was perfectly frightful. But never again!

6 December. The first night of the *Pitman's Pay* is over! After months of thought & weeks & weeks of hard work, my first real play to be really produced! And it went splendidly; I could see that by the way Hope spoke of

The Pitman's Pay Act 1: 'Here's to the Lancashire delegate, and a national union of all the pitmen!'

The Pitman's Pay Act III: Shafto: 'There'll never be another pitman's union'

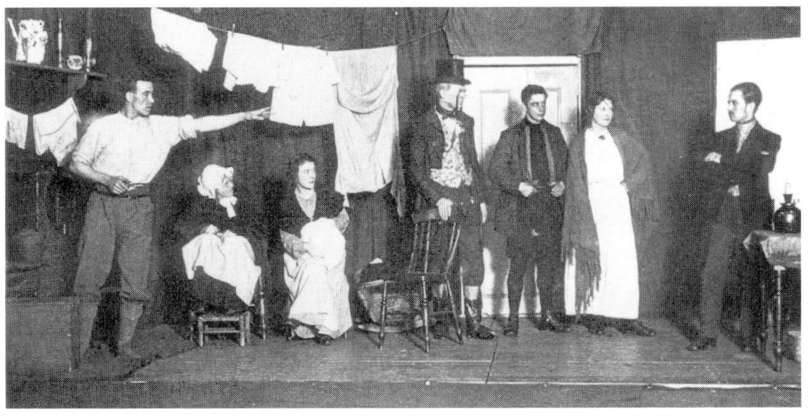

The Pitman's Pay Act IV: 'There she stands, your own spy Mr Forster'

it afterwards. I can trust Hope. And indeed I thought it went well myself. Everyone did splendidly except … who didn't turn up! And Stan had fortunately learnt his part, in response to my anxious appeal on the last rehearsal night, so it didn't really matter… . Everyone of the cast did well – wonderfully! Never was a producer so well supported by everyone. Dresses, scenery everything appeared as if by magic … .

Sylvie made lots of the clothes; … .

8 December 4.00a.m. The worst of it – indeed the only bad thing – is that somehow I can't sleep after this play. I wake about three, when the pitmen begin to pass to work, with a horrible tummy-ache, & can't go to sleep for ages … . I was on in the second act as a woman in the crowd … .

Aunt Camie & a huge party from Ashfield were there the second night; I don't think any of my other relations or special friends have been. But … will be coming to the Newcastle performances next week.

I was called every night … Also I had to make speeches … .

The second night was much the fullest – they took £4.12/- at the door all in sixpennies this makes 184 people; with the cast, who are mostly there part of the time that makes nearly 200. I suppose a few more could have been wedged in but it was quite as full as is comfortable. Last night again, the takings were huge £3. 19/-.

I have enjoyed it, I *have* … .

27 December. I have got such a nice letter from Comrade Jack Lawson M.P. about the *Pitman's Pay*. I do so like praise & appreciation. I try not to be greedy of it, but I am rather.

29 December. I got the contract from the Publishers today & sent it back signed. I wonder if they will be able to sell any? … .The PP was published this week,but there were no reviews & I sore doubt they'll (sic) be none … Both the New Leader & the *M.G.* (*Manchester Guardian*) have simply put it in as a book received … .

10 March 1922. Went to Chopwell in a chara to do PP … . They were kind to us … there was a large & intelligent audience … very good supper … .

17 March. Went to Bill Quay to do PP; this was the last & worst of our country performances; a horrible dirty inconvenient picture hall, a huge noisy, ill-mannered audience, every possible difficulty in entrances & exits, & dressing accommodation, stage space & sitting generally … . The local comrades were very nice & kind … . But the men made frightfully long speeches. They were just starting a local Labour Party & this was to raise funds … . I afterwards heard that it made a deep impression on the more serious-minded members of the audience, & we have been asked to do it at Wardley in consequence … . Also two … made a pilgrimage to Hepburn's grave & decided to tidy it up themselves as a mark of respect & gratitude.

16 May. Wednesday. Last production of PP for the season, at Felling, on Monday 14th! (On Saturday I laid a foundation stone: Sunday I presided at the SSS (Socialist Sunday School) … . Tuesday came to London! … . I was wearing my new navy-blue coat-frock, with short coat to match. It is quite loose at the waist & very comfortable; it has a little waistcoat of mixy red blue green white & black design, very bright, to relieve the darkness, & I was also wearing a string of light blue venetian beads which Aunt C. gave me on my birthday; they were very much admired. My hat is brown with a painted design in blues & greens & mauves, & an orange lining & orange trimming, what Doris calls tubes – going once round & ending in long hanging streams like mantling rather. These are pretty but a nuisance in a wind. On the tops of buses I have to tuck them into my collar, or else be such a forward hussy as to tickle perfect strangers. For the Foundation Stone laying I pinned & sewed it up into a round bobble, as I knew it would be nothing but a bother there on the hilltop. I was glad that day that I put it on, for all the other ladies had very brilliant hats. In London I wore grey stockings, black shoes, grey gauntlets gloves, brown handbag, an umbrella, & the grey scarf I bought for M.s funeral was a great comfort – so cosy on bus tops. That's all! For one hardly goes into under-clothes, though I must add my black & red foulard underskirt with the scalloped edge, because it is new too … .

4 June … . It is due to Hope's work while I was away that the books are well forward this month. But as she is going to a Friend's Peace Conference at Leeds, I shall evidently have to do the a/cs myself to make up … . Went to Mat. & Child Welf. Com. in afternoon; a larger number of applications than for some time. Then the shop till about 6.15, when I had a second tea at the Socialist Cafe & met Sylvie at Lit. & Phil. to go to (a play) … . I *must* work harder … . I have been making up a ridiculous railway Indian melodrama in 2 Acts! … .

16 June. … . Another rushing morning at the Shop but then Saturdays always are a rush. Did a perfectly beastly estimate for Hedley's handbills for a sandcastle competition. Well Turnbull has been away a whole week, so there is only one more week of it, & it really hasn't been so bad. And in a way I quite enjoy being cock of the roost & directing everything again. It is much more amusing than all this endless book-keeping … . J. came to tea & brought the wonderful banner design she has been doing for me. *Our* ILP Banner! Ah, how splendid it will be if only it comes off! … .

6 July. A perfect day – for the sea with at least two bathes; or a garden; but very trying at the Quay, with a weary old dredger clattering & groaning just outside the shop. Yesterday I worked like a slave – today I slacked half the time! A delightful evening poring over the patterns sent by one of the embroidery places (for an ILP banner), I seem to have made a most happy

choice in this case. Oh my beautiful banner, if I can only bring you off!
6 August, Bank Holiday. About the finest Bank Holiday I can remember … . did some more to my dear banner – a real joy, embroidering on my golden silk in the shadow of the wall on the green lawn in the sunny garden! … walked to Black Fell to the Gateshead ILP Federations Reunion. The views were glorious; … there was a fine crowd – three or four hundred, about half women; & in addition crowds of jolly kids. I went in memory of Thomas Hepburn & the great meetings they used to hold in the old days … .

My new dress came on Saturday; fawn silk brocaded with a fairly large flower pattern; quite long white sleeves, cross-over front, with the deep V filled with ninon to match. The dress is meant to be long-waisted but I simply let it come to my real waist.
18 August. Hope & I deep in the Banner … has lent us an enormous rug frame, & I have stretched the banner, at full width & almost full depth; it looks fine but almost too big to reach to embroider … Yesterday I read "Christmas Tree Land", one of the nicest stories in the world; it made me feel very happy. I found it looking for books for the SSS which is starting a library. Alas! our store is sore depleted! The Play Centre made sad havoc with many old favourites.
19 August. Worked hard at my banner & have half one side-panel tacked out … . It is most fascinating work … .
13 August. News from Brian that he is due back on the 25th! It is near! I have a little cold & slept badly; & there is so much on hand! … .Thurs. Booked passage for Sweden on *Thule*; sails 28th this month at 3p.m. ILP at night; Elsa to tennis.
17 August. An old very deaf man came into the shop this afternoon. He began by asking Turnbull if he was a Dodds, as lots of old friends do. Then he said his name was Robertson, & his father was foreman many years ago. He was a sailor himself; a nice old soul; he knew Father a bit, he said, but he remembered M.S. Dodds[3] [Ruth's grandfather] very well. He said he was 76. I asked Father about him tonight but he could not remember a foreman of that name. Before Richard Donaldson the foreman was Wm Stewart, before him John Rock Jones, then Father thinks there may have been one he has forgotten; before that it was Philip Aiden, who was there in '65 when Father began his apprenticeship. Of the very early foremen he could only remember hearing of one called Dodds, not a relation & a very deaf man.
19 August. Still no play; yet I did many things today, though I feel as if I had done nothing. I took a good deal of exercise! I walked over to the Camp on Hillhead with Sylvie … . I had three sets with Sylvie in the afternoon! I did some banner & began to stitch on the black band of the centre panel. (Hope has finished Husbandry [presumably one of the themes]). I wrote two

invitations to tennis & typed two pages of the Pilgrimage Play. I wrote out the ILP minutes. I read a little but hadn't much time for that. But oh how I wish I had written some play … .
20 August. Had a wire from Brian saying he had arrived (from working in Japan) & gone to town (London). Molly & Bob arrived at Ashfield in the evening.
21 August. Grand expedition of Betty & Bob, with attendant Mothers & Aunts to (1) 61 Quayside (2) Trinity House – Interval with large late lunch – (3) Old Castle. Rehearsal of *Hindle Wakes*, & the LP & TC [Labour Party & Trades Council] meeting at which the new agent was selected. Scotsman called Barr.
22 August. … finished my Robert Aske tragedy … .
23 August. … . Got it (the play) posted … & met … Sylvie & Molly for my theatre party to *Lilac Time*. We all enjoyed it immensely; & … I enjoyed it even as much as in London, because I saw so much better, though the singing was not quite so perfectly heavenly … I'm going to stick in one of the pictures from the advance notice opposite, because the first act was one of the prettiest settings I have ever seen, & also to keep a little souvenir of the most charming opera, as good in its way as the *Beggar's Opera,* & for the same reason, the individual charm of it – different from everything else & preserving this time through the airs the very flavour of the particular time & place.
3 September. Very busy day preparing for sailing [for Sweden] on Tues. Went to a Milk Com. at 2.30 after a hurried lunch, & then right on home, to find that Brian was really coming home at six. There has been a frightful earthquake in Japan; how lucky he came home before it … [arrived] earlier than he said. He's so big & fat! Grown enormous & so much older-looking, but just as great a dear as ever. He gave us all very lovely lined kimonos, mine grey & pink with a flame-coloured lining; … of course he's very anxious about his friends. He went down to Ashfield after supper – a full family meal with Father & all five of us just filling the table in the old way.
4 September. Packing all the morning; went to the Quay for an hour or so before S. came with the baggage & the taxi. Hope, Molly, Bob & Aunt Camie also turned up to see us off & afterwards Brian … . Bob was delighted with the ship – & very pretty & clean & nice the *Thule* is I must admit: & the Swedish Captain & crew very affable. there were very few other passengers, but the two other ladies at our table, a Glasgow girl & an old Swede, were very nice indeed. We didn't sail till 9.20 when it was quite dark, & all the lights of the town were blotted out down the bend of the river. I said to All Saint's clock the last landmark I could see, "Good-by, All Saints! Good-by home." We soon went to bed but not to sleep.
5 September. Very sick all night & all the next day. Sylvie too felt ill, though

she was not sick. She got up for tea on this day, but I simply lay in bed. It was not a good passage & not a very bad one but grey cold wet & windy … .
6 September. We both saw the golden sunrise through our porthole with great delight. Sleep again till light & went on deck before breakfast in the glorious sunshine … the Swedish coast just in sight … Gothenburgh [sic] … is a charming place, clean & fresh, trees abound, even the station smelling of fruit & flowers. Alma was waiting on the Quay. We *were* glad to see her … train at 12.30. A lovely sunny day for a lovely journey; woods lakes, low rocky hills, birch thickets, red wooden farms, great fir forests, flowers, blue eyes & fair honest faces – Sweden is something like that. Dark when we reached Stockholm, with the golden lights on the waters & came to Wrangelsberg,.. where Alma & her mother stay at a select boarding house kept by a baroness.

[description of holiday museum visits, opera, film, river trips, shopping etc]

18 October. It seems impossible to write every day in a diary once the Dramatic season has started because one is out late so much … . Then came *Pygmalion*, Monday, & Tues. of last week & this. It has been a huge success. I am too sleepy to write any more. I was up so late last night tidying away props. Today I was at the Unemployment Exchange all the morning; but worked at the Shop till seven, like a good girl to make up.
19 October. … . Hope's first rehearsal of *Dear Brutus* went well … . The Club have asked me to produce the *Northerners*; I was offended when they didn't (secretly of course) & now that they have (as second choice & because, as Sylvie says, there is no one else) I dont much want to do it. But I have accepted with enthusiasm so as not to show the wrong spirit. Sylvie is to act Ruth – a part I wanted for myself, or rather saw myself in long years ago … . I dont want it now, though; much too strenuous! All the queer stage effects & so forth will be fun, but it means a terrible lot of hard work!
20 October. … . Went to dinner at Ashfield … . Then took Camie to a long Peace Conference; writing notes for her is very exhausting. Mr Mosley[5], Lord Curzon's son-in law is rather lovely, over six feet tall & like a guardsman … Hope took Camie home & I had rather a jolly time at tea with Mr Hudson & Dr Williams & Mrs Fields & some more – there were comrades from all over Durham.
21 October. … went to Town Hall meeting (packed) to hear Mosley & Hudson again. Great enthusiasm.
26 October. Came to Oxford with Hope to visit her friends
29 October. Glorious morning. Home; wrote some of Act II in the train. Canvassed for Peter in the evening.
1 November. Peter defeated; five Labour gains & two seats held – the

majority on the Council at last.
2 November. I wish one could be as keen before an election as one is after it. I want to remember to read this next September & October & buck up & canvas like mad as a result. I feel as if I could now; when I was doing it I felt as if nothing could make me, much as I wanted Peter to get in. Now I am sorry I didn't do better; I always am sorry; & I know beforehand that I will be & still I cant do it. My life is all made of broken resolutions & if my good intentions paved Gateshead instead of Hell we should have the finest streets in the country.
8 December. ... *Mastersingers* for the first time; perfectly splendid! ... the Hans Sachs simply perfect. Everything well done, even better than *Aida* on Monday, which we greatly enjoyed, too, but of course the operas are not to be compared ... .
10 December. What a silly paragraph (above)! How feeble & inadequate. When a great new pleasure has been suddenly & completely revealed to you, you ought to hold your breath & wait a bit instead of slopping over into breathless, silly-sounding raptures. You want time to think & think, & dwell on it all again before you begin to find the right words. I was half asleep & wild with all sorts excitement when I wrote that ...
21 December. By misfortune I have had another great treat like unto the last (Sylvie's Christmas present to Molly who couldn't go with rooms booked in London) ... . So I spent half yesterday travelling to London & am now spending most of today travelling back; I never did anything quite so wildly extravagant before, but oh, how well worth it! How extraordinary that money should be able to buy such pleasures! Most immoral it really is! ... . The train was late but we got in about 2 & went straight from the hotel to Wyndham's for *The Rose & the Ring* a pantomime an excellent choice ... For *Hassan* at (Her Majesty's theatre) we had excellent seats in the third row of the Dress Circle. And now I dont know how to describe *Hassan* ... it was better than good, it was a worthy expression of Fletcher's masterpiece ... . [lengthy description]
3 January 1924. I must end my diary with a sorrow; poor Father's speech is suddenly much worse – I suppose another stroke, I hope a very slight one. The Dr thinks he may recover the power almost completely, but of course that is not certain. Pray God it may be so. My darling Daddy! He is so splendidly brave & cheerful & resigned ... .
10 January. Father is making excellent progress, can speak much better & we hope may be downstairs next week ... .
24 January. 11.30 p.m. After the Branch at which it was decided to nominate John Beckett[4] to the LP & TC as proposed ILP candidate for Gateshead ... And I hope he will go through in spite of the opposition of the present J.B.

James Stuart Barr, our quaint little Scots agent. Should have been rehearsing *The Golden Apple*, Hope's play, but it had to wait upon so solemn an occasion. Both H [Hope] & S [Sylvia] turned up most faithfully to support the Exec. Com. who had an easier triumph than they expected.

I finished my old diary weeks ago, & had no mind to start a new at first, with worry over Father, who is down again & much much better, though still slow of speech; & later on too busy with *The Northumbrian*.

Brian is coming to the office instead of Hope & it is very nice to have him … .

12 February. Various troubles. Poor Father has a bad eye, & Uncle Eustace is very ill, after wearing himself out over a bad case. He should have retired long ago! Poor Aunt E. has to do the dispensing & the sight of one of *her* eyes has failed. I think Father is a little better in other ways, but progress is slow. Brian has heard of a job in London … & has been up to apply for it … .

I have been off work a few days with various minor ills including swelled face. This has given me time really to finish [play].

13 February. … . I want to get on with:

(1) Paper for ILP

(2) Trial By Faith (my next play I expect).

7 March. … . After a long morning at the shop … I revised a copy of *The Hilltop* during lunch & sent it off to Uncle Fred. I have also sent a copy to the Drama League … . After tea at Fenwicks S. & I went to see the *Merry-go-Round* partly an Austrian film, it was not nearly so good as *Scaramouche* which we saw yesterday … .

11 March. 23rd night of the *Golden Apple*. Went ever so much better. I was better on the 2nd night, [?] much better, [?] was ill & rather poor. We doubted whether she wld come so I was ready to do her part, & Sylvia mine. I should have liked the experience … .

13 March. Went to Alnwick with Hope … we are staying at the *White Swan*, not very comfortable.

14 March. Went to read at the Castle … a room prepared for us with a fire in the grate a very Victorian room … . On the table was note paper & ink, & all the Record books that Mr H (keeper) had brought from the library for us – transcripts of rolls in red morocco bindings, very fat & heavy but beautifully written & fully indexed. Of course they are all in Latin with many abbreviations so I could only look up the places in the index & mark any important looking references with slips for Hope to take what she wanted from afterwards. It is dull work but not unpleasant & makes one very sleepy. We went out to lunch at the hotel & take a short walk in the middle of the day, & worked again till tea which we had at a cafe … .

15 March. … . Worked harder than ever, returning after tea. Once we met the Duke in his motor, driving out as we were crossing the barbican. It was very

picturesque in the castle after dark, with the lanterns lighted over the gates & the windows lit up … nearly finishing the Assize Rolls which Hope says are the most important. It was very eerie when we were alone there as dusk fell & the owls began to call in the park, & the office people had long gone away so we were the only folk in that part of that great queer place. Castles are very cold & very full of passages I conclude from my slight experience of this one.
16 March. … . However the Castle servants fortunately said that they couldn't do with us on Sunday so we had a whole day to play … . In the afternoon we rested over our drawing-room fire & I wrote a scenario of a … play … an early tea & took the train to Alnmouth to visit … we had a good stroll round first, along the High Links & back by the Low. This perfect day ended in a gorgeous sunset … .
17 March. I write on the train on the way home. We paid our last visit to our room in the castle this morning & made some show of finishing off. More remains than has been attempted!
23 March. … . Worked at the banner nearly all day & finished The Commonwealth of Nations … . Progress at last, but how little!
9 April. Last night of *She Stoops To Conquer*, which has been a great success; packed houses last two nights. Total receipts round about £18! The Banner has really got on a lot since the last entry, the side panels are more than half done & the centre piece, the rising sun, well forward; remains the name, the bottom scroll & emblems, the fringe, borders & general making-up. The great thing is to finish it somehow; what matter how it looks? The early pride & joy is gone, but dogged determination remains. It must be finished by May Day.
23 April. … . It must be finished by May Day! Still ten days! And all is well ahead except the name which is only just started. Dear little Mr Cockburn is going to make it up for me – my tremendous Banner. Work work work! That is the great thing. I worked hard at it during the holidays … . I gave up two possible motor runs for it! And spring just beginning! Never let anyone say I make no sacrifices for the Cause! Today I've had a hard day – paying a/cs at the Quay, which I hate; home & banner 4.30 to 6.30; Audit … 7 to 8, up to Wrekenton to a dance where the Elders asked me to give prizes at 9. (I walked up). Home by eleven, walking down Church Road from the train. I like going up the hill, but the Jazz Band was awful. Now must sleep to be ready for Banner, work, opera tomorrow.
27 April. Worked at Banner. Had cold & was tired; ran short of gold, which has been on order some time. Dramatic Club meeting; MH very bitter about his production. Its always the successful show there is the most trouble about.
28 April. … . I got soaked hunting round the town for gold cord. None right. Mrs Madden & Edie Jardine came & helped. Bottom border all sewn on by night. I had two committees, afternoon M & CW [Mothers & Children

Welfare] & Ed [Education]. Came home with my face swelling! The others at the opera … (miserable) … worked at the banner till 10.30 or after.
29 April. Could hardly see for swelled face but gold had come so worked at "Independent Labour Party" all day – the last to be finished; got the last gold on about nine at night.
30 April. Finished at last. Hope did black outlining all the morning; I was too tired & sore even to help after I got up. It looked fine spread out. Hope took it to Mr Cockburn before dinner … .
1 May. It was presented to the Branch & received with enthusiasm. Hope & S. went to bring me all the details; My face is going down; Dr McNaughton came late on Wednes. & prescribed Barley water mostly.
3 May. Cold & bleak for the procession; but our wagon was very jolly & the Banner looked fine.
Friday … off to the Lakes.
5 June. Strenuous day. Ed. sub-committee, quite good; I always enjoy the secondary meeting with Fred Tait in the Chair. He has been adopted for West Cumberland & is going to Penrith for Whitsun. Afterwards to the Branch; was asked again to stand for the Council in November & said I would not refuse.
19 June. At the Branch; very hot & full. They decided that my name be sent on to the LP & TC for a candidate for the Town Council in November, together with Mrs Biltcliffe & Mr Scott … . George Bosomworth's comment "God help you!"… .
Midsummer Eve – the Eve of St John. A lovely night; spent part of the evening marking the court with Brian & part putting finishing touches to my new … smock & skirt in silver grey tussau [silk], for tennis etc.
11 July. Aunt Poppy has been very ill since Wednesday. I suppose it is probably the end. The weather is very hot. I wonder if she will linger long, poor dear. She is not in pain, & more peaceful today; restless & uncomfortable last night. Aunt Camie is bearing up very well, considering … .

She is conscious when she is awake – at least partly so, & talking just in the usual way, just as thoughtful & kind to the people about her …
12 July. Aunt Poppy died about one o'clock today; she slept peacfully away … . She would have been 85 on Aug. 2nd. I remember perfectly giving her a tiny scent bottle (which she had previously given me) as a birthday present at Bamburgh when I must have been four years old, as it was before my mother died … . I suppose she had more influence over me in the most impressionable days of childhood than any other being except perhaps my father. She was always my fairy godmother in those days, & I owe her more than I shall ever understand. She had a long & very happy life; she made her happiness herself. I should like to write much about her & jot down many

recollections of hers that she told me, & many recollections of my own of her. Never was so gentle a soul – so good, so cheerful; never was silliness so closely mixed with a strong vein of shrewdness … . Hers was an interesting life only because *she* was interesting. I will write more of this another time … whenever she spoke (about times past) she went a long, long way back. Her late middle life, when I was with her most, she never appeared to recollect at all; she never spoke of Alnmouth or Glenridding House – only of earlier or more recent times … . When I try to remember all about Aunt Poppy, it is like trying to remember the whole of my life; very nearly, especially the holiday times. I am not going to reproach myself with being a bad niece to her; certainly I might have been better. But except when I was at the hateful time of life – between twelve & sixteen – "the difficult age" … I really think I did my best on the whole … I did love her very much & where my love failed, I tried to make believe. It is very foolish to let any sort of regret mingle with happy recollections of past times, & it is fatal to clear-headedness to sentimentalise the past, & imagine one was happier than one was. Mine was a singularly happy childhood, & yet to be truthful, it was the least happy part of my life. The passions were too acute, the sensitiveness too great. Aunt Poppy was always my confidante … .
5 June. … . Primary Com. at 6.30. I arrived late, but succeeded in raising swimming for Girls again.
7 June. … . Went to meeting after cutting the roses & took some. I was not altogether in tune with some of the speakers. Mr Gillie sees connections between certain parts of our spiritual life that seem to me quite distinct; but I dare say he is quite right; this time it was the joy of fulfilment in God – the finding of the Holy Grail – & the sense of shame, of being a woman, of having made a fool of yourself. To me these experiences seem quite apart; caused by different circumstances, leading to different ends … . But legend agrees with Mr Gillie: it was Parsaval [sic] "The Fool" who was destined to find the Holy Grail. Mr Chadwick, the meeting-house caretaker, was very nice to me while I was waiting for Hope; she was at a preparatory meeting. He gave me a book out of the Library & showed me the graveyard & all the mission rooms. He is my idea of an ideal Friend. *Mem* to bring him violas for his garden, (the old Friends' grave-yard).

In the afternoon went to Newburn by car, meeting the Drama Club for picnic … very successful. A good turnup in the end – 22. Walked along the river past George Stephenson's cottage to Wylam & Ovingham. Glorious. The hawthorn & broom in full flower; the meadows gold & silver & the clovers beginning. Tea at the Hermitage a lovely old market garden on the brink of Horsely Wood; we walked through it after tea – lovely, lovely place! O green leaves! And scents & white cowparsnip & silver birches. Home by

train as we are no late birds & got in quite late enough at 9.30.
9 June. Signed partnership agreement with Brian. He is off to London on Aero Club business but returns tomorrow. Things very slack at the Quayside.
… . Busy with *Labour News* stuff: four outside pages nearly complete. Went to Sunniside & back by bus & fixed with Mrs Berry for the hot water for the picnic on Saturday. Then to Bensham Grove (the Sunniside bus passes the door) for final Dress Rehearsal of *Peer Gynt*. Troll dance went badly, all the rest well. Then to Westfield; swept studio … Home by 10.30. Now for my psalm & then to sleep.
11 June. … More *Labour News*; it quite interferes with my work at times, I'm afraid, but not seriously. Only things that can wait. It was 103 in the sun at the Quayside.
13 June. *News, News, News*. Three times to Wilson's (printers) & all checked & "put to bed" at last! I hope it will be considered a good number. I *have toiled* at it. Rather on the heavy side but how can I help that? … .
14 June. Wednesday. Quiet day at home. Read Quaker Book – *Later Periods*. Very interesting – The day before Miss R & Miss EE had interviewed me about my application for membership of the Society of Friends. I hope I can become good enough I feel my unworthiness very much. I wish I was calm & good.
16 June. Day of sorrow & repentance & I'm afraid anger against S. for making me feel selfish & in the wrong. Of course it is not her fault that I *am* . Very wrong & thoughtless of me to have arranged my holiday without considering her enough. Well, it is all spoilt now, & I have had a miserable day. But that does not make the wrong right, nor will she accept any atonement; she remains, as ever the absolutely right one, & I the abased acknowledged selfish pig. This is the wrong spirit I know; but it is hard to be made to repent so often by a person who is *never* sorry & regards it as pure weakness in you to be so. I am praying to God to make me better & bring me into the right spirit, but I dont get on. I'm afraid even my repentence is really only vexation at giving her such a score over me which she may use for years … . I never thought, beforehand, that she would say it was unfair to leave her for a week with Father & Brian; she never said so when I first proposed Harbottle. It *is* unfair, if she feels it is so; & I would so *gladly* stay in the comfort & peace at home; rather even than going back to the dear hills. It wld be a *real* holiday for me; & I like helping Father; its nervous work but it makes me feel good. It *is* a waste that she cant be induced to change over. And all the time my sense of humour tells me I am making a fool of myself; & S. was only in a temper & got all she wanted by vexing me at the moment; & did not really want me to cry all day over it. If only I could think of something else! Why do my quarrels with S. darken the world so, always? I

must get used to them if we are to have a peaceful old age together. This may not be religion but its common sense.
17 June. I see where I have gone wrong now. One ought not to grudge other people the pleasure of triumphing over one; I ought not to grudge Sylvia the pleasure of calling me selfish & Hope the pleasure of calling me a fool. They would be less happy if they had no one to look down on; I ought to be pleased to give them that much satisfaction.

[Harbottle holiday with Hope]

4 July. Father's birthday. Got home late owing to doing a/cs, & also staying on to buy him some new ties for a present. Wasn't home till nearly 3 & found he was in the sitting-room having had a heart attack just as he was coming in from the garden. He was wonderfully cheery all things considered … . After tea Hope went to the Garage, got a taxi to Ashfield & brought back Aunt Poppy's carrying chair … . the driver seemed a good strong lad & very kindly & sensibly offered to get another young man from the Garage, which he did & they managed to carry him up [stairs] between them.
5 July. Father continues to improve. Good news from Sylvie (on holiday with Molly); Hugh has got a temporary appointment from the Egyptian Gov. to inspect locomotives in Belgium for 5 months at £50 a month; he may get more work if he gives satisfaction.
13 July. Hot & stuffy. *News* nearly ready … . They told me at meeting yesterday that I was accepted. Dear God, help me to be worthy – … . Was reading old diaries before supper & as old Friends might say "was singularly impressed by the goodness of the Lord towards me in times past"… [recalling] the night in Blemara Park [Lake District], which completed my change of heart, the choice of the narrow path, so beset with thorns & briars. "Woe unto me when all men shall praise me!" said St Joan; & it was one of the most moving speeches in the play. The passionate desire I have had ever since childhood, to be always praised & admired by every one, is only a delusion, not only impossible but even bad for me to dream about. It was true with the Friends, as well, that when all men praised them they weakened & went astray; when all men reviled them they were doing their great works – … . It is better to do right than be popular & much more lasting.
15 July. The *News* is out today – a dull number …. But I must practise a Quaker calmness in all the little ills of life. I find it hard, especially when I miss trams; though rage at that is utterly thrown away & vexes only oneself.
8 August … . I have been elected chairman of the Ghd. ILP Am. Dram. Club! [Gateshead Independent Labour Party Amateur Dramatic Club]
15th August. My resolution to write … & diary alternate nights has quickly

broken down. Everything breaks down the week the *News* comes out – except my iron determination to get it out somehow.
Thurs. Had to spend morning in writing article to fill up news.
19 August. Molly & Bob arrived at Ashfield today; also Brian & Helen turned up late at the end of their strange wild motor tour ... [they] are full of their new house. It is not finished yet they are choosing the walls & fireplaces ... .
20 August. Went to see the new house in Hawthorn Rd – very nice indeed. Coloured glass in the tops of the windows was the only rather glaring disadvantage ... . Tonight bad news – Aunt Louie poorly, feared slight stroke. Poor dears! Its awfully sad when the old people gradually break up one after another like this. It makes these early middle years very sad ones; I look forward – selfishly, I was going to say – but why selfishly? Naturally enough & without wishing my loved old ones anything but peaceful old age & no pain – I look forward to the twenty or so years that should come between the old people getting away & our own old age & break up. Those are the years when we should be able to do one's best work ... .
28 August. One night this week I was reading an old diary of Grandfather Mawson's written in 1834 when he was a chemist's apprentice in Penrith, about 19 years old. More of this later But he made his entry once a week on Monday, & I seem to be falling into the same habit, too ... .
3 October. Should have been helping at Friends' sale & doing a troll in Peer Gynt – to say nothing of *work*, posting the Red Ledger & editing the news! But instead I went to B'ghm to meet Aunt C. visiting Elsa on the way. A perfect day, & journey fairly comfortable but full ... . Went to the Repertory Theatre at night, by bus; a lovely sunset; then darkness falling; The Bull Ring on Sat. night – lights, stalls, crowds & crowds of people – a strange & wonderful sight. Then the nut brown inlaid interior of the Rep & the *Philanderer* [by George Bernard Shaw] '93 dress, very amusing tho' slight. A nice house, a nice audience, an interesting night. The clocks changed ... .
27 October. In the middle of the election – addressed 2 back-street meetings ... yesterday – back Hewson Street & Asylum Square. Three indoor meetings tonight – two at Wrekenton, in the Institute & the Schools – one in Sheriff Hill Schools. The County meeting poor but both ours very good for Mun. Elections. Hope has been to *Othello* ... she & I went to *Tristan & Isolde* on Monday; BNOC [British National Opera Company?] It was glorious. What a strange world! Canvassed Pimlico this aft. ... . It is not right that I should have all the music. The people in Asylum Square might have music too, if they had a chance ... still such places are a sin against the skies, a denial of God. Smells too & little water in the taps, & too much through the roofs is a *hate* a refusal of love. Dear God, make me worthy of the music & all the great joys you give me; help me to conquer my laziness & my putting off & my

blindness & my deafness & thoughtlessness to others. Give me more love; give me more sympathy & more power to show it
22 November. The By Election was, I think, on the 22nd. The result was
Wm Brerton Thompson R.A. 2,060
(The Sausage King)
Ruth Dodds (Labour) 1,576
There are 5,234 Electors
12 January 1926. Brian Mawson Dodds was married to Margaret Helen Nielson, in London, very quietly … . No guests. They went off to Monte Carlo for a fortnight.
16 April. Last night of the four nights run of *Pitman's Pay*. It has left me with exactly the same frustrated feeling as the first production – that it might have been so much better. Probably authors think just the same about all-star London productions! Sleep!

May Day 1926
Another May Day with troubles in Industry & threat of a General Strike on Tues. … . Helped with a very successful wagon for the Procession – Peace Unites the World … I did the dresses. Peace in white, with gold circlet & palm-branch, & flowing white veil sat on a high throne at the back. All the wagon & seats were covered with bright Royal blue sateen. White streams from Peace were held by the five Continents sitting on the front part of the wagon at a lower level than Peace. They were in scarlet & green mostly – America a Red Indian, brown & scarlet, Africa a nigger king in scarlet coat & checked trousers, with a gold crown round his top-hat; Australia in the middle, Digger in red shirt, & on higher seats further back Europe, peasant-girl in green & yellow & Asia, Jap in green & scarlet … the band out in its new uniforms; the banner in form; the South Ward turned up well & followed the banner. I hope "Peace" was a good omen!
Sunday. Went a ramble with Agnes's friends the Tyneside Sunday Ramblers; … walked about 12 to 13 miles; footsore but not tired; all on the *flat*! Father took quite an interest in my adventures. He is now permanently confined to bed, poor dear. But wonderfully cheery, considering, bless him.
9 May. I was 36 yesterday. The big strike began on Tuesday May 4th. May Day seems years ago. Our men & girls are all out except the apprentice little George Lloyd. The weather has been very cold with showers of rain & hail all the time. On Tues. I went to the Settlement & helped with the mothers & babies.
Wednes. Ned Scott came in; he is on the Central Strike Com & suggested a special number of the *Labour News*. I set to work at once. That night I went to the Co-optimists with Hope, but they were rather stupid & we left after the first

half … . Otherwise I went to 11 Bensham Rd, to the meeting of Ghd No 1 N.U.R. [National Union of Railwaymen], Ned Scott's branch; it was very exciting. They were in great spirits & showed me all the telegrams, & news from all round the district saying the men were solid. Thurs. & Friday I spent getting & writing up news – Leazes Terrace a *square* which I went *all round*, looking for No. 57, starting from No. 1. – Burt Hall, Wilson's, & all to walk round to in addition to walking in & out! … . Thurs, branch in evening … . On my birthday had a sort of quarrel with Brian. I'm afraid he has found my beastly cheerfulness all the week very trying. I did not mean to provoke him:[5] Baldwin himself asks us all to be calm & cheerful; & so we are on my side! It is a terrible thing to see a big, cheery man like that so frightened. Oh dear men are babies! They thought so little of the inconceivable horrors of the war, because it was done by the Governments, all decently & in order. Now they think it is revolution when the best organised men go on strike. I have agreed to leave the business & give him my share. God bless him, my own dear brother. He has not really treated me ill; I give what I give of free will & choice. He did not mean to be so brutal to me; he lost control. I was very unhappy & *very* tired last night … . The Browning love-letters got me through a dreary wakeful night; they are heavenly! Tonight I feel heaps & heaps better … . Hope & Sylvie were so sweet & dear to me. It was Father being worse, & then the lock-out & then the Strike, & then working so hard for the *News*, tired of it, & wished I was out of it; & now I do not want to go. I cannot believe yet that soon I shall go there no more. I go about telling myself at odd times, & trying to think what I shall do now. But I have never been very good at making up my mind or shaping my own future, & everything is confusion, from which the only clear thing that emerges is that it will be very hard to get any paid work; & if I give up that it will be fatally easy to waste myself over a dozen different pursuits. Hope's WEA [Worker's Education Association] Summer School last fortnight in July.

11 May. … . There was a frightful storm of rain about 9.30, so I waited till after ten, when the rain had stopped before walking in. I wanted guidance from God as to what to do next; but it suddenly came over me, as I was walking in, that as long as you do something honest, it does not matter so much what you do as the spirit you do it in. Brian is not exactly horrid to me now; I don't think he knows what to say. Turnbull is still worried, but less so than he was. He is more reasonable than Brian. I shall be sorrier to say goodbye to him for good than almost anything alse. I must try to cheer up; I have been feeling low & mimsey all day; my comrades are saying I'm down-hearted! – But it's not the fault of the strike. I am weary of their old strike & wish it was over – & yet – & yet – it is rather glorious too … . Swept Studio tonight. I was so low at dinner time that I could not face my own thoughts &

got a tiny book, an essay on nonsense, to occupy them, at the Lit. & Phil.
12 May. so the Strike has really ended on this odd day. To begin with it was very fine, & I felt in somewhat better spirits, – angrier & less weepy. I still do not "get" the idea of leaving the business & doing something else very well; … I have been trying to cheer myself up with the idea of leaving the business & doing *nothing*; but I cant *believe* in that … If only it had happened before Saturday, I might still be settled, too. But its no good crying over spilt milk. Got away about 4.30 & went to the NUR No1 Branch at 111 Bensham Rd … . News confirmed by the Strike Com., but they were waiting instructions from their own Ex. Com. Found a cartoonist for the *Labour News*. They were all very jolly & nice … saying they wld claim to have won the strike. Rushed home in a tram, too! the first for eight days … .

I am so glad & thankful that our TUC had the sense not to stand on dignity, & were ready to be first to give way when anything was to be gained by it. That showed the right spirit … .
13 May. Now before anyone can confuse the issues in my mind I want to write down my first impression, my earliest feeling – that the Great Standstill has been a fine & successful piece of work, a great demonstration. Whatever may happen now our people have proved that the General Strike *is* a weapon of peace & can be so handled. It ought to be done & could be done without any such hateful incidents as the stoning of trains & the derailing of the express; … . And this within ten years of a great War, which weakens the morale of all the people! The workers stood together, they were very nearly solid – 75 to 80% I should say – they trusted their leaders, they preserved order, they were willing to carry on the vital services, & did carry on (for instance) the sanitary, house-building & health services without any break … . It was a sight to see the *Manchester City*, a great meat-boat, unloading opposite our shop for two long warm days, by voluntary labour, & the dock labourers, the roughest class in the world, standing peacefully watching. Oh the faces in the streets – how they are warped & scarred & made hideous by our ugly life & conditions! Looking in the faces alone explains all our troubles; looking at our towns alone explains our narrow hearts & restricted ideas … .
Friday I was wrong after all in my cheerful first thoughts, as I feared I might be all the time I was writing them. But the trouble has come where I was never expecting it. The employers are demanding the general reduction in wages now & prolonging the stoppage from their side until they get it. This appears to be completely true on the railways, partly true in the printing trade, & uncertain, various among the rest. The trams are working again – some say at a reduction, but I think not. The transport men no one seems certain about; there was a rumour last night that the Northern 'buses would stop at midnight,

but even if it had been agreed at a meeting no one knew whether it would happen. There was a baton charge in Gateshead yesterday – the Spen miners were charged, as some think, by Durham County police; two are rumoured killed, but I continue to think not. Eyewitnesses report the attack unprovoked; in any case far too much force must have been used; the people so far have not been at all unruly. Will Lawther & the Chairman of the Blaydon UDC were up at the police court & fined £50 each. They are going to prison for 2 months, so I am told, as they cannot pay. In usual miners manner some of their Spen friends had marched in with bands & banner to show their support & were attacked by the police going home. Impossible to hear the truth of these things; but the band & banner were smashed up & many people hurt. And *our* people & unarmed.

Yes, the trams are running as usual but still no trains. I am in great confusion with the *Labour News* first trying to carry on, then not knowing what to do. Probably another strike bulletin will be best as the trouble still continues … . Everything is doubtful except the spirit of our people; that is simply marvellous. Last night with this hanging over us, a full Branch earnestly listened to an address on Finance & belatedly argued it; from 8.15 to 10. All the excitement of strike & lock-out & brutal violence had to stand over till after. Then the talk – oh the talk after was good! Our people are reasonable – even Fergie, to my surprise … . Was the country on the verge of civil war? God only knows, but talking to our ILPers one cannot believe it, & they rather more than most were the men at the head of the strike. Was the country "solid"? Here in the north it was to all intents & purposes. Our people had weeks & weeks of fight in them yet. Were the TUC partly afraid of other parts or were they misinformed? What was the response of the engineers? Good here, certainly … . Were the TUC simply tricked by the Government? I think so … simply the same old confidence trick of all time played by "honest" Mr Baldwin. Had they some warning of the employers intentions or did they hope to get back before that plan was complete? Madness, if that was it! Better have held out for the time at least … . We play *Pitman's Pay* in Town Hall on Sat. … I thank God for my good comrades & my good sisters, & my dear home.

Sunday. In the course of Friday & still more yesterday the face of things changed again, almost completely. But I will go back to Friday May 14th … decided to put off our Lakes walking tour till after Whitsun … . The papers were more reassuring – Railway negotiations in progress in London, & all sorts of fair promises from Baldwin, & denials by the Rly Cos.of the attack on wages & intended victimisation. Home to tea after a wild wander round the town in the sunshine wondering what is to become of me next. Then to Westfield to fix up PP dresses, but too restless to work, I went along to 111 instead & sat listening to Ned Scott's Committee (he is chairman of No. 1 NUR Ghd) & talking to one & another … . The news of the settlement had come through, but no definite orders to resume work from the local Strike Com. The newspaper & broadcast terms much resented, but the telegram "Re-instatement assured, no victimisation" – "seemed all right" they said. What has evidently happened is that the Railway Cos & other employers took the calling-off of the General Strike to be "Complete Collapse" "Absolute Surrender", etc, announced by the papers, & gleefully prepared to cut up the inanimate remains of trade unionism, after getting the men to sign any terms they pleased. They expected a stampede back to work, such as did occur in some sections of the transport workers. But the truth was that the railwaymen were more solid than at the beginning of the Strike; there was no general stampede & the stand on "no victimisation" quickly brought the Cos. back into a more reasonable frame of mind. And the transport workers … quickly came out again in those branches where reductions or victimisation did occur. I enjoyed more than I can say to see the NUR Ghd No. 1 Branch at work. Nice, jolly fellows! I am *proud* of our movement … . Home about 9.30 … more of my dear darling Browning love letters.

15 May. The day I ought to have gone to the Lakes! (special performance of *Pitman's Pay)* … There was a huge crowd in the hall; – admission free but by tickets distributed to No. 2 & 3 NUR branches – women as well as men in plenty & a very jolly appreciative audience; good listeners too, in spite of carrying babies. I dont know that the old show has ever gone better or even so well; but it has grown so familiar that I scarcely attach any meaning to the words now. Also I was tired & never in my life felt less inclined to produce a play … I cannot say what began as a weary duty ended as a pleasure – I think it did, or very nearly so – or wld have done so if I had not been forced to make a speech – however I posted Billy in the wings to strike up the Red Flag when I called for it, & with a sure end in view I managed to return thanks articulately, & to say that the moral of the play was that the good cause can never be defeated … . Is it victory or defeat? … no coal settlement … wld turn it into *real* defeat!

16 May. Molly came a day early … She is very sympathetic about Brian & the business. The more sympathy I get, the happier I feel. I *was* so miserable the first week, I cld scarcely think about it without crying. Now I have told several people & kept quite calm all the while.

Whit Monday … . Here's a motto from the Browning letters – if I could only feel as if the business was a prison, instead of feeling that it is or was my own niche in the world, my own work!

"If you take a man from prison & set him free – do you not probably cause a signal interruption to his previously all-engrossing occupation, & sole labour of love, of carving bone boxes, making chains of cherry-stones, & other such time-beguiling occupations – does he ever take up that business with the old alacrity? No! But he begins ploughing, building – (castles he makes, no bone-boxes now). I may plough & build – but there, leave them as they are!"

Of course he was referring to the transforming power of love; but though no great passion has ever come into my life I dont think I can be said … to "lack love" … I am both loving & beloved. And if I could devote myself to plays in the right spirit – plays written for the glory of God – that might be castle building. But to make it pay – that's the rub … .

26 May. Will this month never end? It is very dreary at the Quay, & I often can't help crying, even now when nobody is looking … every now & then, either at home or the shop, the thing suddenly comes over me again, like a dark black cloud, when I've nothing much to absorb me. Come, come, Ruth! This is not manly! This is not to have a quiet soul.

1 June. – the glorious first. Not so glorious as July will be. I am looking forward to my month of leisure. And yet all the time I am hardly less miserable about the parting than I was at first! This is very wrong; if I thought of God more, as a Quaker should, I should not feel so sore & angry & desolate, nor cry or half-cry so much when people are not looking.

THE PITMAN'S PAY

A HISTORICAL PLAY
IN FOUR ACTS

By
RUTH DODDS

WITH ACKNOWLEDGMENTS
TO THE SHADE OF MR. THOMAS WILSON,
THE POET OF MY NATIVE VILLAGE,
FROM WHOSE MASTERPIECE
I HAVE LIFTED
MY TITLE.

1923
LONDON
THE LABOUR PUBLISHING COMPANY, LTD.
6, TAVISTOCK SQUARE.

Title page of The Pitman's Pay

CHAPTER SEVEN: JUNE 1926 – APRIL 1928

Seeking work

13 June. … . Back to the dreary thought of a new life to begin & an old life to say goodbye to, & so many well-worn, familiar things to do for the last time! Back also to Labour Party rows.
16 June. This was the night appointed for the great burst-up of the ILP. But it didn't come off – everything offensive was expunged & all is to be forgiven & forgotten.
14 June. To London to look for a job … . Not much hope. Went to revue by Mrs Ewer's School; quite gay & amusing; but did not see her, as I wished.
15 June. Peace Pilgrimage to Hyde Park; very good. Folk-dancing in evening by the Serpentine – perfectly charming … .
17 June. Drama League – no luck. Old Vic – no luck. Mrs Ewers, no luck. St Pancras people's theatre producer did not keep appointment with me. Liberty's in afternoon; lovely. Tea on terrace (of House of Lords) with Mr & Mrs JB [Gateshead MP and wife]. Strawberries. Saw Baldwin etc.
16 June. Still no luck in morning but Miss Briggs of BDL (British Drama League) kind & helpful … [saw] *Granite* for matinee. Very good show. Evening meal in Hyde Park … . Went to the *Light of Asia* film at the Philharmonic & thought it very fine … .
18 June. … to Molly's
20 June. Home again!
30 June. Left the Business, as requested to by my partner BMD [brother Brian] on 8th May last. I went in Sept. 1915 & started at 5/- a week. The last days were unspeakably wretched. I *must* get more work or do some for myself. At night we played *The Pitman's Pay* to a full theatre at Houghton-le-Spring. Very enthusiastic. We believe we raised about £20 for the Miners' Relief Fund. Very jolly party in bus. Got back early (11.20) but very tired … .
3 July. Started to learn typewriting by touch. Am reading E.B.B's [Elizabeth Barrett Browning] letters as a sequel to the love-letters, but get on slowly. The first part is dull.
5 July. … . Did *Pitman's Pay* at Ouston. Good audience; small but decent Hall.
4 July. Torrents of rain all day. I was very tired & slack. Corrected proofs for *Labour News* …. Repeat performance at Ouston; poor things, they are dreadfully badly off there. It was nice playing to them & giving them a little pleasure. A letter from Brian waiting when I came home; would not read it tonight, as I want to sleep; but I glanced at it & it begins with an apology. Wretched business! As soon as I get over it a bit, it developes a new stage & throws me back; tears & misery are much more tiring than plays & politics! I

have found that out in the last two months anyway. It is to be hoped they do make my plays better; there is not much comfort else. Of course I do forgive him; I am sorry for him, the poor dear silly boy; to get into such a mess! But I am weary of the whole thing.

7th July. He does not repent, after all, though he has sent me a belated apology. Men hardly ever do, at any rate to a woman. I suppose, though it never struck me before, that sex is at the root of the trouble. He would not have treated another man so; & another woman could not have treated me so. If I had been a brother he would never have come back; if he had been a sister he would have been able to work with me – probably able to take second place. Sylvie was right in thinking that he would improve his offer if I held out a bit. She understands him better than I do … It is a shame always to let Hope do Father's breakfast. But I do his bed. And now that I am sleeping better it is so nice in bed in the morning! The time flies away in writing letters & listening for Father; nothing done! … .

9 July. More *News*. Went to Steve Wilson's [printers] in the afternoon & on to town. Had no time to look at the Sales. Went to *Man & Superman* at full length … . It started at 5 & went on till 10.45! Still I enjoyed it

14 July. *Labour News* out today. Now I shall hope to have a little peace; but it has all been most unsatisfactory & I hate the new format … .Then to Ashfield. We had a lovely meeting in the garden on Monday when Ald. Smith spoke on the WEA. Now they are going to form a class with Hope as tutor in Social History.

15 July. Sales in the morning. Got some things for the miners'children but spent far more on myself.

18 July. Wrote & worked at typing … . Primary Committee in evening. Ald Hayes gave me post-dated cheques – well, better than nothing.

19 July. Spent all morning at Shipcote Girls' school … . I quite liked Miss Burgham, the head, a woman devoted body & soul to her work. The staff were delightful. Afternoon at the Arts & Crafts Exhibition at Armstrong College Art School, which I enjoyed much … .

22nd July. … . I dreamt about the business last night & woke up half-crying & half-saying "It *cant* be true I am never going back any more – it *cant* be true!"

23 July. Had a delightful visit to Askew Road Schools – we did Oakwellgate yesterday … . We agreed that Oakwellgate was the worst …

26 July. Sat. Hope went to Cambridge. A warm, wet sunny morning I visited an ex soldier to see he had a wife & count his children, for fear he had made a mistake in filling in his form; got Father's medicine; walked home through the Park, which is charming – more flowery than I remember it … .

I met Peter Howcroft at 1.15 & he took me to Walbottle to hear A.J.Cook speak … in the Banky Fields – a fine playground with a fair stretch of level … All was jolly & friendly – men women & children … from the high ground we saw the country for miles around … Cook – a fine old man of Peter's age – they were boys together; with the old-fashioned Northumbrian tongue in him – more dignified & more ancient than ordinary Tyneside … after the rush to greet him & while they were in the very act of carrying him to the platform shoulder high, the rain began! I listened perhaps 30 minutes in the wet; he is a fine speaker, & without being at all handsome, not half so ugly as the newspapers make him. A more intellectual face than I expected – much. Very fine gesticulations, very forceful speaker & yet arresting – in spite of the wet & the distance, difficulty in seeing & hearing; shouting of children, constant movement – in spite of all I was impressed … .

… to Mrs Joicey at Beacon Lough with a parcel of woolies knitted by Hope & Sylvie for her fund of garments. She was very pleased & gave me a cup of coffee & a rose & showed me the garden, which was lovely – so I got the treat & the others did the work … . A Communist spoke long, long long in the playing field, all in the golden afternoon. Went to Council at night; rather sickening; but I must face out November & try not to let the Party down; but for the shame of that I would throw it up now as some have done … . I do like Ned Scott; he is one of the sort that encourages one to go on; he has lost his job on the railway, perhaps for good, thro' the Strike.

15 August. With the *News* out yesterday, the first rush of the month is over & I must now concentrate on preparations for London. I must make lists! Of what I want & of whom I want to see. I still live in a sad rush & I am horrified to think that for the last two years or so my most frequent prayer has been "Lord give me strength to fulfil my obligations" – a sure sign that I have wilfully taken on far more than I could efficiently perform. Now I must think seriously a bit & try to reduce my chaos to something like order. I am reading a splendid book on the *Art of Thinking* by Graham Wallace, & it has made me repent my slovenly life & especially my slovenly mind. I dont suppose I can do much about it, at my age, but I'll try … .

I think I am missing the business subconsciously a good deal, though I dont think about it much. I am worried & nervy & had a dreadful cry on Thursday, when a trifle put me out at the Branch. I am also silly enough to be nervous about going to London. Strangers frighten me, & the idea of looking for work terrifies me … . My dreams have been bad for the last two months or more … I am in a state of strong reaction against the Labour Party. I think it is the moors I really need. The London holiday will be nice but not quite what's wanted … . I long to finish my play – my poor play – I think the mechanical effort of learning touch typing takes it out of me to a ridiculous extent. But once it becomes really mechanical it will be an enormous help in every way. I

must make my London arrangements now. How I hate the mechanics of life!
17 August. … . I am reading *Early English Lyrics*. I am miserable; I am happy; I am wearying for my business; I have far too much to do; I hate politics; but I cannot live without them. I love books but when I read I fear I am wasting my time, & once I read I forget. I long to get rid of the *Labour News*; yet if only I could make it better, I might almost love it – at least it might become like the business used to be, a sort of mainstay. Dear God, give this girl more sense … .
23 September. I feel so strange coming back from a holiday & not going back to the business – it is unnatural, like a dream – something gone wrong.
25 September. This silly feeling … has not by any means left me, but attacks me whenever my brain is unemployed even if my hands are busy. I have been busy since getting home, though I have not done much that my soul approves, except typing a few sheets of index for Hope … .

Also on Wed. the day we arrived, I went to a ward meeting at Ashfield. Packed, especially with women. Hope & I were at *Romeo & Juliet* for this is the BNOC Festival week. I went to *Parsifal* on Thurs. & to *Hansel & Gretel* last night. Both fine & a nice contrast … . *Parsifal* was really beautiful; yet both *The Mastersingers & Tristram (sic) & Isolda* gave me more intense pleasure … .
23 October. I am in the middle of the Election Campaign & enjoying it too, largely thanks to Ned Scott, who has been a huge big help … .
4 November. The election over, I feel rather used up. But it has been much nicer than usual, because the weather was so much finer & because I was able to do a lot during the daylight instead of struggling round in the dark. I am a bit disappointed this time, more so than ever before; it would have been such a nice occupation the Council work, would have gradually taken the place of the business, being rather the same sort of thing – figures & people to be judged by their capacity for their special work … . never mind I shall have more time for plays. When I count my blessings, it does seem wrong to be cross; even the election has brought me in heaps more funny friends. Next thing is the *School for Scandal*. *The World the Flesh & the Devil* is off. Also I am busy with the next *Labour News* It is heavenly to have fires in the sitting room & a gas-stove in my room. …. I have read a lot lately, having more time to read. I have read *Bleak House & The Ring & the Book* during the election campaign … .
7 November. It has been a lovely fine day. I got up *very* late alas! And wasted some time reading a little book of Hope's – literary essays. Hardly had I got to work on *School for Scandal* dresses etc when Jack Short turned up on *News* business. Then to Ashfield … . Delicious dinner – I'm turning a dreadful gourmand but make a rule against 2nd helps! Then up the hill to

mass demonstration … to Mrs Tait's to order Sylvie a pair of moccassins as a Christmas – birthday present. The (Tait) twins delightful – … she came down with me to the Windmill Hills; quite a good demonstration; heaps of police; the Chief Constable accosted me & we had a long argument on the influence of environment on character. He told me the story of his life – he is so exactly like the quintessence of policeman that you can hardly believe in a thing so like itself … . Sylvie had a nice birthday when I got in … . Then to evening meeting Hope spoke about "We cannot fall lower than the arms of God however far we fall." Then to the Town Hall, packed; I received a sympathetic clap when I appeared, as the highest loser … .

8 November. … . Went to Sheriff Hill after a busy morning over the *News* & the play. Had a jolly time at the Soup Kitchen … went to Sheriff Hill Women's Section & had a very confused time … . I wish I had not been landed with these weary women's meetings … .

11 November. … . Went to West Hartlepool & found the two old dears very well. Had a nice shopping with Aunte Edie & went to a wonderful new oriental cafe – the Andora – with gold tables & hand-painted walls & marvellous Eastern embroideries – furnished by a W.H. millionairess to give a friend a start in life – regardless of expense & ordered in Bond Street! The chairs were goldy-green basket work, & there were ash trays of glowing French glass, orange & greeny-blue, on the tables. The china was charming Chinese flowery designs in greens, pinks & blues. The coffee was excellent … . Played Patience in the aft. *Mem.* to send her some Patience cards. I was vexed to have to go & pleased that I went.

… . Coming home I never saw such fireworks as the engine made – like one long glorious Guy Fawkes display nearly all the way home – glowing golden cinders swirling through the air, some curling to earth like meteors, some streaming upwards like fireflies – sometimes, when we went fast, shooting by in long golden streamers, like the shower of gold. It was really beautiful, though dazzling & wearying to the eyes – showers of fire against the dark dunes & the dark sea. And they "lay" too! – thick on platform or roof of anything dry, glowing on the ground. All the result of poor coal I suppose!

10 November. A long busy confused day. To Wilson's [printers] in the morning … . Steve told me the news – Wardill Mayor, Fibbens & Sleigh knocked off, & Maccoy & Thubron co-opted; they evidently daren't force by-elections. Fred Tait & I are knocked off the Education Committee, as I expected, & Miss Tooke & Mrs Allen put on … .

15 November. I cannot write about the proposed mining settlement. It makes me too angry & miserable. Hope's Marley Hill Class was reduced to 4 because the Miners were at the Lodge meeting voting … .

16 November. And yet what a lucky woman I am! lying here in my comfy bed, enjoying my pretty room – every detail of it – my gas fire on; my dearest sisters, my pleasant thoughts, my good comrades, my busy full life! Above all my happiness here at home in every little thing in life – all the little troubles are nought, even the things I have thought real troubles are not worth a single cry. The only real trouble is darling Father's helplessness; *in* my home that is. And the only *real* trouble outside is not lost business or lost Council majority – oh dear no! but the terrible distress among my friends the miners, & now these shameful terms – shameful to owners & government, that is .... How to help? I wish God would show me how best to help.

20 November. I ought to be composing my mind for Sunday; but God will understand. Really & truly I am trying hard. Today I went to see Helen & Brian, & Hope went with me to help me out; & Sylvie was rather cross with me – but all that's neither here nor there. Wed. Thurs & Friday I had rehearsals (for *School for Scandal*) none of them bad – some excellent in parts. But the news all the week – the miners rejecting those wicked terms, as well they might, & the lies of the press & the cowardly half-truths of the M.G. (Manchester Guardian) – I did think it wld have stood by the Liberal Coal Commission Report ... . Team Colliery has broken away, & poor Peter is rather like a colonel whose regiment has run away in action – crushed with grief & shame ... . He had a meeting from 6 to 12 on Thursday – "pleading with them", as he says. Today he had been at the demonstration at Birtley ... .

23 November. ... . on Monday to a Women's Section meeting in that dreary school-room with the oil-lamps & the blackleaded stove. I heard that Peter, at the colliery, had had an encounter with the manager, who swore at him, for trying to keep the men out – ... & told him he was a marked man; & that the Superintendant of Police went to him, Jim Elder & another, as they were talking together & warned them that if they spoke a word or stayed there any longer they wld be arrested ... . As I was waiting at the terminus, I suddenly noticed that all the men who were standing there (& they have stood there in crowds ever since I can remember) were moving away, in different directions. It was because three policemen were espied in the distance coming down the street ... – it made me feel queer. Afterwards I told about it at Kibblesworth to a nice old couple in the Aged Miners Homes, ending rather tritely- "& we call this a free country." "Ay", said the old man "you're free to go barefoot when you have no boots." I want to see Peter & hear the truth.

This is Tuesday night & I have heard so many different tales at the women's meeting – that there were 50, 100, 150 men working at the Betty Pit. That there were only 5,7,9. I think there is some confusion between men working & men hewing. As soon as a pit opens up they count all the safety men as men now at work even tho' they never were out ... . Women's Section wore me out. It always leaves me feeling like a chewed rag. But I ought not to

think so much about myself when I am all right among so much all wrong. That old lady over 70 said she had never had a scullery house before! … .
27 November. Went to Ncle People's Theatre production of *Troilus & Cressida*. Really very good … .
28 November. … meeting after tea Town Hall, when at last I saw Peter Howcroft & we walked home in the rain & he told me all about it. It was all true about his encounter with the Manager & the police superintendent. The Manager (Colonel Davies) swore at him & said he'd made a clean sweep of the men … & that he'd never get taken on there again. The superintendent told him, more briefly, that if he even spoke to one of the men he'd spend the night in Durham Goal … .
3 December. … . At night took Helen & Brian to the theatre. It's years since I went to the Dress Circle! It was a cold night. The play primitive, but not so silly as I had expected. The company good … . I am not going to bother about those young people any more; they cant say now that I never spoke to them again because of the business. But if we are to have any further intercourse its up to them to begin it. SD [Sylvia] was furious with me about it; "they rob you of half your income & you buy them expensive theatre seats!" Well, that's not quite fair of course; but I love her to stick up for me, bless her. Dear God, help me to forgive my debtors – & always to keep my temper.
23 January 1927. Nearly a month since I wrote! … bad leg was the beginning of an attack of cold or flu or something which finally got me down on New Year's Day (when Hope went to London) & kept me in the house for ten days.
26 January. Sales in the morning. Bought new grey crocodile shoes 42/- reduced from 63/- New felt hat, pale blue 10/- Petticoat 20/- reduced from 35/6 & two prs stockings. I am almost fitted out for London … .
20 June. … . (on the 11th) Father was rather restless & exacting all day, But I did not realise he was so much worse … . Next day we had the Dr & he said it was another stoppage in the brain. He continues to eat well & read a little, but cannot get up or raise himself without help. Then I was to take Aunt Camie to Oxford on the Friday & Sylvia away in the Island! It was a very worrying time. In the end we arranged for a nurse to come while I was away. But S. came home on Friday afternoon & it was really a great relief to me, for I'm afraid Hope would have worried herself to death in sole charge. Now I am at Oxford with Aunt Camie at the Oxenford Hotel; we spent one night at Peterboro'. So far all has gone pretty well, & I had good or goodish news from home today; at any rate he is no worse; … . I think Camie is enjoying it.
25 June. I came home yesterday – a wild tempestuous Midsummer day. On Thursday I saw the OUDS (Oxford Union Dramatic Society) do *The Tempest* in Worcester garden (the Provost's garden) in front of the famous pond, with

swans & ducks swimming up & down behind the actors & all the birds singing joyfully in the trees round about when the play began … .
8 July. … . How I have wasted my best time, & not even won the material success I sought. I have lost my little business that was to have made the money to finance my plays! And now I cannot even find energy & brain to write plays. I chew my way through life in a foolish & aimless half-content. Really I must buck up! I am not worthy to be a Quaker & to be a Socialist. I have lost my place in the work a day world & become a parasite. Well I must make myself a new place in the theatre, maybe, but anywhere that I could do needed work. If only I could get over this sense of utter futility!
9 July A lovely day. Picnic to Finchale [priory] with Hope's WEA Class. The Office of Works are making it beautiful … .
16 July. Sylvie & I had a great day. We went to Leeds to see the Miracle play "King Robert of Sicily" performed in Kirkstall Abbey.
16 July. Polam Hall Darlington … Quaker Summer Settlement … . I was doubtful about coming & came as a duty; now I am glad.
31 July. The two addresses given on Saturday morning were full of the joy of work; Industry, commerce, helping the world to fulfil its needs by the work of its hands is a most fascinating pursuit for any man or woman. For this reason I think that the managing classes in industry are among the happiest & most fully developed of human beings; but they have crushing responsibilities & they have great temptations … the evening lecturer … never once mentioned the word competition. Now, I entered my father's business much later in life than is usual, at the age of twenty-five. My character, of course, was fixed, & my opinions on many subjects, but not on the subjects of trade & industry which I had hardly considered at all. I therefore went into business with a perfectly open mind, & with a tremendous enthusiasm both for service to the community & for my own particular business, & for my own little family firm, which is a tiny affair employing less than twenty people … During the ten years I was in industry, I found that competition was still the ruling spirit there. It is true that the trade I was engaged in, the printing trade, is one of many small masters & especially keen competition, but I am quite convinced that what I saw there is also applicable to many large industries, & generally speaking, to industry as a whole – there are exceptions – the post office & municipal services for instance … . The degradation of the workers by poverty is a horrible thing, but the degradation of the rich by riches is not a bit prettier … . Only those who have tried to be strictly honest in a highly competitive business can have any idea how hard it is. I never attempted a profit -sharing scheme; one of the greatest reasons I did not was because even when I was in complete practical control I always had people who strongly objected to revealing the details of the balance sheet to the workers, & exactly

like Mr Ford, I felt that to give a bonus without showing the figures would increase & not decrease distrust. So we gave a yearly Christmas box instead, which is not at all the same thing.

To show the difficulty of bare honesty take the question of pricing. When I was in the business, I had a costing system which was not perfect, since nothing human is perfect, but was as good as I could get it & was overhauled from time to time to keep it up to date. During the later years of the War & the Boom this worked very well. I priced all orders & all estimates on the same basis with the same rate of profit on both. To the best of my ability it was a fair price. The workers all got trade union wages, & the workers with more than ten years service got a little more, according to length of service. But when the slump set in there was a different story. I could only get orders at a competitive price by cutting down profits. Therefore, there were two prices at least, one for customers who asked for an estimate & one the "fair price" for those who did not. I felt this to be wrong but I was driven to it. It is easy to make out a case for taking a job that shows no profit at all; it keeps your machines busy, it keeps your men off short time & in better heart. But surely you can see how great the temptation becomes in such cases to take the profit where you can get it, & put a bit on to Peter, because you have charged too little to Paul. People who yield to this are actually overcharging their best & most trustful customers to subsidise those who refuse to pay a fair price, & you are gradually on the drift towards rule of thumb charging which amounts to charging each customer as much as you think he'll pay. But besides the customers, how are you behaving to your competitors? The invariable answer is that you are only treating them as badly as they do you. But if nobody ever attempts anything better it is clear that things will get worse & worse. If you want to know how it is that competition in the printing industry is so keen, the explanation partly is that the trade is not thoroughly organised & that in non-union shops girls are employed on work which the men trade unionists claim is theirs, for half or even a third of the men's wages. There are several unions in the trade & the most powerful one has no women members & does not concern itself with women's pay, so that even in nominally union shops it is rare for the *girls* to get trade union wages … . With so many varying factors, especially considering the number of small printing works, with infinite variety in efficiency of organisation, it is no wonder that any batch of printers' estimates show such startling variety … . I always had the idea that I could keep sufficient trade on quality & straight dealing, even if my prices were a little higher than others. I still believe I could have done so. However that faith has not been put to complete proof as I left the busines last year.

Promptings or suggestions which seemed to come to me during the Week-end Settlement:

(1) Further work, probably literary, giving a picture of mining life & trying to express the miners' view of the world …
(2) Help to young people between school-age & marriage.
(3) More active work for children, especially:-
 (a) in the schools, by bearing testimony against War.
 (b) by means of the Holiday Camp movement.
(4) Greater earnestness & concentration on:-
 (a) my own work
 (b) my Socialist work
 (c) any work for Friends, or at any rate in attendance.

15 August. Grisedale Bridge [Lakes] It is funny coming back in the summer holidays, with the limes in flower & scent & the potatoes blossoming, white & mauve. There is not at all the same rapture in coming back that there used to be; & yet it is very pleasant & happy all the same.
16 August. … . The Lake was nearly over the boat-landing last night & must, I should say, be quite over it today. But I have not been down through the mushy fields to see … . On Saturday we had a gorgeous day & walked to Angle Tarn & down by Hayeswater … . We paddled twice, once at lunch time in a tiny wee beck beside Angle Tarn, & once half-way home, in the Angle Tarn Beck just where it reaches Patterdale after an exciting series of falls over the crags. It was full hot sun; Hartsop was looking quaint & sweet; all the becks were full, but clear; the tortoiseshell butterflies were on the purple thistles.
17 August. A perfect day of sunshine, blue sky, white clouds, warm still, yet with a tiny cool breeze. A truly fairy day. I cannot bear to miss a minute of it … . We set off with sandwiches in the boat quite early & reached Aira Force landing at about eleven, after a lovely row down the Lake; all the colours so intense, the fields an intense light green; the sky very blue & the clouds very white & the rocks very purple-grey … . We bought chocolates at the tea hut from a talkative old lady. We went the lower way to the fell; there were a lot of visitors, but the charm of that wooded dene cannot be spoilt; the oaks clinging to the rifted crags, the honeysuckle climbing on tree-tops below your feet in the gully; the boiling of the brown water in creamy foam over the mossy rocks … (on the fell) you can see almost the whole length of the lake – a small piece at each end only cut off. The long line of the Pennines with Cross Fell plain to see bounded the view to Eastward; Great Mell Fell loomed into sight. Birk Fell & Sallow & Hallin were looking their best, with High Street very fine & aloof behind & all the fells at the head of the Lake from St Sunday to round to Angle Tarn Pikes very majestic … . If I could only keep in my mind the briskness & sparkle of the sky, the sweep of the passing clouds, the silver-grey glitter of the

lake in the sun, the glorious hotness of full sunshine; the grateful coolth of the passing shadows! And a thing to be remarked is that the bracken, vivid green in the morning light, had turned into a shimmery grey-green, with a silver touch under the light of high noon. Up this way too there was ragwort. We turned the corner of the hill just beyond a stone seat marked "A Thankoffering 1905", which commanded the whole view I have described of nearly the whole lake; from this spot there was also a steep way down into the low path. I want to go that way some day. Round the corner we came into a charming little valley – quite remote, with both trees & bracken slopes. Then we climbed up behind the outmost projecting rubble, hoping to see deer, but did not go high enough for them & returned to the path well below the Thankoffering seat, down a steep & stony hillside, Bob (nephew) flying joyfully ahead. Molly & I would have liked to explore to the end of the path, but he was panting to be back on the Lake, which certainly looked very attractive, blue down & silver-grey up. We had a pleasant row back & landed on the big Island … . After tea – & we were hungry! – we had to go out again; it was too gorgeous to stay in. I walked down to Silver Point by the high path that goes behind Silver Hill. It was glorious with the golden light blazing on the lake … . I was glad to walk quietly home again by the low road, & watch once again the beautiful shining evening close in on Patterdale & the sunlight creep higher & higher up Place Fell, leaving the whole valley in shadow, & notice the strange effect on Black Crag when the sun was glowing on the haze that clings to the hilltop when it no longer touched the side of it all. Peace, peace; & the song of the stream, & the owls calling in the trees round the house when darkness fell; & a bright star among the pines; & the light in the northern sky gleaming silver on the still lake.

5 September. Kew. Today I saw Winnie at her Nursing Home 202 Bedford Hill, hard by Tooting Bec Common. *And* the precious baby who is to be my godson. He is a fine boy, plain, & his face a good deal marked, poor fellow (surely they ought to have been able to avoid that?) but healed up now, & he has good eyes & masses of dark hair – almost wavy! … . Uncle Fred had an old cousin to tea, a little old white-haired lady called Mary Wilkins; she was one of Aunt Edie's bridesmaids! She is small & shabby & gentle & very sweet, with bright brown eyes, & pink in her delicately-wrinkled cheeks, & a pretty soft Irish voice with the tiniest trace of an Irish brogue. She is an old friend of Father's & he visited her once in her Irish home – Edenfield in Co. Down … . she has two sons & a daughter married & eight grandchildren, & it is great days when they come to London & can be shown the sights; for she is a sightseer to hobby, a real definite calling; she has specialised … in the City churches … . She asked me to go with her & I accepted with enthusiasm.

6 September. So on this day I met her at the Temple at noon – at the District station that is, & we walked alone to the Temple through the embankment Gardens … . We did the Temple first – the Church which was stuffy, but the effigies of the knights in the round church were fine … . The Middle Temple Hall is especially fine & has a magnificent 16th C screen … . We saw most of the Courts – Fountain & Figtree & Pump & Goldsmith's Tomb & King's Bench Walk, & the famous gardens – rather filled up with the tents & marquees of a *Daily Express* gardeners' garden party. This funny little bird-like, tireless old lady is an *Express* reader! Then we went up Fleet Street past the *Punch* office. By this time it was raining & I bought a gamp … Cheapside. I suppose it was here that the churches began but I forget those I only saw without going into … . The first I went into was St Mary le Bow – a Wren church, with subdued brownish glass – better outside than in; like most Wren churches … . Once in Threadneedle Street we threaded our way to St Helen's "The Westminster Abbey of the City." It is the old Priory Church of a convent of nuns –- the church-yard beautiful, & quiet & retired just out of the roar of traffic. Many fine tombs – Then we went on to St Ethelburga's, the quaintest of all, with steps in front, & a printing office (amateur) & a fountain garden (tiny) behind it – all so very very wee! We had a cup of tea in the Lyons opposite – good big hot strong cups which were most refreshing. We ought to have lunched in St Paul's Churchyard instead of the portico, but it was raining too hard … . Mrs Wilkins was very indignant at the recent proposal to sell some of the city churches to provide larger stipends for poor clergy, gloriously defeated in the House of Commons. She said they were all used & useful, & from what I saw it is quite true. Then we went on to All Hallows, basking by the Tower, passing several Wren churches by the way … a newly excavated crypt, dedicated to St Francis. It is beautiful but frightfully "high" … . One thing that amused me was the theatrical effect of arc-lamps *outside* the East Window, so that in dingy city weather they could turn on a little appropriate religious stainglass light! All this time it rained & rained. We would have gone to the Tower Gardens if it had been fine … . The day was dark & dreary as November … . Mrs Wilkins simply did not mind, scarcely seemed to notice; so we both enjoyed every minute of the day … .

2 November. Today I gave Peter Howcroft my lucky £200, which has already been given on the "ask it not again" principle three separate times & always comes back. Last Monday … it came back from Molly, who used most of her Cerebos win from Aunt Camie that way. I never expected it back from her; & now I dont see however it is to come back from Peter; but I hope it will bring him luck. It was to rescue him from the mines, where I was afraid he would kill himself, that I gave it to him

3 November. First night of *Doctor's Dilemma*. Went very well, & we had a better house than for a long time – £3 …

4 November. The second night was even slightly better than the first ... Sylvie is very busy getting the electric light arrangements made – another result of our windfall.

Dear God save me from the sin of wanting to please everyone.

5 November. ... . The last night of DD went best of all & we had a fine audience a £4.10/- audience ... .

10 November. Bob pronounced to have scarlet fever ... . Molly has a nurse & reports that he is going on all right though his temperature is still high. Spent last night at West H. keeping Aunt Edie company ... more snow.

11 November. The electricians very troublesome all this cold day putting in the electric light & making draughts. Good news from Molly. Bob getting on well ... . Went to Bensham Clinic in the afternoon, writing down babies' weights ... small clinic owing to the snow & cold. Ashfield to tea. Branch at night – quite a good Branch. The triumphant Moderates have turned me off the Maternity Committee

12 November. This is my week for attending to Father – but that is no excuse really for my lazy habits. It's true I was obliged to lose a good deal of time over the West Hartlepool visit, but I could easily have made it up again by reading the newspapers less & working more. My whole life's a disgrace because my mind is slipshod – I have no regular habits – except the habit of being late for everything. I did get up a tiny bit earlier & work a tiny bit harder today. I finished my article answering Lundi, the solicitor who has been sending me vague threatening letters because of an article I had in the election issue of the *News* about the Rent Case. He thinks I'm scared of him! – I'll show him! ... . to the Health Office & I have agreed to do voluntary work at the ... Clinic every Thursday. This is sure to prove a nuisance like all regular engagements, but I think I can manage; & I am sick at being turned off after seven – or is it eight? years. And I have done no wrong – only been keener & worked harder than the others. Its a shame ... . Then I went to Westfield – briefly – & home to dinner. Worked a bit on the *News* ... went to Wilson's again ... in the early evening; Westfield again & home to supper; worked at minutes & letters in evening. A busy empty day! Dear God help me to do better & to fulfil my obligations – all of them – & always in the right spirit. It is still snowy.

12 November. A rushing tiresome day; but good news from Molly about Bob. The men not done yet. Some hail & some shopping, & a good deal of *Labour News*.

16 November. Second rehearsal of *The Pressed Man*. Perfectly awful but got almost through. A lovely day in weather. Electric light almost finished. I ought not to be so cross when I have everything so nice at home.

17 November. Town shopping; bought hats at Bainbridges toy bazaar – a

Dickens & a Highwayman … . Ordered green linoleum for my room surround. Afternoon at clinic; lovely babies. Branch at night; not bad. Peter walked home – his first time at Branch for ages. His notice is withdrawn, so he wants to go back to the pit.

19 November. A crowded inconclusive sort of day. Went to town in the morning, after delaying too long reading the MG [Manchester Guardian] by a lovely fire. The MG is little better than a snare! … . A quiet evening at home. Poor Father's mouth bad. Peter in most of the evening. H & S at a play … . Peter has promised to leave the Pit at New Year.

20 November. Meeting – They spoke mostly on humility – much to my condition, as I had been bemoaning my pride & self-satisfaction the night before … .

21 November. The bedside electric lights have come – called limpets, with ugly pink shades – but they are not yet installed. Tomorrow, O little candle which hast lighted my diary-writing so long & so inadequately, we shall part, only to meet in times when the juice fails. … . Have worked pretty hard at some Robin Hood dresses a lady from Shrewsbury wants to hire [from the theatre wardrobe which Sylvia and Ruth ran]

26 November. Another day gone & nothing done! How easily cld I fill this page with vain repining at my useless life! Yet I did a lot – wrote minutes & saw *Faust* & had a rehearsal. Only – only – I never get anything *finished*. I fritter away a morning on half a dozen things instead of doing one & then done with it … .

28 November. Sent off Robin Hood costumes. Worked at dresses for play nearly all day. Women's section & Bazaar Com at night. Life is tiresome, somehow. I think a course of Jane Austen would be good for me, but have no time. …

8 December. The first night of *Pressed Man*. Went pretty well on the whole. Last act weak … . The high brows & go-getters may sniff at me & my company & my audience but I maintain it is well worth doing & I will not grudge the best I can give, though only to amuse by playing at the greatest of theatres, these lads & lasses that spend all day in monotonous work in the factories & offices & workshops. It must do them good & widen their horizons & give them the taste in some measure, for intelligent enjoyment, & an understanding of the theatre. And I am sure it does all these things for me. God has given me a very humble place in my chosen art, & I have wasted many idle thoughts on how to win success, but now I am content with this, the lowest & least success, that the world would mock at as much less than expensive failure. No matter if they maul my poor plays about, no matter if it keeps me from any sort of advance in other directions. It is the task in hand; & my reward is that its a perfect scream! Its good to give fun & have fun too.

13 January 1928. More *News* which seems to cut across everything. Also I am doing Father in the mornings tho' that doesn't really take long. He is much better & more cheerful … . It is really because I am amusing myself so much that I never have any time. S & I went to *Hindle Wakes*. It was splendid, the best British film that I've seen for a long time … . Very poorly attended ILP Town Hall meeting … in evening, which I left early & came back in time to rehearse "Pirates" for Hope … . Then (shame!) I read Granville Barker on my dear Brutus till midnight. I love Brutus better than Hamlet – he was my first love … I admit he is not such an interesting man, not so various, not so brilliant, not so appealing … . I suppose he's more my sort … .

15 January. … . Tea at Ashfield. Aunt C. talks incessantly of Josephine Butler [campaigner for women's causes, especially against the Contagious Diseases Acts in the 1870s] whom she knew & whose life she is reading.

6 February. Another desperate sort of day. Got *Pressed Man* sent off to Norman Southern the President of the Ncl Rep Theatre, but I doubt it will have no luck. I used to dance with him years ago. I believe he was at my 21st birthday dance … I remember thinking he had much more mind than most of my partners … .

7 February. Started well, but has ended horribly; dear God, help me to be kinder & more loving & not so cross about trifles.

8 February. One darn thing after another … . God send me more sense of humour.

10 February. Yesterday I spent most all day worrying over the production of *Pressed Man* at Washington. I pressed out the dresses & it took so long that I had no time for dinner, but ate some biscuits I had in the studio, & then went straight to the Clinic. I saw the Doctor. There really is to be a new clinic at Sheriff Hill. I have worked for another for years & years. It poured with rain & I got drenched going home … . The performance at Washington was much worse then many a nightmare. But all things come to an end at last. I got home by 11.30, which was early and I dont care. *Pressed Man* has been more or less a washout all through – a great contrast to *Pitman's Pay*. But I believe in it still & will try to push it still. Why, the *Rivals* was a failure when it first came out.

14 February. A worrying rushing week … . It has not taken the Rep. long to reject the *Pressed Man* this time. It came back today … . As I have never been loved I think I have wanted, unconsciously, to put the things in me which I fancy to be loveable into my plays, so that people might love them. But it is no good. People dont like my plays; either I am wrong about thinking there is something in me worth expressing, or else God has denied me the skill to express it. But I dont think I shall ever be able to believe this, however much failure & common sense tell me so. I think I shall go on writing plays always. And the thing I most long for is time to write more. I was going to write five between 35 & 40 & already I am two plays behind. *Pressed Man* is the 35 one; *Trial of Faith* (not finished) is the 36 one. 37 one is not started, & I ought to begin the 38 one this year! … .

18 February. It is Saturday night, which good Quakers ought to spend in prayer & meditation. But somehow I never manage it! I like meditation, but I am too sleepy at night to concentrate & sleepier still in the morning, & between times there is never a minute of time. I will try to meditate tomorrow as I shall miss both meetings.

24 February. A rushing disagreeable week. I have been working very hard at *Rivals*, but have got no thanks at all from Hope, who has done nothing but scold me from beginning to end. Wednes. was Aunt Edie's 81st birthday … .

3 March. Last night of *The Rivals* … *three* good houses! Miss Dorothy Jewson [Labour M.P. Norwich 1918-1922] is staying with us, but we were all at the play & all missed her … . I have a long walk tomorrow.

6 March. It was a nice walk. Sunday morning turned out fine, though grey & Peter, Ned, & Tom & I went up through Kibblesworth & round, & down by Old Ravensworth. All the larks were singing & we saw seagulls & thrushes & robins & tits & several yellow-yowlies. We discussed birds & Communists & the County Elections. Not a single Labour card was to be seen in Kibblesworth – all Stott, the colliery official who is running against the Checkweighman. None of the people dare say we'll vote for Elder. Never was a place so completely under the fear of one man. Work, politics, education, religion, – body mind & soul – all dictated by the all-powerful manager Mr Strong. Miss Jewson's meeting at night – a crowded picture hall, a sheaf of scarlet tulips from the Women Workers she organised during the War. I was tired that night & am tired still. On Monday I didn't do much. I sent off *Robert Aske* & the *Pressed Man*, too, to the York Settlement players. Today I sent the PM to Williams, suggesting it for his Village stories … . Today I have spent most of a cold but fine day working for Elder (it is election day in the County) & hunting for 3 lost theatre seats, which are gone. Sylvie set off for London by bus. I hope she is safe there by now, & has reached Kew. I quite enjoyed being among the miners & their wives again. It was a heavy poll. The Old Toll-house just beyond Harlow Green is delightful inside. The old kitchen fireplace, with its shining black bricks, the great fire (notwithstanding the mucky coal) the shining brasses, the three fine boys, one just in, all black from the pit – a little chap who hardly looked 12 though he must be 14, & the neat clever mother, though with rather a careworn face & father – cheerful in spite of a recent illness & operation – "Q Graham" is his pit name & he was explaining how he would have got on the Parish Council only he lost the election by 9 votes because folks turned out to vote for Q & didn't know who to vote for when they got the paper because they none of them knew his name was Harker. And Granny, impressive in black by the fireside, & a younger daughter visiting with a lovely twelvemonth's boy well able to toddle & full of fun … . Paint I the pitman's interiors never so kindly, I shall never make one so delightful and surprising as I have found the truth. Yet why should they please me so much? I dont know, but they delight my heart like poetry. Our hostess in her neat black silk, with a black apron ornamented with large blue roses, & her bobbed hair flying in a brown halo, just touched with grey & her kind anxious face, with its faded prettiness, was a real picture of something hard to put into words.

… . Poor Uncle Eustace is much worse; I'm afraid it is only a matter of time with him now … .

8 March. … . went to the Clinic in the afternoon. Only 12 babies weighed & 2 of them had whooping-cough poor mites. Home to tea, where a cheerful youth from Cambridge was talking to Sylvia. He is really a protégé of Hope's, called Galbraith, a very nice boy, I should say man, who is reading history at Emmanuel. He quite cheered the day up. Made a poster for Lansbury after he had gone. Was rather worried about Father who has a cough, as well as Uncle E. Branch at night & the Children's Fancy Dress Dance … .

9 March. Went to West Hartlepool after a worried night. A very sad visit. Marriage is a creepy thing – all those years of companionship, ties of love, custom, affection. I am glad my [?] did not lie that way, after all. Oh, dear God, life is so sad – so sad!

15 March. … . Today Aunt Camie has sent me Aunt Poppy's picture of Rebecca at the Well, embroidered by Poppy's mother – Aunt Jane Mawson (Née Cameron) … .

28 April. I have just got back from a fortnight in London to find that Uncle Eustace died this morning. I am glad he is out of his pain, but I'm afraid Aunt Edie will feel the reaction terribly after all these months of strenuous nursing. Certainly I am one of those who is very glad he ever lived. He taught me how to walk on the hills & I can never give thanks enough for that. It will never be possible for me to go among the Lake's Mountains without often thinking of him … . He was a good man, a kind doctor, a dear uncle to me, & he had a very happy life … .

Now I will try & remember my adventures in London & enter them, roughly under their dates. I never had a minute there … .

16 April. Got up at six on a cold grey morning, feeling very poorly & reluctant to go. Had a bad cough. However, obstinacy won & I pushed off. … Holland Park … a comfortable house … a nice landlady … gave me tea

which I was badly needing. There is a gas stove in my room with a 1/- metre ... after supper pushed off to the College for Norman Marshall's lecture on crowd work at nine ... an interesting lecture ... .
17 April. Sunday. This was finer but still cold – bitterly cold. I started off for meeting, but it began to snow a little, & I was so mimsey & full off coughs that I turned tail & sat over my gas stove all morning reading ... . After midday dinner went to the College for Mr Houseman's reading ... . I had to go out in the middle I had such a fit of coughing ... wondered if I should get pneumonia ... . They gave a marvellously good tea for 6d at the College hostel ... bread & buns & jam & cakes ... .
18 April. I got more jujubes & an umbrella. It was cold & wet. Mr Marshall's discussion lecture was very good & then we rehearsed *Possession* a bit. Lunch is good for 1/- but not so good in proportion as the tea! In the afternoon Mrs Whitworth lectured on Play writing. Not very interesting. After tea there are more rehearsals ... after that I managed to rush to Victoria on a 46 bus to buy the cough cure ... White Pine Syrup, which can only be obtained at Read's in Victoria St. I dined well ... but did not struggle round to the College for the choir-speaking demonstration. I wrote letters by my nice gas-stove instead.
19 April. There has come a nice high-school mistress to the boarding house called Miss Hillsden; she is very pretty & jolly. The people at the school are nearly all women – about ten to one man I should say – all well dressed & mostly nice-looking; a few older people ... & one or two authors ... Most of the rest are the high school mistres type – the best kind – very intellectually alive, charming & jolly ... . The afternoon lecture was Miss Craig on makeup ... .
20 April. This was a quiet day & my cough really began to improve. We rehearsed ... in the morning. The night before I had gone to Miss Craig's rehearsal of 2 scenes from *Macbeth* – the most advanced of anything I had seen so far. She is not too bad really ... . In the afternoon began a series of lectures on the stage-management side by Mr Wm Simmons, a very nice man but with such a sleepy voice that we could hardly keep awake ... . It must have been on this day that I met Miss Park who had come for the second week of the School, wandering at Holland Walk at midnight, seeking the College – I took her in charge & we struck up a nice acquaintance. She is a delightfully jolly girl, a clergyman's daughter of North Lincs. teaches at Yarmouth & goes regularly to the Norwich Madder-market theatre ... .
23 April. ... . Went on to *Harold* at the Court Sloane Square, the only thing I saw alone. I enjoyed it much ... .
26 April. This was the day of the performances. Mr Simmons gave us more about gesture ... advised us to observe & make notes of gestures really seen ... a rush after lunch to dress & make up for the competitions, which came

immediately after the plays ... my dress was a good deal admired thpough Miss Craig criticised it severely on the grounds of historical inaccuracy ... . However, I felt sure in my own mind that I looked the nicest, so I did not care. The dress was made for stage effect at the cheapest possible expenditure. She admired the quilted petticoat & the shoes, which I made myself – at any rate made the quilted petticoat & painted the scarlet shoes & gold buckles.
27 April. Last morning criticism & discussion took place in the garden as it was so fine & warm ... . I did a lot of shopping of the looking into shop windows kind. All I actually bought was some beads, in Regent St ... one lovely girl, dressed so beautifully in grey, looking as I would look if I could, made me feel ashamed of being so shabby; & the next moment a woman passed so shabby that I was ashamed of being so smart. So passes the world.
8 May. My birthday – A lovely cake, large cheque & 2 "Everyday Books" – Roman & Saxon from Camie. Other nice books too. A Cambridge Medieval Anthology Vol 1 from Hope & the *Bridge of St Luis Rey* from Sylvie ... . Tea at Ashfield – Aunt C busy turning out old pictures. Has found quite a nice portrait of Granny's mother Grandmamma Swan.

J.B. Melville, the eminent barrister who was elected Labour MP for Gateshead at the 1929 general election and appointed Solicitor-General.

Labour supporters congratulate Herbert Evans after his by-election victory on 8 June 1931 – Ruth Dodds is on extreme right.

CHAPTER EIGHT: JUNE 1928 – DECEMBER 1930

Politics, plays and pleasures

16 June. … . John Beckett [Labour M.P. for Gateshead] is rumoured to refuse to stand again – & evidently its true … .
17 June. Got copy of John's letter of resignation at breakfast. Very thin excuses … . When I got to Steve's he told me the scandal about Mrs Bouchier.[1] But after worrying over it off & on all day, I have decided not to believe it – not unless his wife divorces him. It will be soon enough to believe it then … . An Ex. Com. tonight, George White goes too. That means another Agent & another business manager for the *News*. It never rains but it pours! However I went into town this morning & had a lovely strawberry ice. Also strawberries for tea.
18 June. I slept badly, worrying on over the leader to accompany Beckett's letter of resignation. It came out in the end as a model of discretion but a bit feeble like the letter itself … .
19 July. I spent all the morning on my bed reading … because my monthly time had begun … . I went to the clinic in the afternoon & was tired, in pain, & uncomfortable. I thought it would never end. There were 32 babies, & an Irish nurse … .
21 July. … . I am carrying on a very quaint correspondence with George White [agent] about friendship. He hates me, according to Ned Scott, but I think Ned is mistaken; in any case I never gave him cause & if it is so I wld like to find out why. But he goes with John Beckett, so probably I never shall find out why. Probably he does not know himself; I suspect that he is drawn to me because he is rather a snob & fancies that I am a lady; & repelled because, hang it all, I'm only a woman anyhow & yet dare to treat him as an equal … .
23 August. … . Branch meeting. About 70 to 80 members present. A good meeting on the whole; very respectable discussion. Decided to nominate & ask Hugh Dalton. (Walked home with Peter, who *is* a comfort.) … . Fred Tait was the only other name proposed. He was there in very good form.
24 August. Wrote Dalton[2] … .
27 August. Went to Edmondbyers to the Taits Camp with Peter & Sylvia. We had a great day really but taking Sylvia for walks with the comrades is not altogether a success. The trouble is getting home. I like to get home about eight; the comrades, who think you ought to make the most of the country, dont like to get home till about eleven. Sylvia always wants to get home at 4.30! Today we happened to suit unusually well, as Peter wanted to get home to a meeting at 6 – & actually did! But Sylvia was cross because we didn't get in till 5.30, & I thought it wld have improved the day if we had been able to

stop & rest a little instead of going straight ahead. However, it was gorgeous really, & in future I will leave off trying to take S. & take the comrades with the Sunday Ramblers, who, always go very slow. S. is better when we are by ourselves – … .

7 September. … pretty well devoted to the North of England School of Drama for Amateurs until the following week … It was a good school … the Mummers Party on the Sat. night was a huge success – more than 50 dresses … . I have had word that the Sheffield Playgoers are actually rehearsing *The Pressed Man*! I have two plays to dress – *She Stoops* [*to Conquer*] for Oct 13th, & scenes from Dickens for Nov. 1st. Last night at the Branch we decided to nominate Hugh Dalton, although he will probably go to Bishop Auckland.

22 September. A busy tiresome week. I have sent one copy of *Robert Aske* to Miss Craig, one to the Festival Theatre, Cambridge, & one to Matheson Lang who has just produced *Such Men are Dangerous* in London with great success.

23 September. Finished *The Triumph of Youth*, rather a pretty sentimental German fairy story. Then went to Meeting late. Then to a Prop. Com. meeting at Westfield; must give more thought to that bally autumn campaign. Then home to dinner. Typed circulars to speakers – took them to SSS [Speakers Sunday School] … . Ought to have stayed & taken lesson but my whole life is a disgrace & I came home & we had a lovely tea party –

20 October. … . Heard all about sel. con. [selection conference] & new candidate Melville[3] … .

Saw Charlie Chaplin in *the Circus* & bought a new hat. Part of my election address distributed … . Clinic with 29 babies. Made white breeches for officer. Have been cross all day & now repent of it. I find a great comfort in W de la Mare's poetry.

… . My new dress came home; most unquakerish & much too expensive. But I am going to make the best of it now & not worry.

22 November. This has been a busy month – hence the blank. On Nov. 1st were the Municipal Elections. Ned won back the East Ward. That was the only gain. … On the 2nd Sylvie & I went to Sheffield … the shops are good, the Town Hall magnificent, & there is a Labour majority on the City Council. We were pretty comfortable at the Grand Hotel … went to the Lord Mayor's Reception, where I met Mr Gibson the producer, & we got tea … . At night there was a very dull lecture. But we had a good dinner first & there were no good pictures on … tea with the cast of the *Pressed Man* – starving before we got it. Nice young people very. Then the Play. Charmingly staged & dressed – nothing more to be desired there – very well acted & produced. I enjoyed the first two acts thoroughly, but suffered agonies during Act 111, which did not go so well … . The BDL (British Drama League) was there in force & was, naturally, very sniffy; but it was more than I expected that they should even stay for it. The native Sheffielders seemed very enthusiastic … . Now we are at it, hammer & tongs. On the 9th I went to the first Council Meeting; that was pretty good fun. Then the usual rush & strain to get the *News* out. That no sooner over than we have this candidate trouble again – or rather it has been going on for some time … . I must stop as it is midnight … .

Friday. [no other indication of date] I see I have written down almost nothing about all the Parliamentary Candidate trouble; indeed I have kept this journal very scantly during the last few months; & what I write down "in another place" – Branch Minutes, for instance, I naturally cannot be bothered to write here as well. Alas my diary, from long habit is still a sunshine diary, & I write most of holidays & the country, not of work. Politics & plays are my work now since I lost the Shop (which was better for me than either) so actually what I am thinking most about & spending most time upon gets written about least. Enough then that I met Mr & Mrs Melville on Tuesday; heard Morrison the LP Chairman, & liked him; & Henderson (the famous Uncle Arthur[4]), & liked him not at all. That NUDAW [National Union of Allied and Distributive Workers] have triumphed so far & we are to have another Selection on Jan. 8th. It has all been a silly petty business, due to malice of the defeated candidate & his union & (as I cant help guessing) to the fact that the Nat. Ex had calmly made over Gateshead to NUDAW … . Melville defied them on this point; hence their fury with him; but I think he is bound to carry the next conference now … .

2 December. A frosty morning. Spoke in meeting – just to recite " He that is down" in memory of John Bunyan … . Mrs Bruce Glasier[5] here & the other two dreadfully angry with me … . It is so horribly narrow-minded of Hope & S not to be able to endure, even for half an hour, anyone who does not take exactly their view of life. They are letting themselves drift into a hopelessly cut-off position & way of life. Besides, they are so unkind to me, making me regret asking people here & ashamed if I do … .

4 December. Another rushing day; the play being over seems to have left me no better off, as often happens. And so many people want dresses! Went to the Bank, where I am sadly overdrawn, & tho' I transferred £100 from deposit I find now that it is not nearly enough … . It is due to spending £144 on Electric shares; I wish now I hadn't got them. I shall have to sell something if I am to help Ned with his election deposit[6] … suddenly remembered Ned's election introduction & had to switch off onto that. Wrote him a short biography. Tried to be complimentary without being fulsome but it is hard … .

6 December. … . There were 35 babies at the Clinic … . The Branch was

badly attended in spite of important business … . Is it possible that the ILP is really dying? What will become of me? Shall I set up a theatrical costumiers' business? … .
7 December. Ashamed to say I have wasted the whole day (nearly) in reading *Elizabeth & Essex* – Strachey's new book. Fascinating but very horrible. And what a little time separates us from these savages; I know we are still bad enough – … but still, not foxes, but *people* were then torn to pieces for the general amusement … . And I ought to have been working at the *Labour News*! – yes, all day … .
8 December. I got the copy for the Dec. issue – quite a batch – to Wilson's this morning … . I have got most of the Council report blocked out. I am more & more ashamed of my idleness. The contributors have come out strong this month; it is myself that am behind. I have been learning Psalm 15 as a preparation, as this is Sat. night. But alas! I shall miss both meetings again tomorrow … . I have decided to go to Molly's for Xmas. A little quiet after the Bazaar will be very good for me; & I want to play with Bob before he is too old. God bless him!
9 – 10 December. Its very unusual but I cant sleep tonight. I lay till 2.30 trying hard but my nerves all on edge & worrying dreadfully over various mistakes follies & omissions. At last, though very warm & comfortable in body the mental agony forced me to light up & read. I've read all Macaulay's essay on Johnson – poor man, I have detested him for years, & indeed he was detestable. but now I feel a most strong fellowship with him in the matter of indolence & procrastination. Accidie! Accidie! My besetting deadly sin … .
11 December … . I have been seeing rather too much of him (Ned), rather, lately, & getting a little tired of him, as one does of the best of friends. And much too little of Peter, whose wife is ailing, also he is still working on the building estate, down Earl's Drive, past his house. No wonder I get nervy without him to soothe me; he is the most soothing person I know. Four immense chrysanths he gave me ten days ago are still flourishing in the hall. I'm glad that wakeful night I didn't get worrying about my friendship with Ned. I have reassured myself about its propriety a hundred times, but when I do get uneasy it is horrid. However, all is well at present; & it does no good to look ahead for troubles.
15 December … . Wed. Thurs. & Fri. were (ILP) Bazaar days – I was stuck as cashier in the little pay-box in front of the radiator & the emergency exit, & so subject both to keen draughts & intense heat, according to the … wind. The first day I was frozen, the second day baked – which I didn't mind. The first day was tolerably busy – the other two miserably poor. My only comfort was the children – I had an excellent view of the Bran Tub, & the little Xmas tree, which I bought on the stall for 1/- … each day I got it out & decorated it

in front of an admiring half-circle of children … .

20 January 1929. I had a lovely cold lazy holiday on the Island – Christmas & the New Year both. It was great fun to have Molly to talk to & Bob to play with – & to talk to as well – he is remarkably good company. Hugh was very well, too, & actually got a job the day after New Year's Day & went off to Brussels to inspect rails. I had some fine days & some nice walks & it was such a wonderful comfort & change … . Now I am back in the rush again. I have got Peter back, by rather an effort, but Ned is not very well & (as I fancy, perhaps I'm wrong) rather jealous, & I dont feel that I am managing the pair of them at all cleverly. But I cant do without either; at least I wont if I can help it; that's flat. Dear God make me wise enough & nice enough to keep both my friends! This is silly. I have no reason to doubt it really. I think I should like to talk to Peter about religion; I am reading William James' *Varieties of Religious Experience*. I daresay Ned might be interested in it too; but he always has so much to talk about … .

30 January. The week that followed was not less busy though more soberly employed. We had a perfectly hideous Annual General Meeting of the Women's Section, but I got out of the Chair at last for which I am heartliy & humbly thankful; as a sacrifice I have practically agreed to see that the books are kept in order … .

6 February. … . Last night S & I went to MacDonald's[7] big meeting in the new City Hall. It is a fine place; & it was a great occasion – our first absolutely top-notch political meeting … . Ned spoke – very briefly, but quite nicely, & Trevelyan[8] was in the Chair. MacDonald is really rather wonderful – such rarity of tone! … .

15 February. … . Since Monday it has never stopped freezing & pipes & boilers are the only topical subject with all clases of society. I have been getting out the *News* all the week long – harder work than ever as it is now the new *Gateshead Herald*, with twelve smaller pages; & heaps to get in. Poor lamb it is a cold unfriendly world it is coming out into.

19 February. … . This is my week to do Father, though he doesn't take too long.

27 March. I am feeling rather wicked because I have spent so much on clothes lately & not nearly enough on other people's clothes. I'm afraid also I like to indulge my every whim & I dont like to deny myself at all. But sometimes I do though not in a very good spirit. The weekend school, the first I had ever organised went off very well … . Melville & Tom Peacock [a leading member of Gateshead Labour Party, a railwayman and Councillor] … were in good form. I like Melville more & more; he grows on you. His wife is very pleasant to me … . A bumper meeting on Sunday night. How glad I am it is all over. The faithful Mr Cockburn insisted on finishing a new grey coat in time; & it is very nice & has a lovely slippery lining. I hastily got a new green hat at Bainbridges on Saturday, & I *can* congratulate myself on getting a 14/11 one when there was a 29/11 one I liked much more. But my new shoes! – well, shoes always were my weakness … .

26 April. I meant to go to the Lakes … but cold, snow, health (I have suffered from rhuematism, lumbago, & tummy ache this week) & finally my monthly time have prevented. Also Mary [the maid] went off for a week today. I did want to go while the larches were at their greenest. But there is so much to do here. Went to [Bensham] Settlement Handicraft Exhibition. S & I both won prizes – S a glass bowl for embroidered apron; I a milk-jug for King Kasper's gold cup (painted). I am tired.

1 May. A sad distracted May Day. Letters & the Council & No More War Meeting.

5 May. This was the official Labour May Day & for the first time for years I did not attend the demonstration … . I have been trying as hard as I know how to stave off a family row with Brian & Helen – especially Helen – all week. The strain of trying to be both tactful & truthful has been terrible! Today my reward was peace … I have had to sacrifice pride & other things; I have wasted my time abominably & wept foolishly & unneccessarily & lost sleep & neglected my work; but they have responded … .

10 May. Deepdale Hall [Lake District] … .

11 May. This day I woke early to see the mists low on the hills out of each window of my bedroom – the end window which looks on the end of Place Fell … & the front window which looks on Angle Tarn pikes, & ghyll. But they lifted & lifted. Blue sky appeared. By the time I had finished breakfast it promised a fair day. I took sandwiches & went up through the park. All the becks were roaring full after the storm … I was astonished with joy at the scent of the birches. Actually I had forgotten that … I went up Dovedale, up & up. It got hotter & hotter & sunnier… . I lay a long time on the hillside in the sun. It was very good; I ate my sandwiches, of course; time seems longer when you are alone, so this will be like a holiday twice as long as it counts in days. I came down by the lower path, past a most beautiful fall among the birches. But the ashes are all very bare & grey. The birds are brilliant … .

12 May. … it got out just as beautiful a day! I took [book] with me this time & began to read it by a little ghyll, under a rowan tree, where primroses grew thick by the waterfall about two-thirds of the way up to Boredale Hause … . Up on the Hause it was very very sheltered, warm & still. Grey overhead but with blue between … . I held to the hillside & did not touch the houses at Sandwick; but kept on high up round the corner of the mountain to Scalehow Force. From this high path I had lovely views – Cross Fell & Penrith – beacon & town – & Great Mell & Saddleback … . Home along the blue lake by the

Birk Fell track. I never enjoyed it more, nor saw it so lovely. The cuckoo called among the birches … .
13 May. I woke early & saw a golden light along the Eastern summits, shining between them & the heavy clouds above. It is a lovely bedroom. I can watch the postman come up the dale with my letters while I am dressing … . The permanent lodger here called Woods is relief postman & does the other side of the dale … . He plays sometimes in the evening – quite nice things sometimes; once it was *Lilac Time*. My knees were big this morning – my right knee worst. I do not feel it in the least on the level or uphill, but it stabs me every step going down. I meant to go up Caudel Moor but was afraid of the descent. So I went through the Park slowly & it cleared & cleared & grew sunny … I sat me down on a great fallen ash & I read … I came right into the higher of the two pretty larch-plantations above Hartsop which I have so often admired, climbed the wall beyond & so down the nose into the village. This was a delightful bit if only my leg had not been giving me gip! however I enjoyed it in spite of that … .
14 May. Wild & wet – wet & wild … but had a gorgeous wet walk all round Patterdale at night.
15 May. Hurrah it is getting out! I must see about sandwiches. But where oh where? & the last day too! … . I went up the zig-zag on the hill behind the house … . I missed the zag but it did not matter – I was soon up on the warm soft pastures at the top. Then over the top with lovely views into the top of Deepdale & up Patterdale. I struck Trought Head & went over the iron stile & into my beloved Glemara, keeping to the left of the streams the higher side … . On the open hillside with very few trees I saw my seventh squirrel … . I kept round the nose of Birks into Grisedale which was looking glorious & lunched under one of those great chunks of crag that adorn the side of St Sunday … . I went down into the road just below Elm Howe. I did not know where to go next. It was nearly two – too late for any long walk such as up to the tarn. I wanted primroses for Aunt Edie … . So I went down to Grisedale Bridge, crossed the flooded dale to Side Farm … & along the hillside by sheep tracks well above the houses … I crossed the roaring ghyll with some trepidation just below the waterfall & then, climbing what looked a perfectly good stile, tore my skirt to ribbons on the sharp-toothed edge of the wall. So ends my dear old grey coat & skirt which has served me so many many years! … it's a good thing its the last day. To prolong the holiday is useless without a walking suit. Fortunately I can manage in my silk dress & wooly (sic) coat … . After tea I went to Patterdale & after supper down to Bridgend & back through the park as the dusk fell & the thrush sang among the larches & the cuckoo called up the dale. So … I was out practically all day, wandering round, unutterably happy. It is good to be alone & consult nobody's wishes

but your own … .
16 May. … . It was too fine a day to go home on. I must have suspected it was going to be from the first, for I always wrote home that I would be back on Thurs. or Friday; also when I packed up my things, I put enough for one night into my pack. I said goodbye to Mrs Wilkinson & left my fell boots, & promised to come again in October if I could. Then I trailed down the dale with my hat-box in hand & pack on back, in my silk dress, of course, as I had already posted the torn dress home. I posted the hat-box at Patterdale & caught the 10 bus. I had a return to Penrith, but I got off at Gowbarrow, meaning to walk through the Park & get a bus a bit further on when I felt inclined. I went to Aira Force; there was only one other person in the park; the refreshment hut is not open yet, & I had foolishly come without food … I kept too high & scrambled up to the grassy summit of the ridge. Little Mell Fell is just behind. I was glad I did this, though it was very hot, for I looked over into warm, sleepy Matterdale, where the whin was in bloom, & Blencathra & Skiddaw … stood up blue across the wide dale beyond … . It was going down the hill, among the green fields & hedges with all the birds singing that I finally made up my mind that it was too fine to go home today. I lunched at Brackenrigg at 1.30 … . I did not see anywhere suitable (to sit & read to digest large lunch) until I came to Dunmallet … & there was a steamer at the pier. I went on there instead of climbing up among the primroses. It was the last boat up (at 3!!); it had only just begun to run this week … . So I went up to Howtown on it … . I had a delicious tea with little barley-biscuits, fresh-made – the most delicious things I have tasted for a long time. All the Inn was gay with beech-boughs, & great vases of lilac in bud .. & other tall green boughs in all the fireplaces & corners. I was the first guest to arrive … . "I stole a day from duty / And gave it to delight"

These lines came into my head as I walked along the Lakeside road. This has been the perfect pagan holiday. I have considered nobody at all but myself … .
20 May. … . It was not an expensive holiday, that week in the Lakes. I took a little over £6 & bought a 21/- mac. So it only came to a bit over £5, train fare & all, including the expensive extra day at Howtown. Mrs Wilkinson is cheap at 8/6 a day … .
22 May. Spoke at an Election Meeting for Melville – well didn't speak much but was there!
23 May. … . I bought 5 new tiles (for fire place) *Cat & Cream. I Saw three ships, The Dragon fly, & the Peacock*. My lovely Liberty jumper, all green Peacock's Feathers came today, & the new grey stitched silk hat – still a bit tight but now bearable. I do love the jumper! It is too beautiful to wear much.
28 May. … went up to Sheriff Hill & did cottage meetings with the Melvilles;

they came to tea here, & were quite nice & jolly; they had two friends who had brought a car from London to help on Election Day.
30 May. Election Day. Fine, sunny day. Went with Aunt Camie in her taxi to take her to vote. She was very disappointed that things were so quiet … . Went first to Westfield & heard the early results on the wireless – Salford was Labour's first gain! Then to *Chronicle* Office with Peter & listened to those wonderful gains till about 2.15. Very disappointed at Ned's defeat[9] [Ned Scott in Newcastle].
31 May. Was at the Count & took Aunt Camie. What a majority! [Melville][10]
2 June. Kept my promise to Ned Scott & went a ramble with him, with the Sunday Ramblers. It was in Coquetdale, from Felton through the woods to Weldon Bridge; then past Brinkburn, up to Long Framlington & back to Felton by the other side.
6 June. Spent morning writing Council Report – 25 pages! It gets worse & worse! Clinic in aft. – very few babies as it was showering; a little thunder … the Branch. Took rose buttonholes & made 1/10 for ILP Fund. A good Branch, almost excellent … .
9 June. … . Ex. Com. in the morning; but before that I spent an hour cutting & arranging roses. A beautiful Sunday dinner! I wish I wasn't so greedy! I do love Yorkshire pudding; & the glad season of cherry pie has come; but I like cream or even milk with mine & dont get it … .
10 June. Busy with *Gateshead Herald*. Have got to write a lot myself, but the Council Report is very long
13 June. … . Small clinic at Greenesfield. Must start an agitation about the filthiness of that place & the size of the School clinics …
17 June. This was the day they were to start the desecration of Haweswater [The lake was to be made into a reservoir to supply Manchester which involved the flooding of the village of Mardale]. I can hardly bear to think of it … . When I think of the dead unnatural look of Thirlmere … . How I hate those self-righteous Manchester vandals.
18 June. I have just seen *Macbeth* for the first time! It was magnificent. The Old Vic Co are visiting Ncle … .
19 June. … . Twelfth Night … . I enjoyed it very much, but it was not such a thrill as *Macbeth*.
22 June. … . Melville's Victory Social at night; he does not seem to have a swelled head at all, but a row is pending about the Agent, I'm afraid, & he will do well to give in & put up with Harry [Stoddart].
25 June. My first talkie *Show Boat*. Pretty good on the whole … .
11 July. … . While I was at [printers] Father had a heart attack. Seems to be getting over it, but very alarming. It is years since he had one – not since he became quite bedridden. He seemed a little better at night & I went to

Ashfield to reassure Aunt C. & on to Branch.
12 July. He seems just the same this morning. Breathing bad & irregular & rather restless. He is reading a little, however.

Father had another heart attack about six, & died at 9.45.
13 July. It is the most perfect summer morning. There has been a heavy dew. The moon went down & the sun rose on a clear sky. Somehow I could not sleep; I suppose it is nerves & indigestion. It is not grief – I love him too much for that; I thanked God he did not suffer any longer: of course God is on the side of quickly. It has really happened as easily as one could expect … . So many memories – such crowds & crowds of little odd memories of the dearest of all fathers. I found this in Robert Bridges; I dont care for the classical prosody, but I love the meaning:

> What happy bonds together unite you,
> ye living & dead
> Your fadeless love-bloom, your
> manifold memories.
> André Chenier.

It is thirty-four years since Mother died in this room & now they are together, whatever way you look at it – & at peace … . It is such beautiful weather & the garden full of flowers; just as it was when Aunt Poppy died. It is comforting to think of that beautiful Resurrection picture in the Tate, with that clear early-morning sunshine – the first level rays, & such a freshness. Yes, youth & early morning, & young true loves reunited. He was always such an early morning man. He was so good & sweet, & thanked me with his lips for every little thing I did for him as long as he was conscious; I gave him one last kiss that he understood just before he slipped into the unconscious state which lasted 2 or 3 hours; he asked for it; dear darling loving father; how I bless him! Fadeless love manifold memories!
13 July. … . Strange that I dont feel sleepy tonight, though I did not sleep last night. Saw about the registration first thing, & also found out definitely that Brian is away; but not his address … . Mawson was awfully kind & came & advised us what to do & is helping in heaps of ways. We have got in touch with Brian & he & Molly have wired to say they are coming, he tomorrow night & she Monday night. Aunt Edie & Anna … arrived about twelve. She got my warning letter this morning & so expected the worst … after they left went into town & got some mourning at the Sales – a hateful crush & heat. One of the three worst days is over now. We all feel so left in the air – listening for a bell that will not ring … & thinking of meals we dont have to serve. It is better for him – much better; & we shall get used to it in time. Dear God, I thank you for his love for me, by which I know what God's fatherly love to mankind is; & oh, thanks for *all* love for it is beautiful … . Went to

meeting tonight, but somehow it was not a great help, but quite nice. Sylvia & I watered the garden after supper. I recall so many many garden nights with him, watering, weeding, playing ... or tennis. The glow of his cigarette in the dark. Those were golden days ... .

15 July. The third of these hard days over ... . Went into town twice for clothes. Sewed, wrote letters, went to Ashfield for flowers – white carnations, nepeta, irises & spirea, & a great sheaf of canterbury bells, pink & white, with palish blue larkspur & sky blue, & sweet peas too & roses. Molly came about 7 & is a great comfort. Sylvie has been making over a black silk ... .

16 July. Gloriously fine & hot & a little clearer with the wind more southerly. The funeral was at 11.30. Sylvia went to Ashfield to sit with Aunt Camie. Making up the flowers gave us something to do. All garden flowers from Ashfield, or Home House, & a lovely bunch of white carnations & orange geum from Helen's garden ... only one wreath from Ashfield maids ... . Aunt Edie thought it was a good thing to have an open air service instead of going into the Chapel. Bishop Woods, whom Mawson had got, read the service very nicely ... . All father's old Quayside friends ... were there ... some food did us all good; & it is a tremendous relief to have the public part over. We wrote & wrote letters of thanks ... .

17 July. ... . I got into rather a fuss that I had overlooked some flowers sent yesterday. I remembered some pink roses I had never examined, & I thought there may be others, so I went in the morning & satisfied my mind ... . Dr Wardill ... . What a splendid friendship! And what a help he was to Father at the hardest time when he lost mother. I knew that even at the time, I think, tiny child as I was, & realised it more & more as I grew older. Father was 39 when I was born, & I am 39 now when he has left us. It follows then that I only knew him myself in that part of life which I have not reached yet.His younger years, the years that must have seemed the most interesting & active & important to him in many ways, I can only know about by hearsay. There is still time in my own life to get more like him, if only I could. At any rate we must carry on his tradition of kindness & fun & the good life ... . After tea I went to Bensham Grove to a meeting of the Nursery School Com. The school started on Monday, I think, & all seems to be going well so far ... .

29 July. A good day to set to work hard, but I never felt less like work. I am so sleepy & slack. For a fortnight after Father's death I never could be still – not that I was concentrating on my work but always up & doing altering the garden or tidying or something. Now comes the reaction & I want to do nothing but just sit. But it wont do, Ruth; what about those minutes & all those letters! To work ... .

1 August. [Lakes holiday at Buttermere Hotel with Molly & Bob *et al*]

2 August. ... . I have just seen the Keswick coaches – one four-in-hand, two three-in-hand & one pair. From where I sit I can see Great Gable yes, to the summit & Green Gable perking up beside. It was so nice to see all those lovely horses & those genuine real drivers; but it makes the hotel rather crowded … . I am enjoying myself. But when I think of the misery I left behind in Gateshead my heart is sore. They are making hay in the green fields between the two lakes … .

3 August. It rained & rained & rained & I read … . Went up the Hause with Molly. The Moss Force in fine form … .

4 August. More rain. Read … . In a fine interval about noon we had a decent walk all together.

5 August. Bank Holiday. Fine … home

30 October. It is near the end of my fifth election fight. I feel almost hopeful, but as far as I remember I did last time too! … . It is three years since last time, against the same man, Thompson the "food specialist" (or sausage-maker) … . They say he is ill, poor man, but I hope he will soon be all right. I have done more canvassing & held fewer meetings than ever before, & it is harder work – more continuous & slower – but not so trying to the nerves – the speaking is coming a little easier.

31 October. Elections are – well you get used to anything. I half expect to win; but my other half tells me to prepare to second the vote of thanks to the returning officer … .

3 November. I am struggling with the reaction that always follows an election – the longing to be out of the turmoil & the stink & the terribleness of life & back with nothing but books & pictures, writing, dreams & the flickering fire to think about – no speeches, no meetings, no worries. Having won at last – & its the *seventh* year though only the fifth fight – makes it more violent, I think … I dont at all realise that I am a Councillor. It has seemed all wrong, ever since I saw my pile of votes was the highest … . I have a great longing for the hills.

16 November. Saturday. A long stuffy Council meeting but exciting. They turned off all our five Labour Aldermen … there are five bye-elections to fight & we ought to win two or three, which will give us a majority of Councillors – but ten deadweight aldermen is a lot to carry … . I lunched with a crowd of our people at Carrick's, & others went to the Grey Horse. No one went to the Mayor's lunch except Peacock & Hayes, from motives of pride, & Mary Gunn, who I think likes the lunch – drinks & so forth; not that I blame her. Otherwise it must have been all his own side & the officials … .

17 November. We have begun Peter's campaign; I went round the old Asylum with him yesterday. Curious how that place affects me! Had a No More War delegate, a Nottingham girl, staying with us … .

23 November. … . I have been reading *The Faerie Queen* by way of light relaxation … . I wanted to be a Maiden Knight myself & go abroad in silver armour, succouring the weak & saving the oppressed & mixing on terms of equality with the other knights, who would scarcely know, except now & then, that I was a woman at all. Has this romantic dream worked out in real life sitting on the Town Council & making my voice heard at meetings among the men? At any rate there are plenty of wrongs to be righted but how to right them? …. Yesterday I was in the house where I was born & there were six people living in the kitchen – in that one room & it has a stone floor & they pay 7/- a week for it. Of course the chance that I was born in that house makes it neither better nor worse; but there the thing is, not two hundred yards away in my own road … .

24 November. … heroic (mood) varies with a longing for idleness & peace … instead I am going to a Friends' Housing Conference, that sits from ten to nine! This is Peter's election day & alas! it rains. Peter has not got in, & I am dreadfully disappointed! that he should have been beaten by that white slug of a man … & all because it has been such an awful day is too annoying. We have our majority of councillors – Peacock & Hayes are both in – so of actual elected councillors we have 16 to 14 & their ten alderman make it 16 to 24 – five is exactly what we need, & when T… comes out next November, we must have the South Ward again, the East is almost certain, too, & now that we have made breaches in the West Central & Central there are good hopes there … . I wish now I had done more for Peter … . I must try not to let myself be absorbed in the routine of Council work. I must continue to get out into the Ward … . I must remember to try & win over the parts now considered hopeless … I'm afraid I only want to be a popular Councillor. But help me to be a good Councillor & help me not to heed popularity … .

28 November. Since the election it has been the queerest week – complaints, & grievances & committee meetings. I hate people with a grievance! … . On the top of it all the production of *The Best of Both Worlds* … . We had a funny Council meeting on Wednes. – going through the applications for the new Town Clerk … .

2 December. … . Last Friday I had a wild day – Dentist, two films *King of Khyber Rifles, & Gentlemen of the Press* … both talkies & both good in different styles. I find the listening more tiring, however, & I never have the least illusion that the people on the screen are actually speaking. On the whole the old silents, (except for a monotonous orchestral accompaniment) were more of a rest – dream-like, flitting, quietly whirring, grey, remote & yet absorbing. But I have no dislike for the talking films. At night I went to *The Lady With a Lamp*, the first time I have seen Miss Gwen Francon Davies. It was splendid … .

28 December. I went to London immediately aftr the last entry, to a Friends

Conference on Housing. I took so many notes all day, & had such a hard bed at the *Ivanhoe* that I never wrote in my diary. Also I was writing the Council report at all odd times for the *Herald* … . It was my first experience of Friends House [Religious Society of Friends, Euston Road, London] … for any length of time. I like the place. I am shy of Friends & managed badly. Knowing no one, I had nowhere to start; & being tired, run down & nervy I was in no condition to make acquaintances easily. I was dreadfully lonely, but realised it was my own fault; also I had great difficulty in getting enough to eat … The shops were lovely. I had never been in London so near Christmas before except when I was at school. The Conference was very interesting. Perhaps the best thing of all was the Sunday morning meeting for worship in the small meeting house – one of the best & most inspiring I have ever attended. As no one knew me they called me "the Friend from Gateshead" a name which pleased me well … . I spent the last night at 26 Lawn Crescent. Oh the comfort after my hard hotel bed & scant fare! Dear Uncle Fred & Aunt Nellie were well; dear Agnes gave me such a delicious supper … . The nicest part of all was walking through Bloomsbury streets at the enchanted time when the sunset is red at the end of the wide streets & the sky wonderful blue above, & the lights are out … . That's the hour when London takes the heart, with the bare twigs against the sky & the big heavy dark buildings. I went twice to the Museum & spent the time in the M.S. [Manuscript] room – glorious – or buying cards for Christmas – such a number & variety!

The next thing after that was the BDL [British Drama League] Competition. We were working up *Catherine Parr* for it, & had just a week to go when poor Tom Fenwick had an accident at work & lost part of two fingers of his right hand! of course he could not act. The People's Theatre very nobly stepped into the breach with *How He Lied to Her Husband* … .

I'm very glad Christmas is over; it was an awful rush; I scarcely knew where I was & wld never have got through if I hadn't had my photograph taken & sent that round to everyone. That saved me a lot of trouble & expense too. We had the usual party at Ashfield … .

CHAPTER NINE: JANUARY 1930 – NOVEMBER 1931

A lot of Lake District and two Parliamentary Elections

1 January 1930. Toby & I saw the New Year in together in the kitchen where I was getting a little sustenance after a walk up the hill with Peter to a dance at the new Springfield Miners' Welfare Hall. I was supposed to be helping to judge the fancy dresses, but there were almost as many judges as dresses to judge. It was a lovely fine frosty night, stormy & clear. We enjoyed the walk, & he has managed my Christmas parcels beautifully, bless him. I dont know what I should do without him; I find the relief work so trying & he does it nearly all for me ... I have had a deliciously lazy day .... I spent the whole morning in bed – Then to Ashfield to a Turkey dinner, Bri & Helen also there .... It was a lovely dinner & we were all very united.

2 January. Another disgracefully lazy day .... Then I had lunch in town with Hope – her birthday it is, & we saw Douglas Fairbanks in the *Iron Mask* .... Then Camie came to tea – a successful visit ....

9 January. ... . Council meeting in afternoon two till 6.45 & no tea! Got home 7.15. Ward meeting ... .

9 January. What is the good of a bare day-to-day record of happenings of no interest – not even to myself. I think I keep this Journal to convince myself I am not lazy; & its no use because I know I am ... counting meetings & writing as work that's only 7 hours work in the whole day. And now when I meant to write more report, I cant be bothered, And seven hours is about 7 times as long as I generally put in at anything that could be remotely described as work! .... I wish I was a better woman & not so fat too. I did a brave thing yesterday though; I supported a resolution mildly inclining towards favouring Birth Control – a subject I hate & dont want to be mixed up with only my conscience compels. And today I did another – only not so brave – I spoke against all war, including Civil War at the Branch; the would-be Bolshies (odd creatures) oppose all foreign war, but think it wld be rather nice at home! Just to have a shot at the capitalists .... .

5 February. I have been spending a terrible lot on myself – both time & thought & money! First there was the British Drama League Festival – I acted Catherine Parr, & bejewelled Tom Fenwick's Henry V111 dress, & spent heaps of time chasing props hither & thither .... I did go to the monthly meeting & made the housing report .... I did a paper a week past Sunday for the N.W.Ward on Housing. They took it better than the Friends! .... .

4 May. Deepdale Hall Patterdale .... I arrived a week ago last Sunday & have had a most wonderful week. I meant to begin with a summary of the last two months, so that I could consider my life & try to come to some conclusion as to whether it was tending in the right direction. But though it is Sunday morning my mind does not incline to anything so fitting & serious. I would rather go on reading Miss Sitwell's rather ridiculous but amusing life of Pope. Still, many of the interesting things that have happened in the last two months are of a completely frivolous nature. First there was the completion of my beautiful fireplace of Dutch tiles. Here in this plain pastoral farm bedroom, with not even a picture on the walls, only three texts, how elaborate & ultra-civilised does my riot of colour & picture & quaint shape seem … . Another interesting thing at home is the redecorating of the sitting-room, with orange paintwork & a blue dado, to go with the colours in the border of our brown cobweb carpet, & creamy-mixy walls, inclining it to yellowness. There has been a tremendous lot of dramatic activity in the last two months (including the final of the Northern Area British Drama League Festival in which the Progressive Players Gateshead did Fred Chadwick's *Dregs*. Hope & S & Ned Scott went. Hope produced a play & S dressed play after play putting in a big slice of her time. She did eight big productions in March & April) … . Hope has finished her part of the County History[1] & is at last extracting drop by drop the Roman part from three learned but slow & obstinate old gentlemen … . I meant to come here on a Friday but the Carl Rosa's [Opera Company] were coming in the *Flying Dutchman* & I had always wanted to hear it since Father gave me an account of it long ago when I was a little girl … . It was not a very good company but I adored it … . Then there is Friends Meeting. I have been trying hard to do the forget everything, mind absolutely blank, recommended in my mystics book. But no very definite results; except that I like doing it even tho' I dont succeed … . I cannot tell whether this is a misspent life or not.

Now for my nine days here . Summarised.

… . Monday … got so puffed coming up the Park that I began to think my days on the hills were done! … . I was in to tea. It is so nice going up the dale to see the smoke going up from my own chimney & know my fire is lighted for a cosy evening … before supper, my hot meal … I had a much warmer time this year than last with a feather bed & a hot-water-bottle, & my jaeger [sic] dressing gown. I was sometimes too hot but never too cold.

Tuesday … Took lunch & went up by Angle Tarn … a bit of a pull up … I was so pleased with the hilltop views that as I was getting round rather quickly, I struggled on up Kidsty & wandered all round the top, & enjoyed the fine crags on High Street … . Down by Hayeswater & Hartsop

Wednesday. This day it came in very hot. I set out boldly to do Caudale Moor, but as usual, failed. It was so roasting hot! I cld scarcely stagger along under a Burberry & a wooly coat; & in winter combies too. It took me about an hour to get through the Park & Low Wood, … so I spent the day in Dovedale, first going up one side, then the other. It was lovely in the woods &

by the waterfalls & all the tortoise-shell butterflies are coming out in the heat. Then I went round the corner of Little Hartsop Dodd & into the foot of Caiston Glen, & across the Kirkstone Beck by stepping-stones, & saw a shepherd lad with a little fire (which must just have been for amusement) watching his sheep all the day. A pleasant day & oh so warm! But all the time the path up Caudel beck taunted me. Yet I simply *couldn't* get up with that Burberry in my pack! After a very nice tea … I went off to do a little climbing to make up, without any impediments at all. I went up to Boredale Hause in 40 mins, which I call good going!
Thursday. long walk.
Friday. The sun looked into my bed, as usual, & it was another clear blue day. By the way I had gone all the way yesterday in shoes only! But it rested my feet well from my fell boots which were beginning to gall the day before in the heat. Today, I put on fell boots again, to go up Grisedale. I (sent) my little box of primroses for home … from Patterdale P.O. … . I took my thermos full of tea this day & walked down to Patterdale … . I went over by Blemara Park & it was half past eleven or so before I really got going up Grisedale. I felt all the time that I should do Helvellyn & yet I wasn't going to be bound to do it, neither to myself nor anyone … . I lunched by the tarn, which was very blue … I went up by the zig-zag & met two people coming down; I did not really decide to go on to the top till I reached the seat. Then I thought I really would. It is nice to have no one but yourself to consult. On the other hand it sometimes leads me to wander aimlessly all day & regret it afterwards. But why regret it? … . [Helvellyn] very magnificent with his snowy peaks & his rocky ridges, & you feel more intimate when you have just been up him. The view was scarcely as good as from Stybarrow Dodd. Coniston & Windermere were swallowed up in heat-haze … . I met a party of four young girls on the top. They had come up Swirrel & were going down Striding Edge. I soberly went round by the Keppel-Cove zig-zag & the lead mine – rather a dull way & long but I enjoyed going down the right side of Glenridding by the green path in the evening sunshine. I got down about 6.40, too late for tea at Glenridding as I wanted to catch the 7 bus to Patterdale – quite a help on the road … .
3 May. Saturday. I thought it well to rest. It was very hot. I took a load of writing materials & the E.C.P. [Ever Circulating Portfolio – writings collected by friends] which had arrived the day before & went up to the top of the Park.
4 May. Sunday. Went to Birk Fell … had to be home in time for tea at Lane End (with Miss Fry, a Quaker & Mrs Pollard) … I had a lovely tea, a wireless programme & the old ladies are dears … .
18 June. I have not reformed my life because I am forty. Indeed I think I get lazier & lazier. Look at my Journal even! This last written up long after the

event, & then not another entry for weeks!
[Summary of 6 weeks] Visit to Friends Annual Meeting in London with Hope. Paul Robeson in *Othello* … . What are my impressions of Yearly Meeting? … . Hope was good company; but as regards making myself a place in this strange little society where I so strangely find myself a member by my own will & choice, I am still an outsider as ever, & cannot swap genealogies with anyone! – nor am I likely to improve in this respect. The feeling of spiritual & social exclusiveness which at first repelled me so much & made me hesitate so long before joining, I still perceive, but have grown to resent it less & less & even to feel that it is still part of the atmosphere. The amount & variety of the work done by Friends is staggering; I found all this immensely exciting & stimulating, while at the same time I felt my own inadequacy, inefficiency & laziness very keenly. It is not very nice to be made ashamed of yourself, but perhaps it is good for one. I did come away earnestly intending to work harder & do better.
… . on to Winchester & holiday in the New Forest; various visits & conferences including the Friends Industrial & Social Order Council at Oxford.
Council Committees – Town Improvement; Maternity & Health;Library; Education;
11 February 1931. … Mat. & Child Welfare Com., at which I lost my temper & self-control when they again turned down having the food on sale at Sunderland Rd Clinic, after giving me to understand last month that there would be no trouble about it … .
17 February. Shipley Art Gallery Committee in afternoon. I was feeling poorly & slack. Rather an awful local artists collection – & yet still some good things. Education Sub-Committee in evening. That went on until nine. I looked in at Westfield & came out with Ned Scott, who is having a reunion of "The King's Bad Bargains" on Sat. – seven of them who refused to join combatant units in 1915.
19 February. A short Slum Clearance (Sub Committee) at night followed by the ILP … .
20 February. A Towns Meeting on allotments for the unemployed at night … . I am getting keen on the question.
21 February. A little practical allotment work. Went down with Peter to his allotment & sat in the sun, absolutely sheltered from the cold north wind, talking gardens to Peter & Mr Dawson his partner down there … .
It is nice to have Peter back. He is still in rather low spirits over the loss of his money & the failure of his Wicked Contractor, but still more because the landlord wants him to leave his house & the money he might have used to get a new one is gone … . I have made a Good Resolution to read no more novels

in Lent – well knowing that I shant have time! … . Aunt Edie's 84th birthday. Hope & S went to dinner & found her in great form. A joint wireless present … .

I am going to Molly's for Easter & she wants to spend part of the time in London; & instead of looking forward to that first I can think of nothing but Deepdale in May! Yet I love Molly & Bob, & shall be pleased & amused & happy with them It seems ungrateful! But ecstacy is among the hills … .

23 March. I have missed a lot, but nothing very nice. I had a hideous defeat in the Maternity & Child Welfare, which cut me to the heart. Then I reproached myself with being too much concerned for my own success & my own dignity & influence on the committee, & not enough with the welfare of the mothers & babies – who are having a frightful time – the child deaths in the town are appalling … . Now I want to leave the committee – why waste my time & hurt myself so much running my head into a stone wall? It really incapacitated me from work for a whole day – I could think of nothing else … . On Saturday 21st had the first walk of the Good Companions – my own walking party – at present consisting of Agnes, Ned & Self. We only went to Jesmond Dene. I doubt if it will come to anything. I certainly dont mean to take much trouble over it … .

3 May. [Lake District] In Deepdale Park by the Wall … . All the days have been lovely. First on Tuesday, the drive over with Brian & Helen & Sylvia; B & H came on purpose to take me … next day (Wed.) was quite perfect, & I went up Grisedale, through Blemara Park … . (Thursday). I tracked up this ridge … beginning about Wallend … . Lovely views both sides into Patterdale, into Hartsop, into Upper Deepdale & finally into the wild desolation of upper Dovedale. Almost I went on over Fairfield or at least I might have managed Hart Crag; But I did not want to overtire myself & went back … . Friday seemed inclined to be wet & I asked the old ladies from Deepdale End – Miss Pollard & Miss Fry to tea … afterwards they asked me to go & hear the wireless – the pride of Miss Fry's heart; & I heard poor Melville's death reported – a sad accompaniment to my holiday – & a bye-election to go home to! … . (Sat.) A perfect morning … I decided to master Caudalebeck & Caudale Moor at last. I took Mr Lowe at the Bridge into my confidence so that they would know where to look if I was lost! He also told me that the descent to Threshwaite Cove from Stoney Cove was easy; but I doubted him … I actually went by the tongue between the two becks because it looked easier, & also because the beck fascinated me, & I did not want to leave it till I had to. It was a hot pull up & took me nearly two hours. I hated the exertion but I rather loved the hidden pastoral place, folded right in the heart of the hill … I knew the top wld be dull & flat & I was a little appalled to find *how* dull & flat it was. But I got myself to the highest bit (over 2500) called Stoney Cove, & though not in the least like a cove it is an attractive place with heavenly views. First the Scafells, with the jag of Mickledore; & Gable looking very square & isolated, Old Man & his attendants, & Windermere winding away like a dream of beauty among the woods & meadows. The sea had no clear horizon … all the Lakes Fells, I think, were clear from Saddleback & Skiddaw right round to the back of Harter Fell above Mardale. I lunched there on the top at one o'clock, wandering gently round from one view to another, but perhaps loving Windermere & the Scafells (with Bow Fell & Crinkle Crags) the best … (a young man met on the top) said the way down into Threshwaite Cove was very steep & rough & he could not recommend it. This put me somewhat on my metal & when pressed he said that 200 yards was very rough & steep , but if I went he wld advise me to keep near the wall … . I thought I wld have a good look at the plan & turn back if it frightened me at all. I went on from point to point, only seeing so far at a time & always saying to myself – "If I am frightened I shall turn back." There was only one place where I thought I might have to turn back, & by making a traverse away from the wall on the left I got down that too well enough. But the young man was right. It is steep & rough … now however it began to hail, but the nicest hail I ever saw, just a sprinkling & half sunshine all the time. I sheltered under the wall … watching three buzzard hawks hovering among the crags … I shrank from the long strain on the knees down Pasture Beck & went up the back of Thornthwaite Crag, below the summit & so round the head of Hayeswater Gill & up onto the brown back of High Street … . High Street is a dull hill; you want to see over the edges & only can here & there by taking a good deal of trouble; yet the distant views are exquisite & I enjoyed it & even found a bit of the Roman Road that *looked* rather like a Roman Road (just before the Knot). I did not get very tired but I got very hungry. When I got down to the gate below the Knot I wanted to avoid the hard steep stretch on the road from Hayeswater to Hartsop; I tried to work round under Rest Dodd & find a green herd path down to the village; but though I found a good trod through the marshes it lead up (gently) & not down, & soon landed me, as I rather expected, in the track to Angle Tarn. Well I wanted to go to Patterdale for chocolate & other things, so I went on that way … . I got down to Patterdale just as the Hall clock struck six … .

(Monday walk to meet friends walking from Ambleside)

Tuesday. It was showery on the last morning. But I had nearly all day before me, which made me very undecided in my mind. When I was nearly ready to start a tremendous hail-storm swooped down, so that I didn't get off till nearly eleven, & then Fairfield & St Sunday & Greenhow End were all ghostly-grey with the clinging hail, & I crossed the dale in the chill wetness after the storm. I decided the lake-side path. It rained every now & then ... It was hot along the lake, in spite of a high cold wind, because I was carrying so much .... By Sandwich it was beginning to fair up. All Martindale was bright with the cherry-blossom just at its best ....

That is more than two months ago now, & it has been a busy summer. Directly after I got home I got in touch with Dr Mess at the Newcastle Housing Trust, with a view to extending their activities to Ghd. I rather like Miss Jennings, their housing manager .... All this time the Bye-Election Campaign was beginning & after Whit we were in the thick of it, & I did canvassing & meetings & it rained & was horrid. The Good Companions have been walking about alternate Saturday afts .... The Sheriff Hill Clinic have been mounting up & reached the hundred after Race Week.

The saddest thing has been the loss of dear Margaret Joyce .... I have missed her so much. It seems strange, as I saw her so little; but she was there, & I leant on her help & sympathy in all educational matters. Now I have no one like her to help me in the school maze .... I must try to keep the inspiration she gave me & do more for the Nursery School. I have let it fall behind a little recently I have been so busy with the Housing Trust. But all the summer I have been selling roses & other flowers for it; now I must do something more for it for Margaret's sake. Then there was Bob's nervous breakdown. This made us very anxious for a while but he is quite well again now & coming to Sweden after all. Sylvia went & stayed with Molly while he was ill.

Polling day was June 8th & the result was:

Evans 22,893

Headlam 21,501

Lab. maj. 1,392. It was an awful day, wet & miserable. I quite like Major Evans, but he is quite old. We had some very good meetings, but it was a dull campaign .... I have been working pretty hard at the Allotments Committee, too, but so far without any result to mention.

.... Hope & I went to Cambridge for the Social & Industrial Order Council at Westminster College. This was a delicious weekend – roses & limes at Cambridge & lovely weather; & nothing less old-age & hoary to discuss than the state of agriculture. The farming Friends, however ruined, were very delightful, & we both enjoyed the weekend thoroughly .... I have been feeling unsettled ever since. The temptation to go away & live somewhere beautiful & never see Gateshead again! When the best you can do is pretty bad .... Sylvia came home the same day as we did; & Bob came a week later so we have a full house.

27 July. Today I lost my dearest & oldest of Friend of the friends I chose for myself & would never let go again because I loved them. Uncle Fred was Father's friend before he was mine. It was not till I was 17 that I met him at Patterdale. I had just left school & the world was before me & we had this delightful party at Patterdale Hotel – Uncle Eustace & Aunt Edie, Father & Uncle Fred – I forget who else was there – What a delightful beginning it was for a young girl … to make such a friend. I was fascinated by him at once. His long rather shambling strides, his bushy eyebrows, his gentle slightly sarcastic method of speech, yet kind below his sarcasm; then he was an examiner – I was schoolgirl enough to find that thrilling … He had been a Rowing Blue at Cambridge in his youth – & I adored Cambridge where Hope was still in her fourth year. But all these things are only externals. We loved the same poetry & laughed at the same jokes – that goes deeper – I loved him at once & he was sweet & dear enough to let me think he thought me charming – just what 17 (& 41 too!) wants all men to think! … . Uncle Fred gave rather wet kisses when one said greetings & goodbyes, so that it was quite difficult not to wipe your face rather rudely immediately afterwards. I think this & the fact that he was rather fussy in a boat – a great shock to me in an old Blue! – were the only two defects I noticed in his character then or later. We walked on the hills & talked or were silent – he was one of those men that know how to preserve long & happy silences. He said poetry to me – I remember his saying:-

"That time of year thou mayst in me behold … ." in the verandah of Patterdale Hotel where we often sat & talked. I had never heard it before – little savage that I was then. But I amused him with the wide variety of nonsense rhymes of which I then had a large collection … . The Lakes visits ceased for he had a rheumatic knee that pained him, & he could not be content to do less than he was used to do. He & Aunt Nellie had gone for many years to Manesty on Derwentwater … . I stayed with them perhaps half a dozen times at Kew.

24 August. Monday [end of Swedish holiday] … . When we were dining in the train (to Upsala) Sylvia saw something about the fall of the English Government! Imagine how thrilled we were! Here was I only taking my eye off them for a week or two & the Government falling and perhaps a General Election to face as soon as I get home! … then she saw something about a Coalition, & Baldwin & MacDonald both being in the Government.[2] I could hardly believe this; but in Stockholm we got a paper for ourselves & made Alma translate it in our usual conference in her room at night. Alma hates politics & does not seem much interested in any English news except the weather! However we found out the main lines of the astounding fact, & I began to think if we could get rid of MacDonald & Snowden without splitting

the Party, it might be rather a good thing; we could all unite in opposing their beastly economy campaign! It is easier & safer to be in opposition in hard times – perhaps in all times; which is the very reason I supported Mac. as long as he was in favour of the Party policy. Now he's turned against it I think we can part with mutual satisfaction. But oh to have a general election to face up to directly after such a lovely holiday! The flesh is weak & it did seem hard.
25 August. Our last day in ... Stockholm. The morning paper said not a General Election till October anyway & gave a list of the people leaving the Government – almost all our really valuable leaders, from good old Uncle Arthur [Henderson] to Grandfather Lansbury [George Lansbury] to young folks like Graham & Greenwood. But to have Neville Chamberlain at the Ministry of Health again! That's cruel hard ... . After this England dropped out of the paper headlines ... .
29 August. sailed for home ... .
30 August. Another perfect day; & at last I have seen the North Sea in gentle & amiable mood, & taken every meal all through a whole day at sea ... & I have written up almost the whole of this diary ... I have dozed on deck & paced the deck & observed passing ships ... . Now it is nearly ten & we are only about two hours out of the Thames ... re-united Bob with his mother at the Whitehall Hotel ... & caught the Pullman for the north
7 September. It has been a queer week since then. I seem to have spent all the time devouring newspapers. The outlines I had heard or intelligently conjectured abroad, but all the details & the steps that led up to the crash I am only finding out by degrees. Thank God that Henderson & the rest stood firm. There must at one time have been a risk of splitting the Party – & yet not perhaps a great one. They could not have followed MacDonald without giving up everything we stood for, everything that makes the hope of the future – I was going to say that makes this country a possible place to live in. If Socialism died here should I be free to go to live in Sweden? Foolish question! It cannot die here so long as I am here!
21 September. Today we have come off the Gold Standard,[3] thank goodness ... . I have been thinking about very little except the crisis since I got home ... . The political situation is most amusing – quite Gilbertian. The Government which was to save us from the terrible catastrophe of going off the Gold Standard has now saved us again (the second time in three weeks or so!) by going off the Gold Standard! And it was our gallant tars who brought this about according to Snowden; their successful strike against the cuts[4] led foreign countries to withdraw their gold; so the very means taken to save the Gold Standard – unmitigated economy – has been the very means of driving us off it – herein is contradiction contradicted ... .
23 September. Rather a more cheerful letter today, Bob is suffering from a

delusion. It is all very sad & upsetting … .
30 October. Council meeting – horrible. The economy stunt is stopping every good thing. Lectured at Low Fell School at night to a fair audience
1 November. West Hartlepool. Bad news from Molly when I came home. Public & private troubles together – this has been a terribly sad year. Poor old Bob! & *poorest* Molly! Still I hope & pray. Perhaps all will be well in the end … .
4 October. A most *perfect* morning! How I longed to cut & run for the country, but Miss Cox a No More War organiser is here – we took her to please Camie … .
10 October. … . Poor Evans, our Member, died on Monday, & today I half thought of going to … the Memorial Service; but the garden was so gay in the sun that I had no mind for obsequies sad as I am about it all … We are in a whirl of election work, & I have so much to do. But I needed this rest today; & though gardening tires my body I feel the refreshment of mind … .
11 October. Another very beautiful day. I did not go to [Quaker] meeting, though I dont often miss now, when I'm at home. I had an Election Committee in the morning & in the evening the I.L.P. had a special meeting & decided to nominate Steve Wilson [a local printer] for the Parliamentary vacancy … .
12 October. … The tram men are much excited at the prospect of Bevin coming [Ernest Bevin, the creator and general secretary of the Transport and General Workers' Union] … . Then to the Selection Conference at the Co-op. The beginning was inauspicious. The sub. com. met & it was reported that two nominees (Fergie Foster & Wilson) refused to give the undertaking to work with the Parl. L.P. They were therefore ruled out of order, though I urged that they should be heard & the Conference left to decide. However, I was outvoted. It was unfriendly having the meeting in that great gaunt Co-op Hall, filled with clouds & clouds of foul tobacco smoke, so that you could only just discern the faces on the platform through the haze; there seemed to be no ventilation, & though I got one window opened at last it did not have much effect. There were a good many ILP protests against the ruling (on Foster & Wilson) but Pickering managed the meeting wonderfully from the Chair … .

Both the candidates, Bevin & Fisher, were good candidates who might well hold Gateshead. Bevin was a simpler man than I had expected. His preliminary speech was not specially striking, except for an honest sincerity about it. He is a great big man, huge shoulders, massive nubbly face, with something still a little frank & boyish about it, though he must be 45 past. The other man was also big-built, & unusually tall, dark, very full-jowled & younger. His opening statement was much more attractive. He has had a far more varied & interesting life than Bevin & knew how to put his goods in the

GATESHEAD PARLIAMENTARY ELECTION, 1931.

POLLING DAY - - TUESDAY, OCTOBER 27th.
From 8 a.m. to 9 p.m.

ELECTION ADDRESS

OF

ERNEST BEVIN

THE LABOUR CANDIDATE.

Central Committee Rooms :
111, BENSHAM ROAD, GATESHEAD.

Telephone
71776.

Ernest Bevin at Gateshead

window. He is a successful journalist, a Hexham man, claims to be a Tynesider; was in the Navy as an officer during the War; at Marlborough before, Edinburgh, & at Oxford afterwards. Travelled to numerous little wars in the Far & Middle East as reporter. Writes novels. It struck me at once that he would have far more time & energy to give to Gateshead than Bevin, with his great union to look after. Also he was offering more money. But it also struck me on the other side that there was a bit of a pose & a touch of the bully about him; & more than a little of the money touch; in his boasts of his success in life (which I found rather attractive in poor Evans!)the amount he had made, the money factor bulked very large. So I had practically decided for Bevin, because I preferred his personality, before Fisher began to answer questions. On this ground Bevin scored heavily; his experience told of course, but in addition he knew much more about Socialist theory & principle. Fisher seemed weak on the economic side; he is the R.C. nominee, through the N.U.M.G.W. [National Union of Municipal and General Workers] but I do not hold that against him at all; that was where we got Melville from, & I voted for Melville against the Trade Unionist (NUDAW) on that occasion because I thought him the better man for Gateshead. There was one other thing that turned the scale against Fisher, he had never stood for Parliament before; neither had Bevin, but his union Ex. Com. had only just given him permission. Fisher, a free man could easily have got another constituency before now if he had not been waiting for a safe seat; but let educated young successful Socialists like that take on backward constituencies & settle down to win them; if they wont the Party will never grow. Well Bevin was selected by 77 to 46 – two sevens are rather a lucky number; but Fisher polled well. I suppose I ought to have spoiled my paper by voting for Wilson; but I did not because I had got too excited & interested in the other two in the meanwhile.

So the issue is joined & the campaign started. God give Gateshead Good of the result. My hair stinks of foul tobacco smoke as I write this in bed before breakfast … . Rather a sad letter from Molly; she means to make back to Cowes in about a fortnight. Bob the same; it is all very strange & sad.

14 October. … . Adoption meeting at night. We are all tremendously impressed with Bevin, & I think he will be the Leader some day. It was a packed meeting, of course, & Bevin made a magnificent speech. Quite a number of the opposition bubbled in … & the Communists were also present; but the prevailing note was tense enthusiasm. I love great big men with wide shoulders & deep voices, & especially when they are gentle & sincere without a touch of the bully but strong & brave. I hope God will bless Gateshead & bless Bevin too & grant that we never let each other down, but back each other up in true comradeship for long long years, till Bevin's head just beginning to grey, is white with honoured service, & Gateshead is transformed into something nearer the town I want it to be … . I think there is humour & good humour in his face, & that is where MacDonald has always been lacking. I seconded the adoption vote – not very fluently, indeed, but I think audibly & intelligibly. Ned says I spoke for 15 minutes, which surprises me very much, as I did not say a great deal, & I dont see how four times that could ever make an hour's speech … .

28 October. Political life is full of surprises. One of the things I never expected to hear of – the complete wiping out at the polls of a large & enthusiastic Party which seemed outwardly as full of life & kick as ever. Hope says it was because our policy was too tame. Yet the excuse for making an end to poor old Uncle Arthur, for instance, is that he is a dangerous revolutionary! One point is that at any rate there is no one to take our place – we shall come again because there is no other alternative to Toryism for ever. Some people are foretelling it for the rest of this generation but I do not believe that. I believe that the pendulum swings quicker & quicker as time goes on & all the devices of the machine, as Bevin calls it – wireless, stunt press, advertising – cannot stop the swing in our favour, though it may check it. I listened in till midnight at Westfield & so was well prepared for the final disaster – the loss of Gateshead. I went to the count at ten & found a disconsolate & yet wonderfully plucky group of Labour folks – men & women. I was perched up on the platform as usual, with the Tory ladies in front as a matter of right. In spite of the disaster it was an interesting count. Bevin told me at one time that he was down by six to one & had only polled 15,000! As a matter of fact he had polled 21,000 odd. But Magnay [the National Liberal candidate], who is an unattractive personality & will make a thoroughly bad Member, I fancy, had 34,700. So solidly had the non-voting, non-thinking part of the population turned out to support saving their savings & the national no-policy. At the bye-election, poor Evans won with only 1000 more votes.

3 November. … . [municipal elections]. They came off yesterday, & we only saved the North Ward … & lost the Central … & the East – Ned Scott, which is truly a sad blow … . I shall miss him most terribly on the Council, but perhaps he will be able to do more for the I.L.P. I wish I was a better talker – & speaker too – but if we could form a talking group at Westfield we might do some good – but I am timid & fail to hold an audience – not being interesting enough … . I have a nice letter from Bevin, but he will not promise about May Day, & I doubt if we shall ever get him back; still I have hopes.

Diaries missing between November 1931 and 1937. The 1937 diary only relates the Swedish holiday with Sylvia.

Housing conditions on Tyneside in the 1930s. Photograph taken by Bill Brandt on his Northern tour of 1935.

CHAPTER TEN: NOVEMBER 1938 – AUGUST 1939

Last months of Peace; Lakes; end of Westfield Hall connection; Polish crisis brings Swedish holiday to a close

Diary 23 begins Nov. 1938. Unlike previous diaries it contains a summary of year presumably from notes kept.

1938 … . All the year I have been sticking to & sticking up for … the Labour Party … . My best friend [?] has gone away & left me, & seems to want me to disown them too, because they are foul-mouthed, dishonest, self-seeking. But if I leave them because of these things, & perhaps still more because they are so difficult to work with, & turn against you for a trifle, & let you down without rhyme or reason – why where among mortal men shall I find a whole regiment of the polite, the strictly honourable, the public spirited? Why, if one numbers a dozen such people at a time among ones friends, it is a wonderful piece of luck; & we can pick our friends on personal grounds; one cannot pick a political party so. I told Ned last night that he was self-righteous because he thought the Party not good enough for him; but I am just as self-righteous myself, but in me it takes the form of thinking that though the Party may be bad, it will be none the better if I leave it! And all the time I am on the verge of leaving it, over this wretched support of armaments! But I hope God will make it clear to me if & when I must. And George Lansbury [leader of Labour Party 1931-5: a pacifist] is by way of being an earthly guide! Let me count up those who are not just every bit as good but much better men than I, on the Council Group only. Tom Peacock – he has been ill all the last six months, since the estimates went through; dear old Tom. I love him as much when I dont agree with him as when I do. And old gentle Mr Stone, & Bill Barron, & old Bill Tait, & Peter Hancock, & Mrs Hall & Charlie Flynn: Stan Tyrrell has his points, in spite of a careless tongue, & I have great hopes of Ken Hughes, while Jim Hutchie is an old & tried comrade, though a gossip. With myself, that's twelve. The others may all have serious defects in one way or another – principle or temperament – but every one of them has possibilities of doing good work, & some of them great possibilities … .
9 November. Mayor's Day was really a good day. I want to try & recapture a little of its feeling. It was a fine, warm sunny day for Nov. only with a little nip in the wind. I wore my new mohair green frock & my new mohair green coat; but I still have only one old black hat – I've never had time to buy a nice one. I was full of fear & foreboding, not because of the ticklish state of the parties … . I was desperately afraid that our people would make scenes, & whether we won or lost the Party would be let down. But it wasn't! It all went beautifully & the sight of our unanimity confounded the opposition, who

behaved very well, too ... we got four new alderman; & Fergie who was very excited about being an alderman, turned faint & did not shout, & Kegie was cleverly kept quiet by the Mayor & everyone else behaved very nicely; even the displaced aldermen, though rather rude were pleasantly sporting; they knew they would have done the same to us .... I went over to Fenwick's new French Cafe, just opened, & very nice indeed, & had a very good lunch – cold ham & egg mayonaise [sic], & coffee (lots of it) & a tangerine sundae ....

Summary of 1938

It has been a very hard-working year – ... striving & striving & getting no further. Yet that is ungrateful with the New Clinic opened & Deckham Hall & Wrekenton Housing Schemes finished. One always remembers what is still undone, because it is still on one's mind. Spiritually any advance? I dont know .... I hardly like to claim advance. In spiritual matters it takes about all the running *I* can do to stay in the same place, & I am apt to be rather too satisfied with myself even for that!

Now for a narrative; The old people have lost ground – Aunt Camie very feeble now, Aunt Edie quite blinded by a stroke at the end of October & very feeble & helpless ....

The maids have been pretty well & jolly for the year. Flora has got a young man; Mary's enthusiasm for her profession remains unabated. Sublimation in cakes & puddings! .... I am starting this narrative again at Bonscale between Xmas & New Year – not inappropriately, as I dont think I have ever in my life been so often to the Lakes as I have this year. I love it more & more, if that were possible .... There has been the usual round of Council work: I have been a moderately successful Chairman of the Library & Art Gallery Committee & the new Redheugh Branch Library was actually started in Sept; less successful as Chairman of the Higher Education, but passable there; very keen at any rate, as Vice- Chairman of the Housing Com. & a conscientious member of the Health Committee. I have worked hard myself at the Welfare Centres, especially Victoria Rd, & kept the voluntary helpers going with a fair degree of success; this work is getting heavier as it expands. The new Health Centre is tremendously popular. I have not done quite so well with my ward & LP work. The Socialist Soc.[1] has left Westfield Hall to the triumphant ILP & is now meeting at Labour Hall. The Progressive Players are looking for a site for a Little Theatre of their own, & many conferences has Hope had ... about it & many plans have been prepared. Hope is finishing off the last volume of the County History[2]. Sylvia has had a busy year with the wardrobe, especially in spring & autumn. The *Gateshead Herald* has continued its rather uninspired way; but I now have a good helper in Allan Henderson [a young lawyer, actor and writer at the Little Theatre] ....

Green Rigg, Patterdale, in April, after a month with a badly bruised leg … took us for quite a new drive – over by Troutbeck, St John's Vale, Grasmere, Skelwith, Yewdale, Coniston, almost into Broughton & right up the Duddon to Seathwaite. I had never been in Dunnerdale before, only once looked down at it from the top of Wrynose, quite the least characteristic part of it, though fine & desolate. We walked up Tarn Beck, failed to discover the famous gorge, but saw enough of the glorious rocks to be charmed, & also saw a white farm sheltering under a big rock with a notice about boarders on the road. Turner Hall is its name. We thought the situation charming … my plan was to go back to Dunnerdale & stay at the White Farm … . And I did it too! from May 26th to May 30th. It was a great adventure getting there, on a miserably cold & wet day – on beyond Carlisle & through the subsiding Whitehaven tunnel, & along the wild strange coast, with rocky headlands in places & flaky red levels below the hills in others. I could not get further than Millom, & hired a car there which took me up Duddon, still in heavy rain. I did not even know the name of the house then! But there is a little inn at Seathwaite & I meant to go there if the farm would not do. But it turned out to be a delightful place, & Mrs Hartley very kind. Everything very primitive – behind Patterdale standards – but I had a nice sitting-room looking onto the little garden under the crag, & the bed, though bumpy, was sleepable … . How I did enjoy exploring a new place – discovering the gorge & the way up Wallabarrow & all the wonderful rocky barriers, parallel & traverse that split up the valley. I never got to the top of Walna Scar, nor up to the tarn (I saw some poachers coming down from it!) But I had some glorious sunshine, & the rivers & fells shouting full – the stepping-stones, both higher & lower always under water! Splendid views at times of the Scawfells; I was delighted by Birks Bridge; & up beyond Birks (where was one lilac still in full flower by the empty farm) the FC's (Forestry Commission) little plantations had been burned up! Through Grassguards – charming name – I tackled a wild boggy dip under the shoulder of Harter Fell – leaping & even wading the swollen streams. I wanted to look into Eskdale, but managed very little of the descent to it before it came on to rain *heavily* & I turned back; down by the steep Wallabarrow Crag descent – splendid … . I had a particularly nice Friends' Meeting on the Sunday, under an oak on the way to the farm, in a heavy shower. There was a rainbow, & oh the scents! It was a heavenly time of refreshing. Eskdale remains to be explored another time, I hope. I read a nice book about the Wordsworths & enjoyed my quiet fire in the evenings which were generally very wet … .

30 May. After getting off parcels & paying the bill, & admiring the strange old kitchen fireplace, with a grid to riddle the cinders below the grate & a great hole for the fire ashes under the level of the floor, I bravely set off in a mackintosh to meet Ridley on the other side of Wrynose. Years ago I have been at the top of the pass with Sylvia, then the other day at its foot with Mildred & S; now for the miles between! Very interesting it was; though the high fells were in cloud the sun was out about 1.45, when I was lunching in a sandpit at the foot of the final ascent. Below Wallabarrow the vale is mostly wooded & the hills rounded; then come a few outcrops of the nose-shaped rocks; then that magnificent barrier of Wallabarrow where the river runs through the gorge & the Tarn Beck down a wider, but very rocky bed, among charming woods & haughs. My farm is on the flattened bit of the rock barrier, just below Walna Scar & some old quarries. Then for two or three miles the middle reach of the dale is a riot of wonderful rock forms. … Above Birks Bridge the rocks abruptly end, with an outpost rock far above at Castle Howe; & I spent a long time on the rocky hillocks opposite Birks, studying the formation of this wild land. Then up a long upland valley, quite level, Crinkle Crags & Bowfell dominating, in & out of mist; & so up to Dale Head & the foot of Hard Knott. I wrote a P.C. on the bridge in a gale of bitter cold wind, & the post van which I had been playing Hare & Tortoise with all morning took it for me. This farm is Nat. Trust property & I believe you can stay at it; but though it turned a good face to the world it is filthy in the living quarters behind … the sun shone during the last ascent up to the Three Shire Stone; I met a motor coming down & cyclists going up & had to ford many swollen streams, – once I took off shoes & stocking, & it was cold.

I met Ridley [Uncle from Patterdale] at Fell Foot at the gate at the bottom of the pass exactly at 3, as appointed – a miracle! The day was gorgeous by now. The descent from Wrynose is really uninteresting, but how I enjoyed it with the sun beaming & the blue sky shining on me & all the waterfalls sheets of silver! He motored me … to Dungeon Ghyll & we had tea there; afterwards visited a charming rock garden at Ambleside; Windermere was quite as blue as the Mediterranean can possibly be at its bluest; & so over Kirkstone home (Patterdale) … .

All the summer the Greenesfield Health Centre & the other Infant Welfare Clinics have played an ever increasing part in life. The Toddler's room at GHC is a big attraction; we need a large team of voluntary helpers now. On Tuesday I am at the Teams Centre in the morning & usually at GHC in the afternoon, so it is a full day … .

Aunt Edie was gradually getting worse & blinder during the summer, until at length … was obliged to get a night nurse … . Camie had ups & downs, gradually losing ground, but wonderfully bright during her better periods. Talked often of her parents; never leaves her room now. She has a very good nurse.

Tuesday 14 June. I was not long in going away again; this time to Molly's where I had glorious weather … .

Had a hectic July … . Tom Peacock had been seriously ill since Easter, & all this time we were unhappily negotiating the leaving of the Westfield to the triumphant & disagreeable ILP What a trifle after all! And yet the years of work – ! How Tom & Mrs Peacock did *Labour* there! – & I too in my own way, especially for the Dramatic Club, & the Propaganda meetings. There are none now! Goodbye to Heartbreak Hall.

The end of my connection with Westfield is the end of an epoch. We have spent a lot of time there. All my plays have been produced there – & most of them nowhere else. The Progressive Players are still acting there, in spite of the unfriendly attitude of the ILP but Hope has been busy for some time looking for a suitable site for a Little Theatre which Mr Honeyman will design, The house next to the Labour Hall in Walker Terrace would do splendidly, but unfortunately it is not for sale. Plans & talks & views of sites have provided a background to our minds all the summer & autumn. The Socialist Soc., which refuses to die, meets, now at LH not very often, & mostly the Nixons keep it alive.

I was pretty happy in my Council work all the summer – especially working on my dear Housing Com. with good jolly Bill Barron. (Peter I am seeing every now & then but Ned I hardly ever see; he had almost dropped me; I feel just as friendly to him as ever; I'm afraid I made a mistake in taking on the Chair of the Higher Ed., though he urged it. And I dont even care about it! but I do care about him.) There is nearly always trouble on or threatening in the Group & the Party; but I try to convince myself I am used to it. The Clinics keep me busy too. In August I went to Patterdale for a long weekend … Ridley took us some nice drives … . I climbed Place Fell on a very warm damp, rather hazy morning & got very hot. It took me from 10 to 12.25, there & back … .
Sept '38. Hitler's first speech was on the 12th … . It was an evil time. The newsboys went shrieking about the streets long after midnight. The fear of War was bad enough; the sense of having thrown in our lot with the oppressors to encourage trampling on the weak was just as bad. No, the choice was not between that & War! It was simply between joyfully welcoming the crushing of the Czechs & honestly stating the case against it without threatening War … . I listened night after night to the English broadcasts from Prague until Hitler stopped them. It was a strange experience – to hear that quiet voice telling the loss of one thing after another, the gradual disruption of a free state. We all knew, all through the summer that Chamberlain was going to throw the Czechs to the wolves; & yet the way it was finally done, to declarations of eternal peace with the dictators, no acknowledgement of what the sacrificed had lost, & intensified re-armament (against whom?) seemed British hypocrisy parading itself … .

The trenches are still all over the town, keeping the children out of the few play-grounds, months after … .

29 September. Munich. One moment we thought that Chamberlain was going to stand up to Hitler – that was when they dug the trenches. But it is all wrong … .

30 September. Chamberlain's return. I happened to hear this on the wireless, & was astonished at the Press accounts of his marvellous reception – the cheering was not at all ecstatic in my ears – just a sort of courtesy cheer … .

14 October. … . Sylvia was very ill with pleurisy most of October. She went to Stratford with a bad cold & developed it when she came home. Hope nursed her; I helped; I did most of the wardrobe.

23 October. Spoke at Evening Meeting on Silent Worship, the first of three little talks. The others were on Free Ministry & Unity & Peace. I enjoyed preparing them & they helped me very much. I quite liked giving them, too, after the first nervousness; but I always feel grave doubts as to whether anyone so little prepared as myself should speak about religion at all. On the other hand it is true & comforting to think that *anyone* can help another, no matter how sinful & imperfect themselves … . The November Elections were particularly horrid ones, as the Moderates fought them on election & deputation expenses … . Fergie was standing in my ward; I was so frantically busy, with Sylvia's illness & other engagements as well as Council work, that I had a good excuse for not taking much part in it … .

Nov. 28th – Dec. 4th. I wish my Conscience, which is always reproaching me with idleness, would only read this week in my diary. Two lectures on Sweden, at Birtley & Felling, six Committee meetings, clinics fitted in & other party & municipal meetings; no wonder that when I went to *Black Limelight* for relaxation on Saturday night, I was almost too tired to enjoy that neat little thriller; & it went on like that, or worse, till Christmas – I say worse because there were all the Clinic parties, six of them, between Dec. 12th & Christmas, & also an extra E.C. Ward Social because of the Bye-Election after all the agony of the Annual one in November. As extras we had two Basque children for a week-end [refugees from the Spanish Civil War], & I was trying to take a Spanish Food Ship collection amongst the snow-storms. So I felt quite justified in going away for Christmas & New Year for ten days rest. It was a little too late if anything for I developed rather bad rheumatism when I was away (it had begun before) which lingered on for months. I went to Bonscale which is taking visitors again after 7 years … . I had a heavenly time of refreshing.

24 December. Arrived at Penrith in bitter cold & frost; Mr Watson (from Bonscale farm) met me in his funny little car. My green mohair frock & coat are gloriously warm … .

25 December. It was a perfect Xmas morning … . I went up to morning service at the little church on the Hause, but arrived very late! When the old parson prayed for the dying I thought of my two dear old Aunts, Aunt Camie & Aunt Edie, both so near the end of long lives … . The service at Martindale was soon over – I left them to Communion & climbed Hallin Fell up a snowy path; the snow was thin & patchy … . One person had been up & down before me … .

I did not get out of an Xmas Party. Mrs Watson took me to that at the Big House below – Swarthfield, where the two old servants, Susan Nattrass & Mary Bell, entertained them to Xmas Dinner in the finest style, as instructed by their master & mistress. Like most country houses it was terribly cold & doggy, but I liked the two old servants, & we got away at last. I snuggled over my log & wood fire to my hearts content … .

4 January 1939. I came home for the Council & immediately went to the Dr for my rheumatism; also to the Dentist. I had a long course of massage later with Miss Squance which did not cure it … . I found Camie very feeble when I came back, taking no pleasure in anything – only so tired, so tired, though still, bless her heart & soul forever, thankful – much to be thankful for … . It was clear, as it had been for some time, that the end was near. She died on Jan. 9th, early in the morning. Cairns, Nurse & the other maids were there; none of us. It was quite a peaceful end. So the things concerning Ashfield have come to an end. The last of that happy company of sisters gone – for they were on the whole, undoubtedly happy & fortunate. It was odd that Mother, youngest of that family, died first, & Camie the eldest, last … . Day after day we went down, going through all cupboards, sorting, throwing away, giving away, saving, distributing choosing. My greatest find was the coloured engravings of the Great Exhibition of '51, which I had sought for so long. Perhaps the nicest thing was selecting the things for a Victorian Room at the [Saltwell] Park Museum. Also the old letters are often rather charming … . I went once to see Aunt Edie before the end, & Hope went later still … she died just two days before her 92nd birthday, on February 20th … . The Ashfield Sale was on Mch 7th & 8th. The family took all the nicest things, of course. The rest did not fetch much. Now the house stands all empty & spacious. The rooms look rather fine, the garden bursts with green buds – as it always did.

9 March. The £200 which I lend has returned to me again after about 12 years; sadly enough but it has come back. I lent it to Bernard Reed once when he was in a hole in Canada. E.C.M. paid it back – it was long, long ago when she could well manage her own affairs. Then I lent it to the ILP to buy Westfield. They paid it back in a few years – that was Tom Peacock & Oliver Colvin, of course; then I lent it to Molly when Hugh lost his Sth African job

& they were so poor; & she paid it back out of a special gift the Aunts gave us when Cerebos began to do so well. I lent it to Peter Howcroft in or soon after 1926, to get him out of the mines, & now he has paid me back, God bless him! I'm afraid its a sign that he feels he is near the end; he is sore failed … my dear old friend … . I never expect to get it back; yet back it comes … .
25 April. … . Peter's son Tom rang up to say he had died that morning. Dear old Peter! I did & do love him! He was very tired of being so ill – weary he told me last time I saw him that he did not care how soon it was over. He has been such a help to me & meant so much. He was so cheery & kind & true … . I walked in the twilight misty garden & thought & thought & thought of him. One is sorry afterwards one did not make more of ones opportunities. How I love Peter's stories of old days in the mines, old homes in the North! I could have listened to them for ever. I met him first when he was a Municipal candidate for the South Ward in 1919 – that will be 20 years ago come November – the miners' candidate when the miners were so much in the news in the days of the Sankey Commission. How I took to him from the very start & he to me! I was the only woman working in his election. He won by 37 votes! I was at the Count in the old Low Fell Infant School … . We used to walk home along the low lane from Westfield with Joe Mackenzie, under the tall dark trees, winter & summer, light & dark. For years & years we have loved each other with a bright untarnished friendship. He gave me so much … .
27 April. … . [dentist] says my teeth will not last much longer now … . went to Peter's funeral … .
28 April. … . I am much concerned about Conscription & am getting out a "May Day Special", the front page to devoted to Resist Conscription. I am glad the Party have opposed it in the House & pray they keep it up.
7 May … . Glanced through all the letters in Camie's old desk. They date from 1859 – 1866 but mostly 61, 62, 63. Not interesting – a great warning against preserving useless information, as I am doing in my diary here. But why not, if I like it. No one certainly will ever read it but myself, & I doubt very much if I shall – not all of it anyway. But yet I like to have it stored up here … .
31 May. … . I am quite ashamed of all the new clothes I have got – my cupboards have not been so full for ages – but I make Sweden an excuse
18 June. … . The Little Theatre site at the main Park Gates & the top house of Saltwell View is now Hope's, & the Club has left Westfield. Our props are stored at Labour Hall … . I am much involved in a Czech Hostel [for refugees] at Mayfield Low Fell. Plans for Sweden are somewhat further advanced – I have the tickets. I am going to get a holiday Season Ticket & see N'thld this Race Week … . This was a most glorious & memorable Race Week. We walked about 50 miles … .

26 July. Molly arrived safely. Tomorrow she with Sylvia & Elisabeth start their long-planned voyage to Norway to join us a little later on at Stockholm … . They sail in the *Venus* for Bergen tonight.
27 July. Today I had three back teeth out. This is the sort of event that bulks big at the moment & seems so trifling afterwards … .
8 August. Breviksgard Pensionat, Lidingo. It is marvellous to be in Sweden again … .
22 August. … . We had a great war scare about tea time. The posters announced "German Ultimatum to Poland", & unfortunately I know just enough Swedish to understand that. There had just previously been a good deal of excitement over a proposed non-aggression pact between Germany & Russia, which was interpreted by Alma [their Swedish friend] & others to mean that Russia had grown weary of the democracies & thrown in her lot with the Axis. Personally I see no harm in non-aggression pacts, if only nations would observe. Anyway Alma had been in a great fuss on Monday night & to please her I went round to the Consulate & enquired about registration; but there was no rush, no one there but me (though we know from personal experience that Shm. is full of British) & they were exceedingly calm & told me a list of our names & addresses & passport numbers was all that was needed. However, we all kept very calm on Tuesday, & dressed & went to the Opera Kelloren in fine style & had a splendid dinner … .
23 August. Sylvia & I went round to the Consulate again with our list; & again found them very calm. We had thought the news rather bad; but Alma thought it rather better … again they did not urge us to get home at once & were on the whole rather re-assuring; I went round afterwards to Svenske Lloyd & they said the Sat. boat was almost full but there were plenty of berths on the Sunday & Tuesday boats. After a lot of discussion at various times we decided not to alter our plans at present … . I went to the Bank & the exchange had only dropped 3 ore since Sat … except Molly, we went to the pictures to keep up our spirits. We saw a Sacha Guitry film "Champs Elysées" – quite good but oh the heat! … .
24 August. This was the first day when I began to feel, but only at times, that it would soon be impossible to enjoy oneself any longer; that dreadful grip of terror on the heart. But I never felt it for very long at a time; only it is impossible not to face the fact that war may be very near … . We three Doddses went to the Ten O'Clock Concert at the National Museum; the others went to Alma's to listen to Lord Halifax [Foreign Secretary] but the only important news was that the Danish air-route was closed, but one cld still fly by the Amsterdam route. It was much more sensible to go out & listen to music … . We did not stay to the end & walked home in the warm still

delicious night. Alma was very depressed sure that war would come … .
25 August. Today we decided that it was no longer possible to enjoy ourselves under the circumstances & we transferred our tickets to the first available Svenska Lloyd boat, the Britannia, sailing on Tuesday. Sylvia & I also drew all our travellers cheques in Swedish money. We have enough English notes for home comsumption after landing … . Cooks reported that all Danish-English sailings are cancelled, but this seems hard to believe, unless it is because Denmark is so anxious to propitiate Hitler, who thinks this a way of putting pressure on G.B. … we did a lot of shopping … . All the flags were out today & we heard later that it was because the king had returned to Stm. owing to the crisis … .
27 August. … . I wrote rather hastily to Hope & also sent a cheque for £100 to Prof. Reid, so that the refugee hostel will not be left without resources in case I am versunken in the N.Sea which of course is not likely but one never knows … . Now I am on the North Sea, on the Britannia in glorious weather … . Sylvia is having a little difficulty about Alma, who, as usual, says that *now* no one will want to learn English & that she will starve. She last said this because she was losing her work at a big girls school; the City has taken it over from a private company & will only employ certificated teachers. It has always been a handicap to Alma that she had no proper training. So to make up for the loss of school work, Sylvia offered to buy her an annuity of £50 a year. She was very grateful but did nothing about it except make some indirect enquiries about how she could get out of income tax on it! Of course it turned out in the end that no tax is payable on so small a sum. Now comes the threat of war & she is certain she will lose all her private pupils now (I dont see why she should) & starve all over again; & if war is declared it will be difficult to get money sent from England … . Urged by Sylvia she really is approaching an Insurance Company at this last possible moment, & S. & I are going to send her all the money we brought with us & have left over after our trip (this amounts to over £100 in kroner) so that she can begin buying the annuity, or live on the money in case of emergency. This has rather upset & worried Sylvia, who is also unwell at this unfortunate moment. Both my young men are fixed up now, I hope & trust [Austrian refugees Ruth supported at King's College, Durham University] … . & Allan [Henderson, solicitor] is also launched on his career & has given up his municipal ambitions for the present … .
30 August. This day was spent at sea on the SS Britannia. It was a perfect day, warm & sunny. I wrote & read & dreamed wandering about the ship. At dinner the Captain announced that all lights would be put out at 12.30, because the British Admiralty had ordered all lights to be dimmed in territorial waters … .

31 August. … . We were late, & late in getting off, & could only catch the 1.5 at Kings X. The train was fullish – not packed – many babies – as we afterwards realised it was the voluntary evacuation of London – people going to parents in the North. London was sandbagged & trenched, & soldiers drilling in the parks … .

An unemployed workers' rally in Felling Square in the 1930s – Jim Ancrum addresses the meeting.

The Quaker Meeting House in Archbold Terrace, Jesmond, home of the Newcastle Friends since the mid-1960s.

CHAPTER ELEVEN: SEPTEMBER 1939 – MAY 1945

The Second World War

1 September. … . I went to the Clinic, after a rather stunned morning reading the papers. Saw one of the schools marching to the station [for evacuation to rural areas]. Fighting in Poland has begun. Germany has invaded the Corridor. The Health Centre is full of ambulance people. We had a special meeting of the Council at night; nothing much except that they set up a Food Com. & decided to have no ordinary Committees till after Council meeting on the 20th.

2 September (Saturday). The day we ought to have sailed … . England has sent an ultimatum to Germany to withdraw her troops from Poland. No time limit. I spent most of the day at the Health centre helping to evacuate expectant mothers. The mothers with babies & toddlers were leaving too but they met at the schools. Like all war work, or most of it, it was lining up queues & making cups of tea for exhausted workers. The mothers were going to Nth Yorks mostly, the midwives with them. I dont suppose they'll stay long. They'll want to be back to the homes & the men.

3 September. We all three went to Quaker meeting … when we got home we heard about the declaration of War at 11 a.m. So it has come after all our hopes & prayers that good feeling & common sense might prevail. What fools the human race are! The gardens are glorious, the sun shines, there is a tremendous crop of apples, the harvest is golden in the fields & this is what they do! Life is so short, surely we might use it better.

Sept. 4th – 9th. A worried hurrying sort of week & long so long! The four years of the last war were the longest in my life. Disaster has this strange effect of slowing down time. there have been no air raids & no more false alarms here. I am not making much headway with inner life either … .

17 September. Why am I resigning from the Labour Party? Am I really justified? Is it just boredom because I am fed up with it all & dont like Fergie? Feeling as I do at least a half-sympathy with a war against Fascism, is it *really* honest to say my pacifism makes me resign? Is the desire I feel to be out of it, not to be responsible for the bloodshed, not merely moral cowardice? How can I be out of it? Am I not bound to be guilty when all are guilty? Is it just because I said I would resign if & when the Party supported a war?

It is true. I do really & profoundly believe this war & no war can do good; that its bound to make matters worse. But what alternative could I suggest – *now*? (I have suggested many before). I want to make a gesture against it; but what good is an empty gesture like Pilate washing his hands? … . I came back from Sweden, I mean to stay here; I mean to help all the innocent victims as much as I can.

It is only a gesture & no good, but its the only gesture I can make to show I bear testimony for peace; I cant refuse to fight like the men. I also hope to make it clear that the work I hope to do is not done to further the war, but in defiance of war – the things I would have done anyhow; or that *sort* of thing. (Wounds are to be bound up in peace as well as in war).

I want my comrades in the Labour Party to see that I am really in earnest about it. Taking it all round it will be a *giving up* – it will be a release, too, no doubt, but mostly it will be a giving up … . So the letter of resignation I have written had better go. I will pray again; but it seems a little matter to trouble God about with so much real trouble in the world … .

10 October. I am getting through it pretty well ….. The Party were very hateful (it was Fergie no doubt; he uses the Party to hurt his enemies) & made me resign from the Council the next day, which quite took my breath away. It did not happen at all as I expected & my testimony for Peace would have passed quite without notice if I had not screwed myself up to write to the Press about it.[2] The *Journal* gave me a good show & it has made quite a little stir … it is partly sheer relief to be out of the Party – no more ugly stuffy meetings with all the speakers at once ill-natured & wide of the point; no more horrible rowdy evenings on the Council, with everyone at their worst, no more Ward meetings with no Councillor turning up but me & me having to carry it all on my shoulders. No more worry worry worry to get the GH [*Gateshead Herald*] out. And yet & yet – it does mean no more real knowledge of many things I want to know; no more power to press my point, so much work & effort to reach this point – & now all gone – all gone. And the stab the Party gave me when I was so trusting, so anxious to act generously … . I was truly grieved to have deserted my ragged regiment (as they think I have). How can they be anything else but suspicious & ungenerous & unable to respond to affection, when that is the way they were recruited – from the dregs of the unhappy & unemployed. Not all; but enough; they gape after Fergie because he is sensational; they none of them dream of standing up to him, except occasionally on personal interest. I am glad I am out – & sorry. Especially sorry that I could not do better while I was there … .

21 October. … was the official opening of the Mayfield Refugee Hostel. I was pleased & thankful for the sympathy aroused. Then suddenly I got a summons to a GH meeting on Monday night; so if only I could get that out of the road I could go away to the Lakes for the October colours, as I have been longing to do for years, but there is always the November elections. This year there are none, anyhow … . So I slaved over the books all day & took them down at night – & no one would take charge! So much for their blessed new committee! … In the afternoon, Tues Oct 24th I set off in a kind of dream for

Keswick … . I changed at Penrith, just at sunset time; it was red at night; it was odd seeing the Ncle Grammar School boys all about the streets; they are not nearly so fussy about black-out here & the shops were open till the usual times. It was a gorgeous journey from Penrith to Keswick by the light of the moon, nearly full … . I never had so wonderful a journey & all because the carriages were blackout [sic] & I could really see out of the windows for once … . The train was late at Keswick – about 7.45 I suppose; I went to the Royal Oak & a kind man carried my case from the station. It was a warm, but stuffy hotel; & after a good dinner I walked all the way up to Manor Brow, & further too, by moonlight, enjoying the hills & the woodland scents & the peace … .

25 October. A perfect autumn day … . Went up Borrowdale with Margaret & Nell & entertained them to lunch at the Borrowdale Hotel … . M & I walked round Castle Crag – a glorious walk; the trees are more gorgeous than words can say, far more lovely then I could imagine – or even remember. Sometimes I forgot the War altogether; & sometimes I forget my false teeth; but it is lovely to take them out … . [at the Borrowdale Hotel] … a comfortable sort of old-fashioned Lakes hotel with very good beds, hot water in all the rooms, really hot baths, & also hot water bottles if it is the right maids night in; friendly & competent landlady … . It is not far enough up the dale to suit me entirely, but, though dear, it would take a single person, which most boarding houses will not do; & as there were fairly frequent buses to Seatoller & back, the whole dale was very available … . Its outlook, though N.E. is superb – right down the lake to the full expanse of Skiddaw's most beautiful aspect … . There is another woman, about my age but thinner, who is walking on her own. She was caught by the snow on Greenup … the Lakes are new to her … .

29 October. Home.

28 December. Here I am back at Keswick after two months, now at the Manor Hotel for Xmas. Last time was such a stormy windy time. This time has been so very still & peaceful; warm & sunny too for the time of year … . I have a magnificent front room overlooking the terrace & Skiddaw through a fringe of magnificent beeches … .

24 Sunday. … . I went to meeting in Keswick – a quiet but very good meeting; I felt very near the peace of God. I have been practising the period of silence every morning before getting up (as recommended by Penn) with a persistence very unusual with me; perhaps it helps.But my reading every day of *Great Souls at Prayer* broke down hopelessly some time ago.

Christmas Day was gloriously bright & sunny. MAJ & I walked to Walla Crag – the nearest & most obvious walk from here … . The Xmas dinner was very magnificent. There were eleven instead of 14 … we played games afterwards & my Plum Pudding one made a good start … . Mysterious & magic games followed & a memory test called Puff-Puff, & so on. I have learnt some quite good games.

Boxing Day M.A.J. & I (65 & 49) did our big walk today, while the younger generation sat round the fire & grumbled about petrol rations! We caught the 10 am bus up Borrowdale, got out at Thorneythwaite & went up by the green-track side of the Seathwaite valley to the farm. As it was very misty & dark up Grain Gill we went up Styhead Pass, the sky turning blue overhead & the mountains behind glowing with russet red & soft greens & yellows in the sun which did not reach us. Clouds on Skiddaw & Saddleback behind & on Gable (when we saw him) & Great End in front … . We went up to Sprinkling Tarn, lunching in a very sheltered dip on the hause before we reached it between Lingmell, Great End & Seathwaite Fell … . Sprinkling Tarn was frozen … . It was exciting down the Grain Gill way, as I had never been. Lovely views of the Lake in sunshine & blue sky behind. Only a keen wind in our faces made it difficult to look out much because of watering eyes. We caught the 3.30 bus down the valley & had the most gorgeous gold & crimson sunset; & all the high hills had cleared by that time – Great End Gable & Scawfells, & all both ways … .

27 December. Was much colder – frosty morning & frost held all day. MAJ & I did not get off till the 12.10 bus, lunched in the Borrowdale Hotel & did King's How … . We just missed the bus & had tea at the B. H. (Borrowdale Hotel) by a nice fire. It is getting colder & colder … .

28 December. A sense of the letters piling up at home drove me back a day earlier than I had intended … . I paid the very stiff bill & tipped handsomely … .

January 1940 – Dec. 1941 [another summary by R.D.] … . January has been all frost & snow – day after day of frost, day after day of snow – and hardly any sunshine … war & cold & darkness & death. Though it seems the powers of nature are against war as they have made it difficult for men to fight. Everyone had either burst pipes or no water or both; we had two bad bursts & the spare room ceiling down, which conditioned our lives for the whole of February, with men in recasting the whole water system, putting in copper pipes instead of lead, & then the plasterers & carpenters & then the decorators … . spoke at a Women's Peace Conference on Feb. 17th. … . The Sewing Meeting on Tues. went on regularly Jan & Feb … . Trouble at the Hostel (for refugees) continued to brew … . Hope went off to her new flat in the Island [she had recently bought a flat on the Isle of Wight] … . I do not find I have any less to do with being off the Council. I get so tired at home that I come away whenever I can manage it or have an excuse. I have been to a Spanish Tea & a China Conference, & though my book seems to show that I have not been speaking much, I find every speech or lecture a 'costing' service, as Friends say, that I feel as if I had done a lot. Right at the end of Feb. I got three days at Green Rigg [Patterdale] … I got home to all sorts of troubles, but what did it matter? Sylvia went to join Hope at Cowes while I was away.

Apart from the War, one serious trouble has developed during these two months – Hugh got so bad that he was forced to see a Dr at last. He has had a bad cough for years. Now it turns out to be T.B. One lung gone & the other badly affected – Poor old Molly! I am glad she seized time by the forelock & did so much cruising while she could. It is a good thing too that Hope got the flat near her. She is in for a sad hard time. Hugh keeps cheerful & is having gold injections.

2 March. Hostel Annual meeting. Quarrelling among the refugees. Silberstens & Salzers both to go.

6 & 7 March. Every minute these days taken up with the Hostel, the *Herald*, the Wardrobe, Correspondence & meetings – Council on Wed. as a reporter. … . We had servant trouble on top of the bursts & Mary is leaving after all these years.

9 March. … . London for the Friends' Social & Industrial Order Council at Friends House … then to the Island … to see Hope's new flat … . Its funny how little I think about the War when I dont see the papers, in spite of all the soldiers & sailors about … . (flat) is very nice; & the bed they had ordered for me had never come! But Birkett the factotum, said he had a bed in his stores; … & I have slept very comfortably on it ever since!

The flat is lovely – all Heal [a smart London store]; green folk-weave chairs & green carpet, & cream walls & doors – 24 cupboards! – & cream ground folk-weave curtains with pattern in red, buff & black – all over & very gay & pleasing; & the Moorish rugs Hope & I chose – cream & brown & green, with touches of reddish-orange; the polished oak predominates; there are no pictures which I dont like; & it is very warmly central heated; but in all other respects I love it. The side-board-table-bench is a great success. Birkett is a treasure.

11 March. A lovely bright day – sunshine makes the flat nicer still; it is rather nautical with its boards & its balconies over-looking the Solent, & its compactness. Sylvia in her dark cherry coloured slacks fits in well enough; but Hope is the least nautical of mortals! … .

In the aft. all four sisters went to the Townswomen's Guild where Hope gave a good paper on Sir John Oglander of Nunwell; it was very interesting … .

13 March. I have just seen in someone's *Daily Mail* on the boat "Finland Signs Peace Today". This is the first good news for long enough … . One cannot ignore the fact that people do fight & believe it right to do so & that some of them are activated partly at least, by higher motives than love of fighting & desire of domination. Not to recognise this is to distort the truth, as I think the P.P.U. [Peace Pledge Union] do for their own ends … . I was glad too when the Navy broke Norwegian neutrality to save the Altmark men [a German ship, in Norwegian territorial waters, carrying British prisoners of war] … . I saw a news-reel of it – I went on purpose to see what sort of prop. [propaganda] the cinema is putting over. It was not nearly so bad as one would expect & the rescued Altmark men made it almost cheerful … .

9 April. This was one of the horridest days of my life; I have kept on hoping all the time that whatever happened to us Scandinavia would be safe & fairly happy. And now this. First came the news of the Navy mining Norwegian waters, & then the queer story of a German transport on the way to Bergen sunk. Then the definite news that Germany had invaded both Denmark & Norway, & Denmark was not resisting & Copenhagen, the gay fairy-tale city with its copper domes & spires, is in the hands of the Germans; & Oslo has surrendered. I went to the Clinic in the morning & to the last sewing-class in the afternoon. I could not bear to think much; & I was speaking on Swedish Co-operation at the Bensham Guild in the evening … I think of Karin & Alma & I am very miserable.

11 April. … . The naval battles are still quite obscure but I did not listen tonight to the wireless. That is Taboo in our house & one cant often get it alone … . I wrote a little in my anthology – a poem & an aphorism for every day of the year.

18 April I have been listening to the news as often as I could without distressing Hope who hates it. It has been a dreadful week. My dear beautiful Bergen bombed – such a friendly charming town … . I have been so excited by all this that I have sometimes asked myself whether I really am a pacifist at all; but I am, I find, more so than ever; for this shows how useless huge armaments are; with our gigantic fleet, part of it on the coasts of Norway already, hugely outnumbering the German fleet; with our command of the North Sea, with all our famous air patrols, still we could not prevent the Germans seizing Denmark & Norway … [force] is useless – only adds greater horrors to what is in any case a hideous sacrifice – Poland is worse off than Czecha, Norway than Denmark … .

3 May. It is no use pretending to any sort of indifference. I am on the way to London to a Friends Conference, & so miserable over the Norwegian defeat that I could easily cry all the way if I gave way a little … . The working-class reaction to Norway has been "another Gallipoli"; ordinary people have by no means come round to the new idea that Gallipoli was a fine idea too easily abandoned … . I am too unhappy to either write or read. That Norway & Denmark should be suffering so is worst; & next worst is that this hideous failiure is sure to mean a longer war, a longer agony for them & us, & the

Germans too; & that Sweden is most likely to fight against us or at any rate to *be* against us … . I met Hope … . We went to *King Lear* at the Old Vic at night – Gielgud very fine indeed … . A packed house.
Saturday … . Friends' Conference on the Challenge to Freedom – Carl Heath & Margery Fry.
8 May. My birthday, 50. Hugh died early in the morning. Hope had reported him to be failing rapidly. It was quick & quiet. Apparently he had no apprehension & not much pain or discomfort – just drifted away. He was a very kindhearted man & a splendid comic draughtsman; I liked his funny stories, too … a quite kind rather lovely soul; he was a real brother to me; he could be very tiresome but I was proud of him … I'm glad Hope is at Cowes. I'm not going for the funeral & poor Sylvie is not well & living on milk & Bengers food … she is going to Cowes next month … .
9 May. There was nothing in either of our papers to tell of the invasion of the Low Countries; but someone told me … about 10 am. Its a stunning blow, quite stunning. I have not been able to think of much else all day … .
12 May. Whit Sunday. Without any warning all the men refugees between 16 & 60 were arrested & taken away to be interned. The Police came for them about 7.30 am. Mrs Reid rang me about 8.30 & told me & Mrs Bambrough – I got down to Mayfield in time to say goodbye. I gave them some money & they were all taken away in a prison van. Only the Salzers & Mrs Silberstien & Erwin Knoplfler, who is Hungarian are left. At night old Mrs Freudman came (I was out) in terrible distress because they had taken Max. Wolfgang was at Ayton. I dont know yet where they have been taken to. Fortunately the weather is fine though rather cold. The news from Holland & Belgium is rather bad; there has been nothing on the wireless or in the Press about the internment.
Whit Monday. It was a glorious day … . Most people seemed to be keeping it as a holiday, although the schools were all open & carrying out a special examination of the children with a view to a new evacuation. The war news not very good. I dont care for the new Govt. [Churchill replaced Chamberlain as prime minister and formed a Coalition government] nor trust Churchill. The refugees are reported to be at Fenham Barracks.
May 1940. – this has been about the longest month I can remember … . Sylvia was very poorly – she began about a week ago & the Dr put her on a milk diet for a week & at first we thought she was better; but afterwards she began to lose a lot of weight & the Dr still kept her on milk & we began to get alarmed. She was sleeping badly & feeling very uncomfortable … . Miss Bambrough was able to see some of the refugees in Fenham Barracks, & just as we were beginning to get them some of their things, they were moved again on Monday May 20th to an unknown destination.

On Tues 21st Sylvia saw the Dr again, who told her she had better have an Xray on Thursday as she was afraid of ulcers. I had arranged to go up to London … on Wed. May 22nd. I was very alarmed about S. & did not want to go; but she had arranged with Margaret Swanwick to come for a week & keep her company, & urged me to go, so I went, as I did not want her to know how frightened I was.

I had stayed for the unveiling of Tom Peacock's picture on the 21st. … . It was nice but sad. And it was the same day that the news of the big defeat in France [the evacuation of British forces from Dunkirk began on 27 May] became certain & Reynaud told the Senate that the river passages had not been cut at the right time. Treachery? or incompetence? … . So I went to London feeling pretty miserable on two scores … . [Friends meetings] The feeling that we ought not to oppose even that we should support in some degree *this* war *now*, was expressed, & I was glad it came out, for of course a good many Friends must be feeling like that; & perhaps still more, like me, have the feeling come over them at times & dont know whether it is a temptation or a leading [a religious, particularly perhaps a Quaker, concept]. But it seemed quite clear to me, when expressed openly, that it *is* wrong & must be resisted; that terrible times like these are just the test … .

On Friday I got wires from Sylvia & the Dr saying there was no ulcer, that she was to have more to eat, & there was no need for me to go home earlier than I intended. This cheered me up so much & made me so thankful that I stood the war news better. I did decide to go home on Wed. however, instead of going to the Island, where Hope is at the flat.

June 1st to 15th I have done some gardening. Sylvia is as brown as a berry with sunbathing, & is putting on a little weight. Most of this fortnight has been pretty strenuous with refugees. First we wanted to reopen the Hostel for the women now left on their own. (The men are at Huyton near Liverpool, by the way). Then when all that was fixed with the police & we were half cleaned up & had two rooms ready for them, came the H.O. order on Monday 10th that all Austrians & Germans must leave this (& other areas). The next plan was to get a house outside the area & move the Hostel there. This is still pending. Trying for a house at Durham; many difficulties.

Paris fell on Friday the 14th. One of the refugees bequeathed me a big bundle of baby's clothes for Gateshead children – her grandsons from about 0–2. Those poor Jews! He is in Budapest; another daughter in Russia – these poor old people wandering again … .

16 June. I couldn't bear things any longer somehow, so I went off alone into the country to find green pastures & still waters … . I went (as I had often planned) & found Moss Hill, the old house near Naworth which mother's family had as a country residence for some years. Many of Camie's early

sketches were done there … . I got home to the East wind & fog & the news that the French are likely to capitulate. I hope this may mean a short war … .
17 June. The news is confirmed that the French are suing for an Armistice; they brought in an old Fascist soldier, Marshall Petain, a bosom friend of Franco's to do it … .
18 June. It is true about the French. No terms announced yet. I was struck by the "Union" with France "offer", [a suggestion made for indissoluble union of Britian and France – regarded by the latter as humiliating] however unlikely to be accepted, it showed imagination & sent Churchill up in my estimation … . (by the way all idea of taking the Hostel at Durham is quite gone – the 15 women are going to Leeds)
21 June. Spent the morning at Mayfield … sorting out clothes for the refugees … as I was writing up this diary the syrens [sic] went again; I thought they probably would & hurried up to get my bath before midnight. I have been to *Amphytryon 38* at the People's Theatre – it may be their last show (though I hope not) so I made an effort to go & it was very good & over early … . I dashed into town in the afternoon & bought or at least got on appro a new typewriter – two to choose from! I think I shall get an Imperial Good Companion – its such a funny name.

I am lying in bed waiting for the All Clear [the siren announcing the end of an air raid] … .
25 June. Sent off a number of big parcels, & 10/- P.Os to our refugees at Isle of Man … .
26 June. Went to Lakes with Rosamund Mounsey Wood. Her first visit … . Lanty's tarn after supper – a gorgeous blue & orange sky … .
27 June. Angle Tarn with Rosamund & Elsa … Seldom Seen after supper … .
28 June. Along Lakeside path to Howtown. Back by boat … .
29 June. … . Heavy rain going up to Hartsop. Ate our sandwiches at Deepdale Hall … . Got out gorgeous after lunch … home over Arnison Crags & Bleaze End & down by Blemara Park wall … .
30 June. End of June. A roasting day. Nearly all the streams are dried up & all the grass in the hills brown though the bracken is still very green. Lunched in Gowbarrow where they are cutting down & stripping the alders for their bark. Home by bus … . Only one air raid while I was away.
1 July. … . Refugee Committee at night. What a wretched business this internment is! So unnecessarily cruel & stupid. They all want their possessions & food parcels & it is all so difficult & trying when one cant get it to them!
2 July. … was having tea at Bainbridges [a large Newcastle department store, now in Eldon Square, previously situated between Market Street and the Bigg Market] when the first real near-at-home bomb fell! Such a bang! & a smaller

bang just after! No warning. I & lots of others were close up to the plate glass windows; they held but Johnson's next door were shattered! Then we all went down to the packing department in the basement & sat on parcels. The All Clear went in about half an hour – it was about 5.25 when the bomb dropped. There were crowds in the street – everyone going home from work, & a great cloud of black smoke from the river … . We guessed they had been aiming for the bridges. It was odd to see how odd panes of glass, & occasionally a whole shop-front, were shattered, & others – many more – quite untouched. as I went down the Bigg Market a fire-engine went past. I got a tram & saw from the High Level that the Spillers warehouse in the Close was ablaze – great orange flames leaping; the fireman were trying to save the front part. I heard afterwards that two people were killed there but the workmen escaped … . The second bomb (I'm told) fell on Hawthorne's workshop, but the two shifts were changing & both outside, so no one was hurt. The worst was at Jarrow – 11 killed including several children. What a wicked thing it all is!
6 July. … . I rather like the wreaths – like turbans without crowns, that girls are wearing this summer, to keep their hair tidy. All the news is very miserable today. The Gateshead schools are to evacuate on Sunday & Monday.
Tues. & Wed. Busy getting ready for London, & a lot of Refugee business to attend to … . Both Hans Kronberger & Werner Schloss have gone to America … . It is now said that over 6,000 have been sent. I sent P.C.s to all our refugees announcing parcels.

It is strange that ever since the French Capitulation I have had the Marseillaise running in my head. It wont go away. And now the Third Republic is dead & Liberté Egalité, Fraternité no longer the watchword, But "Labour, Family, Fatherland" – God help us! ….
29 July. There was a raid here last night – no warning, the second on Newcastle – bombs dropped on Heaton & along the West Road. I spent a hard morning at Gladstone Terrace, overhauling clothes. We have a good stock of men's in; as Molly sent me Hugh's & an old schoolmaster's daughter has given … his on his death. I got very tired & dirty but have brought home a lot of things that will make into rugs & quilts. More remnants still needed!
30 July. Lent or gave Friend William Carr £50 for his appeal against a fine of £30 for a technical breach of the Aliens regulations – a scandalous fine … . The Stanley Bench are in any case notorious for harsh decisions; it was time someone protested. I dont suppose it will do any good, but I'm glad to fight against this panic perversion of justice in any way, however small.

We expect Molly on Thurs. I do hope she comes & that we dont have bad raids while she is here. Four people were killed or died afterwards of injuries in Sunday night's raid, including wife of caretaker of Heaton Secondary

School. Many people say the damage to property is being minimised; on the other hand rumour exaggerates it – so one cant tell what to believe.
10 August. I think this must have been the day Molly came. She stayed about 3 weeks & was much better when she left, we all thought.
August 1940 … . We had a fair number of air-raid warnings but nothing very near. Sunniside & along the hilltop was about the nearest … . There was much talk of invasion & about the date that Hitler had announced he would dictate peace terms in London (Aug. 15th) – that is if it was true he said so – began the great air raids on London. Many other places have suffered & are suffering still Bristol & Liverpool, for instance, but of course much the most is said about London & it certainly is very bad. Doesn't bear thinking about, in fact; & I wont any more … . Molly could not settle alone, she found, with so many air raids & so much firing. She went to Brian & Helen , & has gone on to Green Rigg [Patterdale]. Hope has finished the last vol. of the County History … . I have begun to write reminiscences, but get on slowly, about the Lakes holidays I have had. I am not doing much for peace … September 1940. Refugees of one sort or another were the chief anxiety this month … . First there were refugees released from internment because of their health. I have had most trouble over Mr Stein, as his guarantor is reluctant & his other friend fussy; but he has a good friend … with whom he is in lodgings. S. Berberich is at Leeds massaging, & Heinz in the Pioneers, & Mr Silberstein is released & with his wife. We have heard from Schloss Wendtner & indirectly from Brassloff in Canada; so only Hans Kronberger remains to be traced. We have helped Prof. Reid to get Knopfler back to college – by providing funds. All the family came out strong.

Then there are the refugees from London, especially Agnes. I took her to Deepdale Hall to recuperate from her London horrors, & she has settled at Patterdale as village dressmaker, grumbling all the time.

October was mostly clinics & rehearsals of the Chinese play, the *Professor From Peking* … .

Professor From Peking at People's Theatre on Dec 11th. Audience about 70. It was rather awful, but I enjoyed the preparations & the whole thing up to the end … . I never got to the Lakes (Borrowdale) as I'd been hoping. I was too poorly after the play, with swollen knees. Then came Christmas … & I got a poisoned leg, very sore; soon after that snow & frost; more trouble at the (Labour) Hall (then 'flu')… . actually went to Keswick on Monday,
10 February. 1941. By Wright's bus over Hartside … . I have a charming room & very comfy bed. Walked … up Castle Head … but was rather wobbly & fell down & bruised myself very badly on rocks … . We get rather a lot of BBC news here but the birds are a great pleasure … .
10 February … had a lovely evening walk, twilight to dark, through the Great

Wood on the slopes of Walla Crag. We got some lovely mosses – the litle fern sort & other kinds. There were many catkins & lovely views of the silvery, misty lake & white soft clouds on the hills, through the bare treetops. Rather a magic time I never saw the high hills again after Tuesday; they were blotted out by the mist … .

23 February. I stayed in most of Sat. which was fine & sunny again, as it was my period & I felt poorly; but I should not have been so lazy all the same. all I did was to make one small cot quilt – *five* thicknesses, 1/4 small blanket, old curtain doubled & two outer layers of new gay but very cheap cotton … .

7 March. First visit to Jordans, a great pilgrimage place for Friends.[1] There is a very pretty old meeting house where my dear old Friends, Herbert Pickles & his wife are caretakers. There is a large Friends Hostel, very comfortable in an old hall & farm, with a quad where the farmyard used to be & a lovely old timbered barn said to have been made from the timbers of the Mayflower. Food & accommodation excellent; the Friends Service Com. have a wing, called the old refectory. It was a place of Quaker meetings from the beginning of Quakerism. We had quite a nice conference there … .

We had disturbed nights hearing the raids on London & some of our meetings were punctuated by gunfire. The planes were flying round all the time … .

10 April. At Green Rigg [Patterdale]. It has taken weeks of arranging to get here for a week but it is done! There were noisy but not (it fortunately seems) very fatal raids on Tyneside on Monday & last night, Wed. So I am very sleepy – as soon as one got dozing last night the guns started again – & such variety of tone & delivery, as well as distance, about six different noises … .

24 April. … . Agnes has written asking me for a map. I found one with "Edwin Dodds April 1892" written on it very big; & on another leaf

"8 Swanwicks and 5 Doddses at Seatoller 9th – 23rd April 1896"

in Father's most vigorous hand so *all* the Swanwicks were there. That was the year Mother died & the time & place I first visited the Lakes. The map is scarcely used. Is it worth keeping out of sentiment? I could so easily buy Agnes a new one. No, let it be used while it is still good enough, let Agnes have it. I will be true to my belief that things unused, no matter how precious, are things wasted. Dear darling Daddy! How nice to think of him.

May & part of June – a Summary – I had a rushed month while H.& S. were away … . Then they all came back, with Molly, who at once went to bed with a cold; & stayed six very cold weeks; all May. I went to London once or twice to I.S.O. [Friends' Industrial And Social Order] Conferences … . Clinics on Tues. & Wed. & sometimes the Toddlers' Room on Thurs as well as Tues. have been about all the justification for my existence! … I addressed a number of small mothers meetings & some Friends Fellowship meetings.

12 June. After the usual efforts to get letters written & ends tied up I managed to get myself off on a Wright's bus for a few days in Borrowdale … . I got a very crowded evening bus to Rosthwaite, & like the Royal Oak there, a homely little place, typical of the smaller Lakes Inn; very comfortable beds & water laid on in the rooms – which has advantages but the big disadvantage that you cant put a basin on the floor & steep your feet! That night I explored a little on hill tracks through Stonethwaite to the old mill at the foot of Coome Gill … came up from Keswick & we had a lovely walk up Lang Strath … a late but delicious tea at Rosthwaite P.O. with jam & scones & cakes & butter ad lib like peacetime! Living is very good at the Royal Oak too … .
14 June … . I spent the day exploring Johnny Wood, between Seatoller & Rosthwaite on a spur of Scawdel Moor. It is a heavenly wood, full of the loveliest ferns at their greenest & freshest; oak & beech, big & little … & great magnificent groups of lady-fern … .
1 September. There was a very bad raid on Newastle. Nearly 200 people were killed in the Shieldfield district. The New Bridge Street Goods Station with its big warehouses was burning for about a week … .
2 October. There was another heavy raid at beginning of Oct. mostly on North & South Shields – two nights running … .
October … . All the time I was busy trying to get Kurt Wendtner back at the College & succeeded in the end. I should have seen the Rector *myself* at *once*.
16 October. … got away with Sylvia for a whole fortnight in the Lakes, starting at Patterdale. We stayed at Deepdale Hall … .
22 October. … . S. & I stayed the night at Green Rigg & then started off on the adventurous part of our trip … a long & often crowded bus journey from Patterdale to Penrith, from Penrith to Keswick, fr Kes. to Ambleside & from Amble up Langdale in a gloriously sunny autumn evening to Dungeon Ghyll Old Hotel. Marvellous sunset crimson on the Pikes, when we walked up to Stool End just before dark. Hotel expensive but very comfortable.
24 October. Very successful day over Wrynose Pass, starting at Blea Tarn … .
25 October. Gorgeously fine & all the woods & hillsides ablaze – I was too hot! Did that lovely walk back of Wallabarrow, then by Grassguards & Birks over the ridge between the two valleys & right down opposite the big falls at the top of Tarn Beck … .
26 October. Fine & clear but gale of bitterly cold wind for our walk over Walna Scar to Coniston. A glorious day all the same. Wonderful views of Scawfell group going up, & a magnificent stretch of wild country once we were over the ridge – shining sea, long inlets, the whole length of Coniston silver at our feet; black moors & … hilly ridges near at hand & wonderful ranges of distant hills far away … a very interesting walk along the side of the

Coniston fells. It was gorgeous by the lake in its autumn colours – everywhere the hollies have been in magnificent berry … . We got the bus from the Waterside Hotel … then again a bus from Ambleside to Keswick. We were lucky to get a little car to carry us & our newly-collected luggage up to the Borrowdale Hotel – a wild & stormy drive … .
28 October. Cold & very windy but clear & bright. Over the Stepping Stones (at Rosthwaite) & up Lobstone Band – in good shelter till we got to the top of the ridge up at the back of Dale Head. Over Scawdel Moor & along Maiden Moor & Narrow Moor & down to the hause between Newlands & Manesty … .
29 October. Too cold & wild for the hilltops so we walked over Honister Pass – not a car on the road! – down Buttermere & back by the Hause & Newlands & Brandelhowe woods. It was a great day … sometimes a struggle to put one foot before the other … hawks overhead … & one snow shower just before we got in. We left next day in miserable weather.

1942 Summary of January to August
What sort of a year has it been so far? War & distress & disaster in the world. Quiet enough for us at Home House – three old sisters growing grey together, quite in the family tradition. We have had no maids & Sylvia has worked very hard at cooking & housework, but says it does her good. She still keeps busy with her wardrobe, but does much less sewing, although we have not yet quite got through our stores of materials. Hope has been very busy with her work as Librarian at the Black Gate for the Ncle Antiquarians. She has done a good deal of other work for them too, papers on Sacred Wells & Sacred Thorns, & William Percy is still unfinished. Molly at Cowes is very busy with W.V.S. & her Townswomen's Guild. Her lecture on Fashion Through the Ages with illustrations from Sylvia's wardrobe was a great success.

I dont seem to have made any progress, spiritual, mental or physical, for a long time … . On the whole one might say that Refugees have rather dominated my life. I am supporting two Austrians at Kings [King's College, Durham University, at Newcastle upon Tyne] – Wendtner & Brassloff – & Brassloff has now been joined by his mother, who works as a cook & is quite self-supporting. Knopfler is doing rather well at Kings but will probably need more funds soon … .

On the whole I have been doing much more for the Society of Friends than ever before – speaking, reading, Committees & so on. It has almost taken the place that the ILP, the Soc. League & the LP work on the Council have held in my life at different times. I wish I could feel I was helping & being helped more. I am seeing a great deal more of Nora Ghillie [d. 1959. A member of Newcastle Friends' Meeting] & going to her Adult School on Tuesdays at the

Meeting House. I think I may in time be some use there. I think the women feel me less remote just because I am less saintly than she; but then I am less likely to do good … .

When I read over this prim record of minor Good Works & fairly Christian Endeavour, I do feel a hypocrite! It seems to have almost nothing to do with the essential me, & yet it is certainly RD who is doing these things & for no reason except that she wants to do them. Potty little things – but the real me is far sillier, & my mind generally babbles nonsense & repeats old rhymes & romantic poetry when I set it free to do as it likes. there is an unfathomable childishness in me that takes joy in all sorts of pretty trifles, & even through this miserable year has kept me more happy than unhappy. I am writing in the train on the way to a conference at Oxford & though I am going through N. Durham, one of the ugliest black patches on the face of the Earth, even here I continually see things that delight me – a field of stooked oats, wheat just ripe, a bed of ragwort, a mass of yellow violas, leeks flowering in an allotment, little black ducks on a colliery pool … . My change of life is not complete yet, & though I am lucky to have no bad pain & no alarming flooding, it is giving me a great deal of discomfort, so that I seldom feel really well & nearly always thoroughly slack & lazy – but I am never quite sure how much of that is just natural laziness.

I am perfectly happy pottering – I think I always have been, & now that there are potatoes to peel & vegetables to pick, I can have an excuse to potter all day over minor household tasks. The newspapers are so small that they are not quite the old snare – & the news is so monotonous, too, & so badly told, that even if there is something & cheerful, like the Moscow Convoys getting through, they make it dull in the telling.

Perhaps the most exciting thing I do now is speaking at religious & other meetings. This does stir me up a great deal & sometimes, after a lot of hard work I enjoy the result & think the audience does too. … another I gave at Great Ayton (Friends School) to the children about Monk Lewis & his Slaves was a great strain … . It is a very nice school as schools go. How I did toil at that little address! Certainly this is what Nora Ghillie calls a *costing* service. When my conscience reproaches me with laziness, I have that defense; & I never refuse an invitation, much as I always wish I had when the date draws near – but I know it wld be sheer laziness & shyness … .

All this travelling about at this awkward time, with buses packed & trains few can be very trying; [train] often an hour or two late; & at the best means walking home after midnight … [war] is the shadow, dominating outward life with rations & points & queues; & tribunals & sending books to C.O.s in Durham Jail; & shoddy clothes & holidays at home; & also dominating inward life with the feeling of everpresent horror … .

Now that I am not very well & also get up at seven alternate weeks to make breakfast, & also travel about so much, I know I ought to go to bed & to sleep earlier; but I cannot give up that hour or two idle reading at night that I love so much; & I cannot even turn it into something directed like family history or essay-writing, which is idle & useless enough for anything – I cannot make myself give up this purely random reading – old books, new thrillers, magazines, children's books, poetry – no method, all madness & caprice – losing my beauty sleep, too, so that my face is – well, showing its years!

... went to York for a Conference ... & met Rosamund; I am in a bit of a fix about her; she has taken a great fancy to me & insists on being my best friend, whether I will or no; this fusses me & gets on my nerves, as demonstrative affection always has from childhood – though of course if I found her exceedingly attractive I shld feel very differently, no doubt. I am hoping that if I go on trying to be kind to her, quite honestly, knowing that she is a better & more hard-working woman than I am, I shall gain that very firm-rooted sort of affection which one gets for people one thoroughly knows & is quite used to. I am ashamed of myself for not returning her, quite undeserved, regard, more warmly; but she is rather plain, has an unattractive laugh, & that kind of unconscious intrusiveness that makes her dump herself on people just when it suits her & not at all when it suits them. We have a very great deal in common – love of the country, for instance, & interest in social work; but she is no reader, so the great subject of books does not bring our minds in touch; she is most interested in people & is rather good at people only not at all sensitive about them which is probably just what is needed for her work as Hospital Almoner ... Hope ... went to the Island & saw about giving up her flat. The navy have taken the block.

There was a heavy raid on April 31st ... just as the attack began a heavy mist came over & blotted out the N.E. So the bombs were scattered over a wide area, more or less at random from Bolam to Beamish. Some fell on Ghd ... I saw from the bus that all the windows were out along the Durham Rd opposite Enfield ... Town Clerk's Offices had been largely wrecked & I began to be very worried about Ned, who firewatches there; & also wonder what had happened to the Little Theatre ... went down after suppper, & found out that two time bombs had gone off in the Park while we were away; nearly all the glass in 3 Saltwell View was broken – but none in the Theatre! The Theatre doors had all been blown open & there was a large piece of tree-trunk & several stones through the roof ... wonderful how little damage was done for the bombs were close at hand ... . Best of all the Policeman told me that there was not a single casualty in Gateshead – not so much as a cut! Unfortunately a lot of children were killed at Beamish by an undetected time

bomb in an empty house.
July … . visited the Friends' War Relief Hostel at Bentinck Rd, in which I am rapidly becoming more & more involved. A nice lot of earnest young men; I did not meet the girls … . On Saturday July 18th it was QM [Quarterly Meeting] at Durham … . I enjoyed it. The two subjects were the hostel & more important, the future of Friends' Schools. Was there to be a Central body for all of them? Were they to accept Government grant? … .

1942 Oct. Eskdale. It was a wild wet autumn that followed a wet cold summer. Sylvia & I went to the Lakes rather late by Wright's bus to Keswick on Oct. 2nd. Next day we went on to the Borrowdale Hotel for a couple of nights. We had a nice walk over Kings How & visited Peace How, N.T. property near Manesty … . Torrents of rain all night. We did not know whether there would be any chance of starting for Eskdale in the morning (Oct. 5th) & the day began with a steady downpour. We packed & sent off parcels – talking about getting trains round to Ravenglass & trying from there. Then, on the way back from posting parcels at Grange it suddenly began to clear! We took a desperate resolution to risk it & started (very late) up the valley in the bus. By the time we got to Seatoller it really was sunny & clear. We blessed our luck (rather too soon) & set off with several other parties up the Seathwaite valley. All the becks were up, of course, the waterfalls roaring white streaks; but when we got to the bridge we found the road beyond under water! There had been a cloudburst up Gillercombe way & the ghylls on this side were worse even than anywhere else. Yet most people pushed on up the yew tree side of the valley & we did too till we came to the flooded Buttermilk Ghyll. We got across somehow & tracked on through the bogs till we came to Piers Ghyll which was ten times no better (as Ned would say). Sylvia took off shoes & stockings & (not without my help & advice) got across fairly dry; but I am afraid of the sharp stones & plodged over in shoes & stockings. I was afraid of the raging waters too & yet determined not to turn back. So we had barely got to the foot of Styhead when it was time to feed. I had a change of stockings – oh how welcome – for the cold waters struck to the heart! We got hot enough climbing the Pass – very wet going up wetter at the top, but dry, rough & stoney dropping down to Wasdale Head – sunshine & cold wind & white leaping waters & the hills with every savage ridge in the wild rocks clear cut. I shall never feel the Scafells such strangers as I used to do, after this day; we became more intimate, distinctly, though we shall never really be old friends, not in this life of mine! I dont think I had been down Sty Head that side, since I crossed it with Uncle Eustace so many years ago … . It is a rough descent … . We had the usual difficulty in the road turning into a stream at the bottom, but found the hotel all right & had a good early tea … . Now came the new part – a lovely long ascent up to the ridge of the screes, with the golden light on the wonderful Scafell crags & gullies; then over the marshes to Burnmoor Tarn, with the sunset red on its waters & lighting up all the wild lonely falls on the marshy end of the Scafell ridge – a strange land of yellow bent-grass with the sunset sky above & the pools giving back the sunset light, & such a rushing of streams. Perfectly awful underfoot – either plodging in the mosses or excruciating for my sore feet on the nubbly stones that in dry weather make fords across the streams; but the path was all stream that day. I got terribly tired the long long descent to Boot, with the light going. At last we came down to a mill by a wooded & rocky gorge, with a light in the window, just as if it was peacetime. Still some way to Boot – & it was just dark when we got there & still a couple of miles to Penny Hill … . It was moderately comfortable at Penny Hill. Food good, beds hard, fires inadequate … cold & wet weather. Most successful day was when we went to see the Gosforth Cross … .

[1943 & 1944 – largely brief summaries of walks, plays, family visits & holidays in Lakes]

July 12th 1944
A very memorable day. I went to the University Congregation for conferring degrees & Hans Kronberger & Kurt Wendtner, the last two of my refugee students received their degrees. Kurt was there & very happy; Hans had gone to London to see about a job … .
17 July – 22 July. One of my great ambitions was fulfilled this week & this made me very happy in spite of all the terrors & horrors of the times. It was the North Eastern Regional Drama Festival & it was held at the Gateshead Little Theatre. I staged 21 plays in 6 days! Teams came from all over Northumberland, Durham & N. Yorkshire – as far as from Goathland on the Whitby moors! – & they all were welcomed heartily & went away satisfied & most of them saying they had never appeared on such a good stage & under such pleasant conditions before. It was really a great week … .

There are confusing accounts of a rising against Hitler from Germany. But one does not know … .
October 18th to 21st Production of *Emma* at the Little Theatre – our first anniversary & our seventh production.

29 April 1945. There have been some hopeful signs lately. The Blackout was ended a week ago … . One night last week I travelled home … in a fully lighted tram. Today there is a rumour of a surrender offer from the Germans to the U.S.A. & G.B. I went to a famine relief meeting yesterday … .

1 May. … . It seems the allies are deliberately choosing to go on fighting – whether through mutual suspicion or spite at Germany or a little of both is not at all clear … .

Still no news of peace. Yesterday it was said that Mussolini had been killed by an Italian mob. Today it is said that Hitler had been killed – the Germans say in action. Roosevelt died in his bed – the advantages of democracy? … . Apart from the fact that every one is rather relieved there will be no question of two Dictators on trial how flat the news falls! I hope that will be some antidote to the cult of the Great Man which spread so between the two wars & was fostered by people like Bernard Shaw who ought to have known better. How much these two men owed to the sensational Press of the world! … . Their rise was so much due to the effect of their picturesque poses on the public mind of the world … . Of course the weakness is in human nature – people wanted the Dictators … . Even Churchill with his drink-sodden face & his shifty record is adored by all the Tory old ladyhood of England – & they are a powerful body. They are influencing the minds of our young ruling class – the lower officer ranks – even when the boys think they are in complete reaction against them. I realise now I am old how much I too have reverted to type – how much influence my aunts really had on me – how superficial was my revolt into Red Imperialism! … .

Gateshead Progressive Players' theatre

Hope Dodds

Ruth Dodds

Sylvia Dodds

Ruth Dodds as oldest inhabitant

Ruth Dodds May 1965

CHAPTER TWELVE: MAY 1945 – NOVEMBER 1974

End of War; a quieter still busy life, loss of friends and family, the last of her line

8 May. Today I am 55 & it is the first of 2 VE days or Victory holidays .... A very busy day – wrote theatre letters in the afternoon. But quite half life goes in housework at present ....
July 1946 Howtown Hotel. [Lakes] A great day it seems likely to be. 83 Labour gains by the one o'clock news & NO LABOUR LOSSES! 265 Labour seats reported later by someone who came in with a wireless on in a car. Like old days – like 1929 – what a long time it has been to wait for anything like that again! .... It was a beautiful sunny morning & Rosamund & I went up Hallin Fell. Glorious views. I came yesterday by bus. The country was looking lovely ... I thought of all the changes along the roadside in the last six years, & how I had been in fair & foul weather, in sunshine & snow .... All the roadblocks gone; & the sign-posts back but not all the P.O. names; all the poles from the big fields gone – except one field where they were all dressed up as scarecrows in sacks! The most lasting scar of war is the felled woodlands, where now the fireweed is making gorgeous purple patches ....

10.30 p.m. So this is the day I have so long worked for & desired, & recently quite despaired of ever living to see. The first majority Socialist Government of this country! I never expected or thought it could come this way – as the result of a great War. That the people should have grasped that ten years of Tory rule led to the War & that it was time for a change – once I would have thought that likely, but '31 & '35 especially made me despair of it. So the King has sent for Attlee & Attlee is forming a Government; & the figures are decisive – no doubt about the verdict of the people; & quite a heavy poll it seems in spite of a bad register .... And that I should hear the result *here* is so odd! hanging over the office door in a typical Lake Inn hall, all hung with brasses & foxes heads & antlers! .... Rosamund is sympathetic & rather scared. I was terribly scared the first two Labour wins, 1924 & 1929; less so now; the alternative is so much worse than we knew then. But I do pray for our people – leaders & followers, yes & opponents, too ....
1 August. Came home yesterday. It was a delightful visit, I've seldom enjoyed one more. Rosamund was in good health & good spirits, & though I feel my bliss amongst the hills best when alone there is a great deal to be said in favour of company. I'm not so inclined to wander at random & waste time over indecisions ....
12 August .... Since then things have taken one of those horrid lurches towards misery & chaos to which world affairs are prone, with the announcement & actual use of this appalling atomic bomb ....

August to Dec. Five months of War over without much feeling of Peace, though of course we are all very thankful that most of the killing has stopped. Unlike the last War & most recent Wars this one is followed by … many State trials both of enemies & traitors. I have never thought that treason should be punishable by death; I mean even less than murder. There are many good results of stopping the fighting & one should think of them. First the prisoners came home from Germany; that is joyful. Now they are coming back from the East; one is thankful but they seem to have suffered more moral damage & learnt less – as far as one can judge. Then the soldiers are trickling home … . Then the refugees are indirectly getting news of home & may hope to be back before very long – if they want to go. … . Gateshead Little Theatre's second birthday Oct. 13th & 25 year – Silver – anniversary booklet, a history of the P.P. was out at the same time … .
[1946 – Very thin summary of some plays produced & some visits.]

1948 – 1958 Generally diary now contains much less detail; summary accounts of holidays, visits, plays produced etc. More about activities – various – for the Friends … .

5 July 1956. … . Rosamund was discharged from the Retreat on June 21st & committed suicide by an overdose of aspirins two days later. I wish I had loved her more Alas! alas! … .
1958 – 1966. As for previous diary mostly Gateshead Little Theatre & visits –
24 July … . At home there was bad news of Brian. His operation was not a success & the disease is spreading. Poor Helen writes very sadly & we all felt distressed since she does not want a fuss made & says the Drs are keeping down the pain … . When all the world was young he used to drive us over those lovely Hexhamshire hills & over Hartside to the Lakes first in the old steam Stanley & then in his Siddeley. That was how we first got to know Northumberland. He was such a charming boy. I have seen very little of him since his marriage. Helen never liked us & perhaps I never made enough effort to overcome her dislike … . But I think she has made him very happy & that is the great thing … .
13 August. Brian's death has affected me much more than I should have expected if I had ever thought about it. We bickered a lot when we were children but I loved & indeed adored him all the same. I used to wish we could be devoted to one another, like a brother & sister in a story, but this naturally did not appeal to a boy who got tired of a little sister always tagging after him, & not wanting to be left out of things. But you dont like people less because you have rows with them. Then when we got older there were the wonderful motor trips … . Most of my memories of him seem trivial. Once in

middle life we came near a quarrel but it was averted [see 1926 – over the business]; I'm glad of that. I think he would have been quite pleased to see more of us these last years; & he wrote us charming letters, like Father's letters. He had the family love of local history which we have all learnt or inherited from Father … . I wonder how the loss of Mother (I was 5 & he was 8) affected us – or rather how it affected him. Of course I know how I felt about it. I always felt & still feel that I loved him more than he did me. But perhaps it was about even really; & better put that I wanted us to be closer friends. Never quite satisfactory? What human relationship is? … as he mellowed this sweet gentle side of his nature appeared more & more clearly. All the people who lived near him & knew him said how kind & helpful he was & how they would miss him … .

1.12.62 Golden Wedding of Ridley (Richard Nicholas) & Elsa (née Rounthwaite) Temperley. [They were often visited by Ruth at Green Rigg Patterdale where they had retired in 1934]. She was a great gardener, had attended a Warwickshire gardening college before her marriage (in 1912) & worked as a market gardener near Reading & in Yorkshire.

July 1963 … . the Dr decided the ills I had been suffering from for the last year were due to diabetes. I went to a specialist the day before my 73rd birthday, which was on May 8th. I had to lose another stone in 2 months & go down to 8 stone after being about 12 stone for years; but in the last six months or so I had already gone down to 9 stone. No more iced cakes for me any more! … .

I did lose the extra stone by July & have been round about 8 stone the rest of the year. The diet is tiresome but I do not miss sweets so much as I expected & Sylvia has been very good especially in feeding me lots of clear soup – which I like very much when home made – *not* at hotels & restaurants! I feel better on the whole – not quite so weak willed & unable to move myself about … . I have not been to London for more than two years! But I went to Patterdale by Wright's bus on July 19th … . Then only two nights at home & went with Hope & Agnes to Dryburgh Abbey Hotel. … . Peaceful & happy time … .

7 December 1963. Ridley Temperley died on Wed. Dec.11th. A dear old friend gone. He was 84. When I was with them in July he was much failed & rather unhappy in his weakness. He had a bad fall in August & after that he was confined to bed, except for tiny walks from one room to another. I spent about a week with them in September … again on Dec. 6th, from Molly's. She was down with flu & Sylvia & I as usual took turns to go over & be with her … . So many happy memories of Ridley! All my life. He was a sweet & satisfying companion on the hills, in the garden, children's Christmas parties at Carlton Terrace; tennis at Home House when summers were summers;

August holidays at Glenridding House, where the Temperleys had stayed in prehistoric times before we ever went there … . And when I came down one lovely sunny morning my admiration at finding Ridley had been up to the top of Helvellyn before breakfast! he came back with a wreath of stagshorn moss round his cap! I thought it the most wonderful moss – I had never seen it before – & it has thrilled me to find it ever since; & he a most wonderful mountaineer. Later he was a great climber in the Andes … . Later he was a splendid partner at dances; then he was courting my cousin Elsa, a golden-haired beauty who had many admirers. Then they were married on a snowy day, the 30th November 1912 & went out to Chile where he had a post with the G.E.C.(?) He was declared medically unfit for the 1914–18 war. Their only child Elisabeth was born in Chile in 1915, the same year as Molly's Bob … . Then the Green Rigg days & many happy visits & grand walks on the fells, exploring odd corners … down to quite little walks & garden work at the end … .

1964 [Summary] *May 8th* I was 74. *May 14th, 15th, 16th* – Three perfect days at Banks with Molly … .

Running the Little Theatre is getting too much for me & I decided to retire next May when I am 75.

1965 Sylvia in hospital for an operation at Christmas … has got through well. *January* Sylvia had a happy homecoming early in January, though she was rather weak as she got an infection at the hospital which put her back just as she was doing so well after the operation. It was a sunny day, the ambulance men carried her upstairs; her room was full of sunshine & flowers … . I was able to manage the cooking & shopping very well & Mrs Lamb came a lot of extra days to help me, until she had serious illness in her own family … . Hope is keeping nicely & helps a lot too … .

May – June … . Really retired on May 29th at the PP [People's Players] Annual General Meeting & seem to have been busier ever since. Am training 3 people to do the job in my place … . The players are lovely to me & gave me glorious flowers & two tokens for Garden & Books £7 & £5! I never expected that. The next thing is the Freeman Ceremony[1] … .

June 29th The Freeman Making Ceremony in Shipley Art Gallery. A lovely fine day & all went off splendidly. I had a new dress made for the occasion. Hope was on the platform with me. Lots of old friends … . Sylvia of course looking very smart & imposing … .

December. Went to Moll's & found her quite nicely – cheerful & working hard at Xmas Cards & presents. She had set about 2 dozen bowls of bulbs herself!… *18 December.* On the last night of *Quiet Wedding* S rang me at the Theatre to say Molly had fallen in the kitchen & broken her femur; she was taken straight to Carlisle Infirmary. It happened about 4 pm & Mr

Freeman ceremony at Shipley Art Gallery, Gateshead, on 29 June 1965

Moses found her about an hour later.
19 December. Bill Dobson most kindly motored me over to see Molly. She is not in pain, brave & cheerful & still smoking. Operation tomorrow.
5 January. 1966 Molly died in Carlisle Infirmary, of bronchitis following her fall. The leg was not mending. Sylvia was with her in the aft. Molly got worse just after S. left – but she has been desperately ill for the last few days. The Hosp. phoned me & I got the 6.20 to Carlisle seeing S at the station getting off the train I went back on. I did not get there till after 8 & she died at 7.25 pm. Everyone is very kind.
10 January. Sylvia & I went to Molly's funeral at Carlisle Crematorium; Michael Rounthwaite kindly drove us there & back … . Everyone is loving & appreciative of her. She has been with me all my life long & I feel part of my roots pulled up by the parting. We loved each other better & better the longer we lived. What happy times I have had these 20 years at the little cottage at Banks … . The Bank [at Brampton] people were kind & helpful. Sylvia & I are both the heirs & the executors … an internment at Lanercost on Jan 13th of the ashes … .
10 June. Though I have had an impulse to write much more about Molly it does not seem likely that I ever will do it. She was too integrated a part of my life & even of myself … . I have just spent a couple of nights at Bell's

Cottage, which she recreated from a very old house to fit herself. She did this to all her homes … .

4 September. I bought Mary Moorman's Life of Wm Wordsworth some weeks ago. A very expensive book but I could not resist. The years during which I read the 5 volumes of the Letters of Wm & Dorothy were among the happiest of my life.

29 November. I think this is the last of these nice linen bound books which I brought from the Quayside when I left it in 1926 – 40 years ago! Incredible! … . If I dont write soon & often I shall certainly never fill this book [she didn't – only about a quarter way] – & why should I? Life is so much memory now that it will be only writing again what I wrote long ago – & now distorted & at second remove! Yet life does go on & the itch to record what is not worth recording is still very strong!

Stupid old thing that I am – I should be using my so short time to write useful letters of loving kindness to others … .

2 June. All these five months gone & I have written for the ECP Ever Circulating Portfolio] instead of my Diary – have had no impulse to write till now. They have been happy months but the weather bad – gales mostly & a lot of cold … .

1969 Sylvia died in Conrad House [a Newcastle nursing home mainly for cancer patients] on April 24th 1969 about 5.20 pm. I had rung up about 3 pm & was told she was rather worse, but no suggestion she was dying; she rapidly went down after that. I was with her every other day that week & she slept a good deal & looked weak but was bright on the Sunday. Sleeping she looked so like Mother.

21 June … . I am still thinking of her almost all the time – sorrow & joy to remember. O Sylvia, Sylvia I keep saying to myself. It is loneliness & company together … . Hope is wonderful to me, so cheerful & calm. I get into a panic about dinner nearly every day & about all the things to do & to remember … .

1971. Brief summary 3/4 page includes the following entries:

Op. in Gen. Hosp. end of January. Feb. first 13 days in hospital, then a fortnight at Close House Nursing Home near Hexham … . Hope not so well; in RVI in August for check up. Picked up in Oct – Nov but not downstairs again.

1972. Hope died on 13th May 1972. Since then (now July 1974) I have lived alone.

My dear friend & helper Ada Lamb comes in every day except Sundays or I should have to go into or find a home of some kind, as I could not keep this big house clean. My sight & hearing is poor but I thank God daily for Ada & for what sight & hearing I still have. Though I am lonely I am not unhappy; I have felt & had too much to do all my life (being naturally lazy & yet with an urge to do things I want to do) & this feeling increases with the langour & slowness of age. Old friends are going rapidly but I have my good younger ones. The attic flat has been let to 2 pleasant young girls for just about a year.

An Ideal Timetable

Early Tea about 7.30 & do the Aga. Ada comes soon after 9 am. try to get up soon after that & be down by 10 – 10.30 except when Ada gives me my breakfast in bed about 9.45. Then try to be down by 11 am.

Phone calls. Letters. Go into garden for a short time. Start dinner about 12. – 12.30. Dinner 1.30.

Rest letters shopping read pm.

Tea at 5 – 5.30

Rest read garden phone.

8 p.m. Tidy up. Supper NOT LATER THAN 9 – 9.30

Bath & bed. Try to be in bed 10.30 – 11.30. Some hope!

1974 Nov.

Not keeping to the Ideal Timetable *at all*! but of course I am going down hill fairly fast. Ada is so good to me. I am a lucky person.

Final entry in diary Nov. 28th 1974

Ode addressed to Accountants

In an Urban Landscape
Strip lights in skyscrapers gleam
Through the grim grey December
While busy commuters
Are feeding computers
To urge us to pay on the Day.

Ruth Dodds died 1 April 1976

PHOTOGRAPH CREDITS BY PAGE

Jim Ancrum Collection (held by Bewick Press, Whitley Bay): 156, 167.

Bewick Press: 168, 187.

Gateshead Public Library Local History Collection: 40, 66.

Mary Melville Collection: 127.

Newcastle City Libaries and Arts Local History Collection: 50

Rounthwaite Family Collection: 18, 19, 20, 21, 22, 23, 24, 25, 26, 27, 28, 65, 89, 128, 188, 189, 190, 191, 192, 197.

ABBREVIATIONS

ILP Independent Labour Party

LP Labour Party

Lit and Phil Literary and Philosophical Society

NUR National Union of Railwaymen

PP Progressive Players

SSS Socialist Sunday School

TC Trades Council

TGWU Transport and General Workers' Union

TUC Trades Union Congress

VAD Voluntary Aid Detachments

REFERENCES

Chapter One

1. Aunt Poppy – Lydia Jane Mawson 1839–1924. She was one of the three unmarried sisters of Ruth's mother, Emily Bryham Mawson (died 1896), who lived at a large property, Ashfield, in Gateshead where the Dodds children spent a lot of time. The other sisters were Camie – Elizabeth Cameron Mawson 1849–1939 and Harry – Harriet Cameron Mawson – 1853-1917.
2 Hugh Rounthwaite 1882–1940 a cousin. Married Ruth's sister Molly March 1913 – see 5 below.
3. Clapham Girls' High School which Ruth attended for the following two years.
4. Aunts – see 1 above.
5. Molly – Mary Muriel Dodds 1881–1966. She attended Gateshead Girls' High School and Bedford College, London University, after which she kept house and helped with her younger sisters and brother until she married Hugh Rounthwaite in 1913. They became engaged in 1903. (I am indebted to Mr Michael Rounthwaite, their cousin, for this and other information about the Dodds Family.)
6. Molly's book – three volumes of cuttings about Newcastle United Football Club 1903 to 1910. The first and third volumes are bound and held in the local collection in Newcastle Central Library. (L796.33 955989A).
7. Mrs Rounthwaite – probably the wife of Henry Morrison Rounthwaite and mother of Hugh (above).
8. Cocoa parties in the evening were a feature of life in the women's colleges at Cambridge at this period. A collection of letters from Hope at Newnham refers to them frequently.
9. Home House in Kell's Lane, Low Fell, home of Ruth, Hope and Sylvia throughout their lives was built by their grandfather in the 1820s. It is a substantial stone property with a large garden where the Dodds maintained a grass tennis court. It is now a residential care home.
10. Uncle Eustace – Eustace Maclean Swanwick 1848–1928, a medical doctor, in practice at The Hartlepools, married to Edith Dodds, sister of Edwin, Ruth's father.
11. Brian – Brian Mawson Dodds 1887–1958. He was educated at Bow Preparatory School, Durham and at Oundle. He worked for a while in the family printing business, M.S.Dodds, 61–63 Quayside, then went into aeroplane manufacture. He was at various naval aeroplane factories

during the 1914–1918 war, and then worked for Short Brothers. He went to Japan after the war with an aeroplane-building instruction mission. When he returned to England he joined Ruth in the family business which she left after arguments in 1926 (See chapter 7). In 1926 he married Margaret Helen Nielson. They had no children.

Chapter 2

1. Anna Swanwick, youngest daughter of Eustace and Edie Swanwick, see note 11 chapter 1.
2. See note 1 chapter 1.
3. Lloyd George's 1909 budget, the 'People's Budget' which introduced a redistribution of wealth through taxation making the budget a tool of social policy. The House of Lords, predominantly Conservative, rejected the budget which resulted in a major constitutional battle between Lords and Commons resolved only by the Parliament Act of 1911. Two general elections were held in 1910 on the budget and the powers of the Lords.
4. Robert Peary, an American explorer, led the expedition which discovered the North Pole in 1909
5. A University friend of Hope's.
6. The Pilgrimage of Grace – a history of the rising led by Robert Aske, against the dissolution of the monasteries during the reign of Henry V111. Ruth and Hope Dodds published what was to be the standard account of this event in 1915.
7. The Literary and Philosophical Society of Newcastle upon Tyne, founded 1792, of which the Dodds family were members and frequent users.
8. see f.n. 5
9. Tilleys – a smart restaurant and tearoom previously in Blackett Street, Newcastle, and with other shops around the town.
10. Molly's baby, Bob.
11. Ruth was local secretary of the National Union of Women's Suffrage Societies but there are very few references to this in the diaries.

Chapter 3

1. Dr Ethel Williams – a Newcastle doctor, socialist and suffragist.
2. Professor Pollard – an eminent historian.
3. *The Pilgrimage of Grace.*

Chapter 4

1. The *Lusitania* – a ship carrying passengers and munitions sunk by the Germans in May 1915. The act produced anti-German riots in England.
2. Armstrong's munitions factory on Scotswood Road, Newcastle upon Tyne.
3. Ruth began to work at the family printing business because several of the men had joined the armed forces.
4. Roger Casement, who had been a British consul, sympathised with the Irish nationalists who planned an armed rising against the British government. He tried to recruit an Irish legion from prisoners of war in Germany to fight the British troops occupying Ireland. His plans miscarried and he was captured before the Easter Rising itself took place. He was hanged for high treason on 3 August 1916.
5. A conference of socialist parties from allied, neutral and enemy states was proposed to be held at Stockholm to consider Russian peace proposals.

Chapter 5

1. The general election of November 1918 resulted in a sweeping victory for the wartime Coalition Government led by Lloyd George. Gateshead, which had unfailingly returned a Liberal was won by a Coalition Conservative.
2. Dora – the Defence of the Realm Act gave the Government far-reaching powers; first enacted in August 1914 it was repeatedly strengthened and continued after the war in the Emergency Powers Act.
3. *The Circular* – the first news sheet published by Gateshead Labour Party. It was developed and extended first by Tom Peacock and then edited by Ruth Dodds as *The Gateshead Herald.* It was published monthly and Ruth was responsible for it until September 1939. It was published by Wilson, a Gateshead printer and ILP member.
4. Westfield Hall, Gateshead, was the headquarters of Gateshead ILP.
5. J.J. Lawson, Labour M.P. Chester-le-Street 1919–1949; First Baron Lawson of Beamish, created 1949.

Chapter 6

1. Margaret Harrison, a Dunston school-teacher, married Tom Gibb (below-2). When she was widowed in 1928 she was employed full-time as one of the two organisers of the Labour Party in the north of England until 1956.

2. Tom Gibb, Labour Party organiser, died Sheffield 1928.
3. Oswald Mosley, at first a member of the Labour Party, but after his radical economic proposals were rejected founded the New Party, then the British Union of Fascists. He was interned during the Second World War.
4. John Beckett was a protegé of Sir Charles Trevelyan and an ILP nominee. He later joined Oswald Mosley's New Party and contested a Midlands seat.
5. This quarrel with her brother arose, she told me, from their different attitudes to the general strike. It resulted in her impulsive severance from the business which she very much regretted.

Chapter 8

1. Mrs Bouchier, an actress, with whom John Beckett had a liaison.
2. Hugh Dalton, Labour M.P. for Peckham, later Chancellor of the Exchequer, was known to want a different seat, but he accepted the nomination for Bishop Auckland, Co. Durham.
3. J.B. Melville, had become the youngest King's Counsel in 1927 and the Labour Party wanted to find him a safe seat to increase their legal strength in the Commons.
4. Arthur Henderson, a leading Labour politician for a long period, known in the Labour movement as 'Uncle Arthur'.
5. Katharine Bruce Glasier writer, speaker and Labour Women's activist.
6. Ned Scott, Gateshead Councillor, and Parliamentary candidate for Newcastle North in 1929.
7. James Ramsay MacDonald, Labour Party leader; Prime Minister 1924–25, 1929–35; M.P. Seaham, Co. Durham 1929–1935.
8. Charles Trevelyan, an important Northumberland landowner, at Board of Education in 1929–1931 Labour government.

Chapter 9

1. Madeleine Hope Dodds wrote large sections of the *Northumberland County History.*
2. When the Labour Government resigned during an economic crisis on 23 August 1931, its leader, MacDonald, remained as Prime Minister of a predominantly Conservative Coalition government.
3. The Coalition government, established ostensibly to 'save the £', suspended the gold standard on 21 September.
4. The sailors of the Atlantic Fleet at Invergordon refused duty in protest

against the cuts in lower-deck pay and the more extreme cuts of over 10% were reduced.

Chapter 10

1. The Socialist Society, which joined with the Socialist League after the secession of the Independent Labour Party from the Labour Party in 1932, was an organisation of intellectuals intended to continue the work of the ILP. Ruth Dodds was the secretary of the Northern Area and Regional Representative on its National Committee. Its papers are in the local history collection at Gateshead Central Library. The League was expelled from the Labour Party on 27 January 1937 largely for its support of a 'unity' campaign with the ILP and the Communist Party. It dissolved itself two months later.
2. Letter from Ruth Dodds to the Editor of the *Newcastle Journal and North Mail,* Wednesday October 4, 1939.
   Sir, I wish to make clear that I have resigned my membership of the Labour Party which has involved me giving up my seat on Gateshead Town Council solely because the Labour Party is giving active support to the present war, while I hold all war to be contrary to the will of God. It is true that the Labour Party has never been completely pacifist and that during the last few years it has been committed to supporting a war against Facism. While war remained hypothetical I did not feel it necessary to make a choice; but now that it is an actual fact, I feel that I cannot remain in a party which is making the same mistake as in 1914 and again backing a war between rival imperialisms under the delusion that it is a war to end war. I shall always be on the side of the common people, and I cannot forget that whoever wins a war the struggling masses of all nations are bound to lose it.
   The home programme of the Labour Party still has my whole-hearted approval, and I shall continue to work for it and for the restoration of those hard-won social advances which are now swept away. For instance, there are now more than 10,000 children left in Gateshead. Six weeks ago there was a free health service for them from birth to 14 years. It is now gone; clinics closed, doctors and dentists idle. If this goes on till Christmas more damage will have been done than by a dozen air raids, though it will not attract any attention.
   This is only one of the ways in which we are sacrificing our children in the hope of destroying our enemies. Our real enemies are injustice, poverty and ignorance on which aggression and greed thrive, and we shall find them at home just as much as abroad. We shall never defeat

them by war, which only makes them stronger, but only by seeking that way of peace which takes away the occasion of all war.

Chapter 11

1. Jordans, in Buckinghamshire, is one of the oldest Quaker Meeting Houses. There are burial grounds where William Penn and his family are buried, and a Conference Centre.

Chapter 12

1. Ruth was the first woman to be made a Freeman of Gateshead and remains the only woman to have been thus honoured in the town.

INDEX